SANTA BARBARA CELEBRITIES

OTHER BOOKS BY CORK MILLNER
Vintage Valley
Sherry—The Golden Wine of Spain
Wines & Wineries of Santa Barbara County
Recipes from the Winemakers

SANTA BARBARA
CELEBRITIES

CONVERSATIONS FROM THE AMERICAN RIVIERA
INTRODUCTION BY JONATHAN WINTERS

by Cork Millner

Santa Barbara Press
1986

Special thanks to Anne Erikson

Cover design by Mary Schlesinger
Cover photos:
The collection of Andrew Velez (Jane Russell),
Cork Millner (Jonathan Winters), John Derek (Bo Derek),
Universal City Studios (Steve Martin),
Hara (Kathy Ireland, James Brolin)
Typography by Jim Cook

Published by
SANTA BARBARA PRESS
815 De la Vina Street
Suite C
Santa Barbara, California 93101

This one's for the whole gang—
Lynda, Kim, Dane and (sure, why not?) Mika

Contents

The Models

The Tennis Ace

Their Honors

Introduction

by Jonathan Winters

I defected to Santa Barbara.

Actors, actresses, writers, artists, all sorts of creative folks escape to Santa Barbara just to live in slow motion, away from the frenzy of the Los Angeles traffic, away from the incredible number of people. We escape just to find a couple of acres where we can relax and slow down the pace of life. In Santa Barbara I see a lot of people sitting, just eating popcorn. That's slow.

Santa Barbara is the retreat I picked out long before I got into show business. My great grandfather visited the city in the late 1800s coming all they way from Dayton, Ohio. Orville and Wilbur Wright also came from Dayton. My father said they were two of the dullest men he had ever met; anybody that had to go all the way to Kittyhawk, South Carolina just to find *air*...

My great-grandfather always said that Santa Barbara, with all its sunshine—probably more than there is now, even the water must have been bluer, the mountains a deeper purple—would be a lovely place to live. He loved it. He didn't stay. He went back to Dayton. But the contact was made.

I first came to Santa Barbara with my grandfather in 1940. We toured the city for a whole day, then he took me to a fig ranch where he had bought a hundred acres. Looking out over those fig trees and the mountains beyond, he told me: "Jonathan, I don't know what you want to do in life, be a farmer, raise avocadoes, be a writer, an actor...but whatever you do, I hope that someday you will think about settling in this beautiful place." I was only thirteen at the time, and I felt—no, I knew—I would come back someday.

It took forty years.

But, I made it, and I love the place. It's like a little village. I can walk around the streets and into the stores without being hassled. The people are fun, I would like to assemble a little group of them to call my own. That would be fun.

You know, I really don't know a lot of people. If I were to die tomorrow, they'd have to rent people to come see the funeral. If you're an actor it's necessary to have massive assemblages at your funeral, just so the newspapers can say, "He had a magnificent showing." At mine there'll be only one person, an auctioneer selling all the stuff I've collected.

I digress. My mind wanders. Must be a power shortage.

Santa Barbara's celebrities are not royalty, although they do love to hold court. For this they are criticized by their spouses: "Well! Everyone certainly centered around you!" Actors tend to draw a crowd. Then, they talk about themselves. I myself am guilty of that. I don't know an actor who isn't. Eventually, you have to stop and say to whoever you are talking to: "Hey, what do you do?" Unfortunately, too many times they will say, "Aw, I don't lead the interesting life you do."

Of course, there's the other guy who says, "I'm the fella who repairs the bushings in the machine at the ball bearing factory. Now, you probably won't be interested in this, but we set those things at 700 of a centimeter, then it revolves every sixteen hours and that forces the ball through the bushing..." ZZZZzzzz....

Santa Barbara's celebrities are invited to a lot of parties because they're supposed to be fascinating people. Now, that's not always true. The magic of the screen can enhance the image of a personality to monumental proportions. You use this close-up shot of an actor's face on this massive silver screen, and the lighting on his face is powerfully dramatic. And in the scene the sea is sending torrents of water against his face...and all that's happening is some prop man twenty feet away is throwing buckets of water at him. Over the tempest of sound effects, the actor is shouting: "Heavy storms bar my passage...only to crash in the gray mist against the shoals and rocks..." And everyone watching this immortal performance is saying "Oh, my gosh, isn't that actor, Wendell Crawford great!" So next he leaps off an eighty foot cliff, runs a dozen bad guys through with a rubber sword, and makes love to five voluptuous ladies in a canoe while being chased by a howling tribe of Apaches.

Then you invite him to dinner.

"Ah, Wendell, what's your next picture?"

"Ah...really don't know...last one was...ah, think it...Greeen Cactus?...I was ...ah, pleased with it...don't know if it's released...soon...though..." ZZZzzzzz....

Actors and actressses are unique. Actually, we're strange. We're strange because of the business we're in. One minute you have this great part in this magnificent movie, and then you're out of work for 261 weeks. That's when you have the choice of speeding off for a twenty day cruise to Catalina Island, or taking your girlfriend—or even your wife—to a Tahitian village so you can sit around taking pictures of each other.

Or, if you want, you can play tennis every day of the week in Santa Barbara, just put on a V-neck sweater and pretend you're Gilbert Roland. Touch up the hair a little, pencil in a thin moustache, and speak Spanish. *"Cómo está...me nomer, Luis...conleatos ah ver tolento."* Of course, someone like Barnaby Conrad, who speaks Spanish, may walk over and that's very dangerous.

I like to simply wander around in Santa Barbara. I walk into beauty parlors just to talk to people. Into grocery stores. Into banks. I asked my bank president if I had any interest built up in my savings account. He said, "Mr. Winters, on an account with less than two dollars..."

I like to put on different costumes when I walk. I may wear my 1800s cavalry uniform with the red-striped pants, or a Cincinnati baseball uniform, a Navy torpedoman's blue jumper, or maybe the Marine camouflage fatigues. My wife Eileen, doesn't understand: "You're no longer the court jester," she says. "You're the village fop."

I wandered into the Santa Barbara zoo the other day. Even without my monkey suit, I'm not comfortable in zoos. Thre is something about seeing a gorilla sitting in a Firestone tire....He looks very human to me. I think if you put a bow tie on him you'd have found a friend for dinner. I look at those deep-set eyes and have the feeling that if that guy ever got out of his cage, he'd be driving a truck to San Francisco using the tire as a seat cushion.

I guess that gorilla is a little like some of us actors, actresses, writers and artists. We're dressed up in a monkey suit most of the time, letting people stare at us. It's nice to be able to get out of the cage and drive up here to Santa Barbara to relax. To be real people

That's what Cork Millner is saying in this book, *Santa Barbara Celebrities*. Even though others look at us like some kind of strange royalty, we *are* real people. It's just that sometimes we are pushed so high on a pedestal that we forget *who* we really are. Cork's book hacks away the tinsel jungle and dims the center spot we live in and shows us, and everyone else, how we really are, how we live, how we feel, how we think.

I like that. So will you.

There is a poem by Rudyard Kipling called, "If." I have always read it to my son and daughter, and I read it to myself sometimes. It says it all:

"If you walk among the kings, but never lose the common touch, then you are a man my son."

Jonathan Winters
Santa Barbara
1986

The Santa Barbara Style

"Santa Barbara reminds me of the French Riviera of the 1940s...I hope they preserve it."
—Baron Philippe de Rothschild

Jonathan Winters is having lunch with his wife, Eileen, and a few friends in the Fountain Court of the Santa Barbara Biltmore Hotel. He is, as usual, dressed in one of his own unusual outfits: this time a baseball jersey with "Cincinnati" emblazoned across the front.

The conversaton centers on his book, an unpublished autobiographical journal titled: *I Couldn't Wait For Success, So I Started Without It*.

"The book's been around to several publishers," Winters is saying. "After reading it, one of them asked me, 'What about your affairs?' I told him—They're in order."

Winters' companions laugh.

At a table next to the window sits comedian Steve Martin talking in hushed tones to an attractive blond woman. Martin wears a sweater, tennis shoes and brilliant red sox with a yellow stripe. Even without the toy arrow through his gray head he is instantly recognizable.

Yet, no one rushes up to either Martin or Winters and bothers them for an autograph. *That* really isn't done. Not in Santa Barbara.

"People are so sensitive to actors here," says actress Eva Marie Saint who, with her television director husband, Jeffrey Hayden, have a weekend retreat on the beach. "People don't approach you. They let you approach them."

To the actors, actresses, models, artists and writers who come to this color-coordinated kingdom by the sea, Santa Barbara is a fantasy come true. Whether they take the city in weekend doses or as a way of life, Santa Barbara is like a Hollywood movie version of the idealized place to live.

The people who visit this scenic, seaside city read like a Who's Who. Ann Landers found it a "fabulous walking city. It seems like there's something special around every corner." Peter Ueberroth said it was "an historic city vibrantly alive with places to go and things to do..." All who come to Santa Barbara find it charming.

And that's part of it: Santa Barbara's style is one of *charm.*.

Driving along palm-lined Cabrillo Boulevard, visitors feel in the sea mist certain romantic stirrings that build from within. They know that each motel will have a view, every lobby a fireplace, every dining table will be bathed in muted candlelight, and that strawberries will always be in season.

12

They know that the moon will glow an extra hour in the cloudless sky, and that the sun will always shine brilliantly in the cobalt sky. (It is not polite to notice the profusion of oil rigs that appear on the horizon like an aircraft carrier task force. *They* are there, Santa Barbarans say, because *we* were overcome by federal tomfoolery.)

The Santa Barbara style is also one of *relaxation*.

Celebrities come to Santa Barbara to get away from the frenzy and expansive energy of the freeway-veined megalopolis of Los Angeles one hundred miles to the south. Santa Barbara and its aristocratic environs, Montecito and Hope Ranch, are relaxing meccas for actors in retreat, and artists and writers in residence. Once an enclave where the very wealthy lived in mysterious walled-off, Gatsby-like estates, Montecito has evolved into private residences of refugees from Hollywood. Robert Mitchum and his wife, Dorothy, live in a modest two bedroom ranch house overlooking the Pacific. When he is not making a film, Mitchum relaxes at home. "I answer the phone," he says, "open the mail, watch the evening news..."

The Santa Barbara style is one of *privacy*.

Dame Judith Anderson, who moved to a Montecito cottage in 1940 (she was the first celebrity to settle there), says, "I wanted to live where it was private. Where I could walk my dogs day and night."

Santa Barbara's lure of privacy, coupled with its Mediterranean atmosphere, and casual California lifestyle, has attracted an amazing melee of celebrities. The San Ysidro Ranch in Montecito, which was once owned by Ronald Coleman, has been the rendezvous for the rich and famous for the last fifty years.

Everyone in Santa Barbara knows that John F. Kennedy and his bride, Jackie, honeymooned at the San Ysidro Ranch. Vivien Leigh and Laurence Olivier were married there in the middle of the night in 1940. Humphrey Bogart and Lauren Bacall wandered happily hand in hand to and from their vine-covered cottage.

"I fell in love with Bogey there," Lauren Bacall recalls. "I can still see him surrounded by all that purple bougainvillea—it was beyond irresistible."

The Santa Barbara style is one of *peace*.

"There is the feeling of the Mediterranean coast here," actress Anne Francis says shading her eyes from the sun and gazing at the Channel Islands which ring the coast like a necklace. "It's lovely with islands in the distance, the mist on the mountains, the palms along the beach—and the solitude." She puts on a pair of dark glasses, for the sun, not for the movie star effect. "Santa Barbara radiates peace to me."

The Santa Barbara style is *beauty*.

Many celebrities maintain a working residence in Hollywood and a relaxing one in Santa Barbara. Actress Eva Marie Saint and husband, Jeffrey Hayden, drive to their waterfront Montecito home "almost every Friday." Brushing her golden hair from her face, she says, "As soon as the mountains behind Montecito come into view, I can see my husband's face lose five years. When we sit on our deck overlooking the ocean, we say, 'no place in the world is more beautiful!' "

Julia Child and her husband, Paul, spend the winter half of the year in an ocean-view condominium in Montecito, the summer half in their home in Cambridge, Massachusetts. "I simply couldn't stand the cold winters any longer," Julia says in her raspy chortle. "Santa Barbara is so warm and beautiful."

Mayor Sheila Lodge says, "I think Santa Barbara is a special place with its climate, its mountains, beaches and beautiful parks. What I hope to do as mayor is insure that all the city's special qualities are preserved forever."

Santa Barbara's celebrities are entranced by these special qualities. To Monte Hale, one of the last singing cowboys of Saturday movie matinee fame, who resides with his wife, Joanne, a condominium away from Julia Child, the city's most special quality is its "home town" atmosphere. In his "Ya'll" Texas drawl, he admits he likes a town where "the barber shop, drugstore and groceries are right there next to one another."

The Santa Barbara style is one of *giving*.

Even though privacy, quiet and leisure are part of the Santa Barbara style of lving, it's not all. Celebrities do much more than appear to idle their time away with midafternoon poolside drinks and black tie patio luncheon buffets. They are also active, working, sharing, and giving members of the community, offering their time and names to a variety of charitable activities.

The 1985 Humane Society's fund raiser drew over twenty movie celebrities who brought along their canine pets. Such actresses as Dame Judith Anderson, Bo Derek, Anne Francis, comedienne Fannie Flagg, composer Neal Hefti and actors John Ireland and James Arness showed their dogs as Jonathan Winters provided the commentary. "I wore my doggie slippers," Winters wagged, rolling his eyes.

The Santa Barbara style is one of *vitality*.

It's easy to label Santa Barbara as an enclave for octogenarians. The old joke, attributed to resident writer Barnaby Conrad, goes: "Santa Barbara is the place where old people go to visit their parents." Actor John Ireland, who is in his mid-sixties once remarked, "I like it here. It's the only place where they call me kid."

Sure, Dame Judith Anderson may be nearing 90, but she never feels she is part of a retirement community. Dame Judith heads to Hollywood twice a week to play Minx Lockridge on NBC's daytime soap "Santa Barbara." Young actors like John Travolta, Bo Derek, and Jane Seymour have added their own vitality to the city's presence.

The Santa Barbara style is like *Hollywood revisited*.

"People do what they want here," says resident novelist Joanna Barnes *(Silverwood)*. "There's no industrial entertaining, no Hollywood hellos. Maybe that's part of the charm. Scan the community; what it's really like is 1930's Hollywood."

Joanna Barnes is right. There's a strong Hollywood aura hanging over Santa Barbara. Perhaps the reason is that the city was once the *original* "Hollywood."

Hollywood was just an ill-tended vineyard in 1912 when Samuel S. Hutchinson, a Chicago film-maker, visited Santa Barbara. "This town has everything!" he exclaimed. "Perfect climate, mountains, islands, the ocean, beautiful beaches, brush country—and those magnificent Montecito estates so reminiscent of French and Italian villas."

Intrigued by this "Riviera of the West," Hutchinson formed the American Film Company, bought an ostrich farm (it was only a ramshackle house which provided a haven for seven scraggly birds) near downtown Santa Barbara, and set-up his Flying A Studios.

Silent film celebrities such as Mary Pickford, D.W. Griffith, Marian Davies, Mary Miles Mintner (then reigning queen of the silents), and Richard Bennett and his daughters Constance and Joan, came to Santa Barbara to make "two reelers" for the Flying A.

Between 1913 and 1918 Santa Barbara turned out over 1,200 movies. They were far from epics; most films were completed in a few days. The *Santa Barbara News-Press* of July 13, 1912 carried a story that said in part: "A new world's record was made today when a thousand foot story was filmed by Flying A in two hours and fifteen minutes. Filming on *The Stranger* began at 9:45 a.m. By noon, the villain was hanged and everybody went home."

Then, suddenly, Hollywood happened. Santa Barbara's star-spangled era faded, its moment in the cinematic sun dimmed.

But the celebrity aura lingered.

Movie people had fallen in love with Santa Barbara. Fatty Arbuckle would gather a group of Hollywood cronies and trek to the Montecito Inn for a relaxing weekend. Others headed for the fashionable El Paseo restaurant in downtown's fabled Street of Spain. During the '30s and '40s, the El Paseo restaurant hosted such glittering stars as Ginger Rogers, Mae West, Tyrone Powers, Fred Astaire and Will Rogers.

The El Paseo's small stage regularly featured the Cansino family, a group of Spanish dancers performing to the music of Xavier Cugat. In the troupe was a young, vibrantly beautiful daughter named Rita Cansino. She eventually rose to stardom under the name— Rita Hayworth.

What makes these names so indelible on the Santa Barbara scene is that the stars returned time after time. This color-coordinated kingdom by the sea held out a mystical hand which beckoned them to come—and relax and enjoy a place far from the hassle of Hollywood.

"We respected their privacy," a former employee of the El Paseo restaurant says. Privacy. Ah...it still attracts a large share of the celebrated. Santa Barbara residents know how to walk the fine line between open-armed hospitality and regard for the individual. It's a trait that's embedded in the city's history.

The Santa Barbara style is one of *history* and *heritage.*

The overall appeal of Santa Barbara didn't happen like some natural wonder rising out of a Miocene upheaval. *People* made it happen. They made it happen by visualizing a city that would be an oasis for the future. Then they went about making that vision come true. While other California cities were being buried beneath billboards, and smothered against the sea by high-rising cement monoliths, or entangled in a web of telephone poles and black wire, Santa Barbara retained its natural qualities.

How?

The clue lies deep within the city's Spanish heritage.

Like no other city on the west coast, Santa Barbara has retained the flavor of Spain within its coastal boundaries. Kenneth Rexroth wrote: "Santa Barbara is the last unspoiled city in a mediterranean climate in the world...the French and Italian Rivieras have become one immense hotdog stand, the Spanish Med a free brothel."

Author Thomas Sanchez, another frequent visitor, called Santa Barbara "the last intact town of substance and size that still has contact with its Spanish heritage...the whole place is a private garden with courtyards rivaling those of Cordoba."

Santa Barbara wears its Spanish heritage well. It was over 450 years ago when Spanish explorer, Juan Cabrillo, first sailed by and sighted the west-facing bank of beaches and mountains along the sea and claimed it for Spain. Perhaps he could visualize a future Spanish-style city with red-tile roofs equal to those of Granada or Seville.

In 1602 the first Spanish sea captain anchored off-shore and gave the city the name she still bears. The date was December 4th, the feast day of Saint Barbara, Patroness of Mariners.

The Spanish sailed away and it was almost two centuries before they returned, this time on foot, establishing a string of missions and forts along the coast.

In 1782 Padre Junípero Serra planted the cross and dedicated the Presidio Real, the Royal Fortress. Four years later the Mission of Santa Barbara was founded. After a century of design and construction changes, coupled with the destructiveness of periodic earthquakes, the "Queen of the Missions" was finally completed, rising skyward in rose-hued splendor.

A tiny pueblo of thatched huts, with thick adobe walls to ward off the summer sun, sprang up around the mission and the presidio. Casa De le Guerra, the home of Spanish-born Jose Del la Guerra, Commandante of the Presidio, was erected in 1827 and became the center of the social life of the city.

Henry Dana, author of *Two Years Before the Mast,* came ashore for a visit, and discovered a rustic court of Spanish settlers who lived and looked like royalty. He called them—Californios.

The era of the "Californios" was short-lived, ending in 1845 when an American colonel named John C. Fremont raised the first American flag in front of the De la Guerra home. The Americans that quickly followed changed the stylish Spanish architecture into undistinguished "Yankee" wooden frame buildings. The red-tile roofs were submerged in a sea of pine siding and cedar slats.

One visiting writer of the time was chagrined by the change. He wrote: "The beauty of these early adobes went unnoticed by the Americans, who carried with them the prevailing Victorian taste for elaborate, jig-saw decorated wooden structures."

Downtown Santa Barbara became a potpourri of ugly, uninspired wood, a western town entangled in its own spurs. By 1925 Santa Barbara was a wasteland of western junk that had spread over the original Spanish architecture like a smothering fungus.

Yet, the Spanish style was submerged, not destroyed. All it needed was something to restore it. A gigantic bulldozer, perhaps. And then it arrived.

June 29, 1925.

The earthquake.

Destructive as it was (although only one life was lost), Santa Barbarans in retrospect have called it "The blessing." The earthquake measured 6.3 on the Richter scale, a sufficient shuddering and violent shaking to level most of the downtown area.

The new Santa Barbara rose like a Phoenix from the splinters and dust of crumbled buildings. The new structures were built in a curiously harmonic hodgepodge of architectural styles: Spanish Colonia, Mission Revival, Mexican Californian and Spanish Moorish. The one single coordinating element was that all the styles were related to a Mediterranean climate.

With the change in architectural style , coupled with the limited space between the sea and mountains, it was necessary to closely monitor the city's growth. Sprawl was banned. Building heights were severely restricted. New housing development was slowed to a trickle when a water moratorium went into effect in 1960. Subsequent plans to increase the city's water flow have been quickly denounced. One local confesses stubbornly "I would rather bathe once a week than vote to bring in new water for new people."

Some long-time residents joke that a wall should be built around the city, and visas required to enter. Yet, tourists and the bikini-clad Pepsi generation are not excluded from visiting. Not far from the exclusive Montecito cemetery (where Ronal Coleman is buried) is East Beach, a mecca for long-legged girls who come to the city for its endless summers, surfing and sustained happiness. There on the sand they languish like breaded porkchops, rising only when challenged by a bronzed surfer to a volley ball game.

Santa Barbara is also the "home" for a ragtag army of drifters in search of an ecological buzz. They assemble next to the freeway for shade and solitude beneath the city's famous Moreton Bay Fig Tree. They shrug, "It's better to starve in a warm climate." One wry wit called lower State Street, which is the center of this drifter's kingdom, "the world's largest open-air psychiatric ward."

Through all these contrasts in lifestyle, Santa Barbara continues to maintain her *own style.* A style that is in part her beauty, charm, peace and privacy. Santa Barbara is not Beverly Hills. It's not Palm Springs. Yet, it does have its own interpretation of luxurious California living.

There are other queen-like resorts throughout the world but none protects herself so well, none spreads her tourquoise shawl so protectively over her people.

None has Santa Barbara's *style.*

Steve Martin and Lily Tomlin in "All of Me."

Steve Martin

A Wild and Serious Guy

I came to a screeching halt when I saw Steve Martin sitting at a table in the El Paseo courtyard. I slipped behind a purple bougainvillea—feeling as ridiculous as Inspector Clouseau—and watched the wild and crazy guy sip coffee. Finally, I stepped from behind the bush and walked to Martin's table. "Uh...Hi, I'm a writer, and I...ah...." The next words sputtered from my mouth without benefit of passing through my brain: "Uh...do you know where I can find Jonathan Winters? *Martin's head swiveled slowly toward me like a macabre scene from the* Exorcist, *and he said: "That's almost* funny."

Even without the toy arrows through his prematurely gray head, Steve Martin is instantly recognizable. And he knows it. "The biggest loss at being a celebrity is that you can't go anywhere as an observer," Martin says. "You can't have fun like everyone else. You can't go to a park, or a zoo, or a patio cafe. People are always watching you, lurking behind trees, bushes..."

Steve Martin is sitting with three friends at an umbrella-shaded table in the El Paseo courtyard in Santa Barbara. He peacefully sips from his cup of coffee and listens to the bubbling water of the patio fountain. Then, Martin *feels* it coming—a Steve Martin fan. He hunches over, pulls the collar of his leather jacket around his neck and shifts his eyes warily behind the jet-black sunglasses.

A fat woman in a print housedress jiggles up to him, fluttering a napkin in one hand, and a ball point pen in the other. She giggles and thrusts them in front of Martin's face. He smiles wanly and scribbles his autograph on the napkin. She blubbers happily then wobbles away across the patio flagstones, a walrus on a rocky beach. Returning to her husband at another table, she whispers, "He didn't even say anything *funny.*"

Steve Martin is expected to be funny—everywhere. Yet, the "wild and crazy guy" that audiences loved on stage is far different from the Steve Martin in person. In a one-on-one situtaton he gives the impression of being sincere and full of enthusiasm. He almost sounds like he is saying "Gee whiz!" to every question he is asked. He would have made a great listener.

Although he is a nice guy, and a "gee whiz" kind of fellow, his interviews tend to be bland. Sure, he is funny on stage, but when he is not performing he's just another run-of-the-mill kinda guy. That is difficult for him. He is always expected to "say something funny."

Martin would like to take the time to be serious, but he can't. That's not his image. To his fans he will always be that happy "jerk" on stage. And that image has threatened his movie career. Although he was the most phenomenally successful stand-up comedian of the 1970s, he has continually had creative problems in transferring his whacky brand of humor to the movies of the 1980s.

"I really want to be successful in motion pictures," he says very seriously. To Martin the movies are like catching lightning in a bottle where it will glimmer on and on, preserved in it's iridescent glow forever.

Unfortunately, his movies haven't electirified critics or audiences. His first movie, "The Jerk," which came from Martin's fertile imagination, was the exception. It was a resounding success, selling $74 million in tickets.

Martin's next movie, *Pennies From Heaven,* an art-deco musical fantasy, confounded audiences and bombed at the box office. Martin aficionados were bewildered by the film which was more somber than funny. The story was based on an old premise about a sheet-music salesman in the 1930s whose unhappy life runs counterpoint to the joyful songs of the period. "I tended to overplay the somberness," Martin admits, "but the humor was there, it came out of the characters. Sometimes a joke was set up half an hour before it arrived, and when it did come, I thought it was very funny." Unfortunately the audience couldn't fathom the delayed humor and the $22 million movie only sold $7.2 million in tickets.

Martin did a little better with *Dead Men Don't Wear Plaid,* which was as much a departure from his comedy style as was "Pennies." Directed by comic buddy, Carl Reiner, the movie's gimmick was to intersperse new scenes with footage from old black-and-white vintage movies. In it Martin "starred" with macho movie images such as Humphrey Bogart and Alan Ladd. Although the premise was a unique and interesting exercise in creativity, the movie was less than well received by Martin fans who expected and wanted that "wild and crazy guy."

In *The Man With Two Brains,* Martin got closer to what his fans wanted. The jokes were zany and the comic bits close to burlesque, and Martin thought it was almost on track. He and the producers were stunned when it only earned $9 million at the box office.

Lonely Guy followed next and went so quickly it only sold $5.5. million in tickets. "It was sort of a stinker," Martin admits.

Martin's search for cinematic success finally came to fruition with the 1984 release, *All of Me,* which made use of his gifts for physical comedy. "I'm very happy with *All of me,*" Martin says. "It's the first film I have done that is funny without having to think about it. It's a drawing-room comedy with a very solid story."

Martin feels that *All of Me* established him as a screen comedian. He wasn't just a fad like Hula Hoops or Pet Rocks. He wasn't just a flash that ignited in the '70s. He was a movie comedy star of the '80s. Most of all he would never have to go back to being a "jerk" on stage again.

The Steve Martin comedy that came out of the '70s was, well—weird. It was labeled silly, brainless and Disneyesque. Newsweek called Martin the "ultimate West Coast wacko" as opposerd to the archetypical EAst Coast neurotic Woody Allen."

Carl Reiner once told Martin that he looked like a guy who looked at Fred Astaire and said, "Hey, I can do that—watch." Pauline Kael said it more succinctly when she described Martin's stage act as a guy acting like a comedian and the audience acting like an audience.

"I always looked at my solo stage comedy as a success of timing," Martin says. "I had the right act at the right time. That's why I was a stage phenomenon rather than just another comedian. It was during the sixties when I started formulating my comic ideas. I knew that the seriousness of the social sixties would eventually pass into the silly 70s, and I was getting ready for it. When it came, I was ready. I was silly, but I was *avant garde*.

"If I had to categorize myself at that time, I would say I had sort of—I wouldn't say gift—but rather a supply of energy on stage. I was real energetic—and real dumb."

It was difficult to focus in on what made Martin's comedy routines work. Anyone who can stand in front of audiences of 20,000 and get them to laugh by turning balloons into animals and singing his one million copy best-selling album, "King Tut," must have something unique going for him. Laughter is one of the most unusual of human responses. No one knows exactly how it works or what brings it on. Surprise seems to elicit laughter. Silliness can also work. Nonsense, in Steve Martin's case, works even better. On stage, he'd say: "Now, the nose-on-the-microphone routine," and he'd put his nose on the head of the microphone then say, "Thank you." Simple and childlike, yet it worked. The audiences always howled.

One of his "funnies" became a staple in his act, a little sanctuary, a relief, something he could thrust into the act when he was experimenting with a new routine and it began to fall flat. He would use it for a sure laugh: "Mind if I smoke?" he'd say, then answer quickly in another voice: "No, mind if I fart?"

"If I just start talking funny-type things and never give the audience a punch line, eventually their tension is going to grow so much they will start laughing on their own," Martin says. "They'll start choosing things to be funny, which is the strongest kind of humor. *They* have determined what is funny, not me. The laugh I like to get is, 'What? I don't know why I am laughing.'

"Beside laughs there is the real thrill of timing. That's the greatest fun of all. When you're resting, waiting, and you've got the next line in your head and you're just waiting for that little intimate moment...things are really flowing. Charged. Like a ballet."

Unlike his stage persona, Martin is a very serious and a very private man. His personal life and his long relationship with Bernadette Peters is taboo talk, as is the time he spent with Linda Ronstadt. His weekend retreat in Santa Barbara, is built like concrete bunker, more ominous than inspiring. It is there that on weekends he goes to ponder his past and future. His biggest obsession, other than his comedy, is collecting 19th century art. He is a serious collector and the walls of his home are filled with paintings by such artists as Edward Hopper, Mary Cassatt, and Winslow Homer.

"The greatest thing I can do with the money I make is buy paintings," he says. "You can never have enough money if you collect art. People like me are an art dealer's dream."

When Martin's busy schedule from movie making permits, he likes to relax in his Santa Barbara home. It is a perfect retreat from frustratons—and from interviews.

He once told an interviewer: "Don't make this interview too nice. You know, those nice interviews are so...I don't know—nice." Like any celebrity who is being interviewed there is the fear that the written story won't portray the way they see *themselves*. It is difficult for celebrities to cope with the writer's—and the public's—image of them. Like Woody Allen, Martin agonizes over meeting people. In interview situations he admits to thinking: "I hope he doesn't ask me that."

How did this basically shy, almost introverted "nice guy" become the goofball who looked like something out of a 1935 Disney cartoon? How did he transform himself into a flippant and flamboyant character who paraded before thousands of people with bunny ears on his head?

"Oh, God, you're not going to get into my past are you?" Martin responds when told it is time to talk about his background. "Nobody gives a shit where I grew up. That's boring. Even I don't give a shit. When I read an interview and it gets to the part where a person grew up, I turn the page."

Although Martin is reluctant to delve into his "boring past," it is interesting to note that his fascination with being a performer began when he was ten years old. That was when he was hired to sell guidebooks at Disneyland. From there he "played" all the amusement parks: at Magic Mountain he demonstrated tricks at their magic shop, then at Knott's Berry Farm's Birdcage Theater he was given the opportunity to do his newly-developed magic act and try out a few comedy routines.

From there he enrolled in Theatre Arts at UCLA, and took a television writing course. In 1968, when he was only 21, he was hired to write comedy for the "Smothers Brothers" show. ("If I wrote anything it was: 'Here's Burl Ives.' " he says. "It was no big deal.") Writing worked for him, and at a weekly salary of $1,500, paid the bills. But, he wanted to be a performer.

"Writing for TV was like learning to swallow swords," he remembers. The closest he got to being a performer on Smothers Brotehrs was the night he played a human head on a silver platter and spouted off with several one-liners.

After the "Smothers Brothers" show was axed by CBS, Martin got a job writing for Sonny & Cher, then Glenn Campbell. He still wanted to perform and finally began to get on the talk shows: "Joey Bishop," "Merv Griffin" and, of course, "The Tonight Show."

"I guess I've been on television a lot," Martin says. "Probably 500 times; the 'Tonight show' thirty-five or forty times. I did a lot of crazy things on that show. One was reading a phone book to make people laugh. I'd pick up a phone book and read: 'Aaron Adams, 717 South Remington.' Of course, there wouldn't be a laugh, but I'd go on—'Bill Black, 982 Montrose Avenue.' Still no laugh, then I'd take out my arrow and put it on my head and read a sillier name like, 'Mary Ann Pinball...' By the time it was over, I'd end up waving a rubber chicken, and then finally say: 'Don't look at me, I didn't write this shit.' "

Before Martin made it as a television comedian he was signed with the William Morris Agency as a writer. "I went in and told them I was leaving television writing to be a performer," Martin says. "They said, 'Don't do it, you'll never make it.' Well, I've heard that line in a dozen movies, so I knew I could make it. Rejection is one of my accomplishments."

Although Martin started out as a comedy writer, he didn't write his own material for his stand-up comedy routines. They just evolved. "I don't know if I could sit down and write a routine that would be funny. My original act came out of a philisophical point of view. A new point of view. I was just a guy up on stage acting like a comedian."

Martin admits that it was a marvelous feeling to be in front of 20,000 hysterically laughing people.

"Yeah, that was a thrill," he says. "But, there is still the thrill of looking back and saying—'I was the biggest comedian in the world.' " He pauses and reflects, "I will be very happy, if when I'm sixty, I can look back and say, 'I was a very funny person in this world.' "

Steve Martin has packed away the arrows-through-the-head, he has deflated his ballooon animals, and he no longer has happy feet. After all, that really wasn't Steve Martin. It wasn't even close. The real Steve Martin is a "wild and *serious* guy."

James Brolin at his beach home in Santa Barbara (Hara)

James Brolin

The Hunkback of Notre Dame

Parrots. Those damn parrots of James Brolin drove me crazy. When I walked up to the door at Brolin's impressive Spanish-styled Montecito estate, I could hear them squawking in protest at my arrival. Brolin led me into the kitchen and settled into a chair. Behind him the two gigantic jungle parrots increased their decibel level of complaint. I asked if we could move to another room. Brolin shrugged at his multi-colored pets and said, "Yeah, I guess they are kind of noisy." He led me into the living room (several blocks away), but even at that distance the incessant protest of the two parrots almost obliterated the taped interview.

"I've been always been cast as a leading man in the movies," James Brolin says. "And it's boring. Maybe I could play Tootsie."

He laughs and discards the idea. "Naw, I could never play Tootsie, but I want to break away from the macho mold and do something really bizarre like...how about playing *The Hunchback of Notre Dame?* Brolin rolls up the sleeve on his plaid cotton shirt and crosses his legs one ankle over the other knee, then spreads his arms wide across the back of the couch. "No, I mean it, I'm serious. I want to do a totally off the wall character part like the hunchback. I know I'm not right for it physically, but I have been workng on that. I do a lot of private rehearsing with physical posture right here at home using a video camera."

It's a little difficult to imagine this tall and tanned actor—the star of such movies as *Amityville Horro, Capricorn One* and *Gable and Lombard*—shuffling around the living room of his Montecito home, his body and face twisted grotesquely, bounding across the couch pretending he is swinging from Notre Dame's bell tower.

"Well, maybe I'm not right for the part," he says, and his face takes on a shy, boyish demeanor. His voice is deeply modulated, warm and friendly. "I sat down and watched the original movie with Lon Chaney, and the classic one with Charles Laughton. Finally, I saw Anthony Quinn's performance, and Quinn was the best by far—and he's lean and Latin!" Brolin spreads his arms in a "why not" gesture and says: "Why not James Brolin? Maybe the idea is so novel and so unique that the audience will watch just to see me screw up." He pauses, then adds, "But, I might just surprise them."

Brolin leans his head back against the couch and sinks his 6'4", 205 pound frame deeper into the cushions. He stares up at the high oak-beamed ceiling of the living room. From the nearby kitchen two parrots screech and squawk in a duet of decibels. From a massive stone fireplace that dominates the living room a shaggy buffalo head looks down in glassy-eyed silence. The living space is huge and looks more like the lobby of a hunting lodge in the Rockies.

James Brolin fits comfortably into the hardwood atmosphere of his home. Ruggedly handsome in a neatly trimmed beard, the forty-three year-old actor physically personifies the he-man image that Hollywood has cast him into. Yet, he is uncomfortable locked into this image of movieland masculinity. "I don't get a great deal of pleasure out of being classified as a 'Hunk.' " he says honestly. "Producers keep casting me with that image in mind and it's tough to get away from it. For years I have been trying to put aside the Dr. Kiley character I played for six years on 'Marcus Welby, M.D.' But to get rid of one image you have to replace it with something stronger."

Brolin hopes that his performance on the successful television series, "Hotel," will give him the power to overcome the limitations of type casting. Based on Arthur Hailey's best-selling novel, "Hotel" the hour long super-soap has got "kind of a Rolls Royce atmosphere," Brolin says. "It's rich and it's real, and it wants to make you laugh and it makes you cry. When I first read the script I knew it was gong to be a big hit. We got the right people and the right writers and the right producer—Aaron Spelling, the most successful television producer in the business."

In "Hotel" Brolin doesn't get the opportunity to break away from his he-man image. He plays the hotel manager, a worldly, knowledgeable individual who is an exceptional organizer. "The manager is a prince in his own majestic city—the Hotel," Brolin says, leaning forward, elbows on his knees. "I used a different technique in developing his character than I did with other parts. Usually I'll write one hundred pages or so on the background of the person I am going to portray. I even place him in hypothetical situations and devise decisions for him. In this case the character was fully developed in the book. All I had to do was walk around the Fairmont Hotel in San Francisco, where the pilot film was shot, and soak up the atmosphere, the same atmosphere the manager had been accustomed to all his life."

An extra enticement was added to "Hotel" to insure a viewing audience. Bette Davis, the matriarch of moviedom, was cast as the hotel owner. Brolin had never met Davis before. "I've met a lot of people in the business and I am not one to overreact; I don't collect autographs. When I was told Miss Davis wished to see me, I was escorted up to the hotel suite, and when the door opened I saw her sitting with two other women at the far, far side of the room. I thought I was there for a brisk chat and tea, but she jumped up and came running across the room and said in that indomitable style of hers: 'Why, Mr. Brolin, how nice to meet you!' We talked, and by the end of the conversation I knew that if we had a bottle of wine between us we would have been like old friends." (Due to ill health, Davis had to give up the role. She was replaced by Anne Baxter, who died in late 1985.)

With the success of "Hotel" it appears that Brolin will be forced to tie up his acting career for five or six years. "That is a lot of time," he says, "But I know what I am getting into—and why. There are a lot of things in life that you *want* to do, and things in life that you *have* to do. A successful television show is a way of recapturing the *power* that will let me do what I want."

Like playing in a feature film called the *Hunchback of Notre Dame?* Brolin grins, big, and the parrots in the kitchen can be heard screeching loudly in approval.

"I love workng in feature films," he says after the parrots have quieted down. "There is an energy there that television doesn't have. Unfortunately, television is like making one mini-movie over and over again with the same people. Of course, some people are great to work with."

"I've worked with Jill Clayburg and I think she's the greatest. She's very disciplined, and she's also very scattered. By that I mean, you really don't know exactly what's going to happen when you act opposite her. Even though you've rehearsed and rehearsed and you know exactly what's coming next, she will do something surprising and you'll have to react to it. It's like a bomb going off in front of the camera, and the scene will really work." He sits up straighter in the couch. "It's like sitting down next to an exciting woman. You don't know what makes her exciting, except you can't guess what she's going to do next. Jill Clayburg is like that on screen."

Brolin played opposite Clayburg in the movie titled, *Gable and Lombard.* Playing the role of Clark Gable was about as close as Brolin has come to doing a character part, even though he portrayed Gable as a he-man from another era. He had a few misgivings about accepting the part.

"I was approached by director Sidney Furie to play Gable," he says. "At first I thought it was absurd that Brolin could become Gable, but Furie kept saying over and over, 'You can do it!' He made me watch every movie Gable had made, and the more I saw of Gable on the screen thé more passionate I became about playing him, not to just mimic his voice and his mannerisms, but to get deep inside him—to duplicate him. I had begun to notice little moves or actions that he did on the screen, and there were a lot of things that I understood or could relate to. I could see that he was a little shy or awkward on screen when he would momentarily let the facade of 'The King' slip away. There was a lot of *me* in Gable's personality."

Unfortunately the movie's producers sensationalized the film, and the critics savaged it. Yet, the public loved it. "People will come up to me and that's the only thing they want to talk about—*Gable and Lombard.* They loved it. So did I."

Brolin loved *Amityville Horror* even more, but for a different reason—he struck paydirt. The film was a smash hit and grossed over 140 million dollars; Brolin had a chunk of the profits. "I normally negotiate for a part of the movie," he says, "but I don't usually end up with that big a chunk. The movie was a financial bonanza and gave me a little of the power I want. I even liked the character I played."

Brolin also seems to like the character he plays in real life. His personal interests mirror the image of masculinity that he is trying to alter on the screen. He has his own airplane, a Cessna 186 "tail dragger" that he uses to release energy, and he races cars, and for several years raised thoroughbred horses. It's a personal lifestyle that has its own built-in excitement and challenges.

"A lot of it is challenging those personal juices," he says, sinking deeper into the sofa. "It has nothing to do with impressing others. Perhaps I am simply trying to impress myself; push myself further than I did yesterday. If that is the macho thing..." he sighs, "then, that's what I am.

"When I was nineteen I wanted to be a test pilot," he continues. "I even tried to join the Navy Aviation Cadet program, but I couldn't fulfill the two year college requirement. I wanted to be one of those rugged individualists who would calmly say—'Buffeting...buffeting...left aileron is coming off, we'll have to redesign it'—just before he creamed it into the ground.

"Yeah, Chuch Yeager, that's who I used to dream about being, that's the one person I would rather be than me. He was the first test pilot to break the speed of sound, even when everyone thought there was an impregnable wall. Yet, he pushed through it and came back and laughed about it. He did incredible things, and there was this look in his eyes that said,

'To hell with it, you put wings on it and I'll fly it anywhere, even beyond the fringe of space.' Yeah, Yeager was some cowboy."

Dreams aside, there are a few things Brolin will not attempt. Hang gliding is one of them. "I once saw this guy trying to get this elephant to water ski," he says. "And the elephant ended upside down in the water chained to two pontoons. If it wasn't for his trunk and figuring out there was air up there...well I look on hang gliding like trying to waterski an elephant."

James Brolin didn't start out to create a macho image when he was in high school in Los Angeles, nor did he envision himself as a movie star. "I couldn't even give a book report in front of class," he remembers. Luckily he was offered a tour of a Hollywood studio when he was fifteen. What he saw was intoxicating. "I guess I thought movies were born out of an egg," he says, "but in the studio I saw all these people working together to create a film. I was fascinated. I left there telling myself I wanted to become a cameraman, but I was told by a cinematographer that it was a family business passed down from one generaton to the next, so I kind of got the idea I could become an actor."

Brolin joined the Drama Department in high school and shortly after appeared in a play. "It was sheer terror," he remembers. "I wasn't that shy, I was just scared." Terrified or not he gave it another try and after graduation he enrolled in UCLA's Theater Arts program. "It was stagnant boredom," he says. "I wasn't learning anything so I quit and enrolled in several actors workshops. I eventually got a couple of television commercials and an agent." Signed by Twentieth Century-Fox Studios, Brolin was occasionally given a line or two in such movies as *Take Her, She's Mine* with Sandra Dee. Then came *Von Ryan's Express* which he was featured in opposite Frank Sinatra. "We filmed in Italy and Spain and I loved it. It was like, 'Join the movies and see the world.' "

Then in 1966 at age twenty-six he was sent to Johannisberg, South Africa with Jacqueline Bisset to star in a low budget film called *Cape Town Affair*. "I was the male protagonist and it was the first time I had the acting reins in my hands. It felt great!"

The phone rings from the kitchen and Brolin gets up and walks out of the living room and down a passageway lined with French windows that open onto a patio. A gardner is trimming the heavy foliage of plants and shrubs that surround a shimmering pool. In the kitchen Brolin picks up the phone and the two parrots cease their squawking and fidget nervously on their pedestals. The kitchen looks like a well-stocked delicatessen with strings of peppers and garlic cloves hanging in profusion from the ceiling's heavy oak beams. Thumb-tacked to a cork bulletin board near the refrigerator are several pictures of Clint Eastwood, a close personal friend of Brolin. There is also a picture of Jane, Brolin's wife of seventeen years. Brolin glances momentarily at his wife's picture then sighs and turns away.

"I suppose the world knows now," he says. "Jane and I have finally decided to separate. We have always had a different kind of marriage, not your normal Ma and Pa Kettle at home kind. We both have different lifestyles and interests. I'm in Los Angeles all week long filming *Hotel,* and she is in San Luis Obispo where she runs a restaurant. She also has her own hobbies such as collecting wild cats, not domestic tabbies but wild mountain lions. She has always had her own identity, and doesn't just want to be known as James Brolin's wife." The Brolins have two sons, Josh and Jess.

Brolin agrees he will have to give up his huge lodge-style home. "It's too big anyway," he admits. "We always lived in the kitchen." Brolin designed the kitchen himself, a warm comfortable space, more like a huge family room. He also designed a new, smaller home that he is building behind the present one. He got his idea for the new house at a restaurant and sketched the plans on a napkin.

Until his marriage settlement is determined, Brolin spends weekends at a small beach house in Santa Barbara. There he can look out over the surf which is only a few yards away and muse about his life—and his future.

"You know, when things are really rotten and everyone's saying it's *not* going to work out fine, I just ease back and remind myself to smile. You see, deep inside I know something they don't know—I know it's going to work out just fine." He pauses, and smiles, real big, and the weight of the last few moments seems to have been lifted from his shoulders. "I *know* I am going to play *The Hunchback of Notre Dame.*"

And the parrots take up their screeching again—and strangely, it sounds like applause.

Don and Elizabeth Murray.

Don Murray

The Quiet Man with Quiet Dreams

During the course of the interview session with actor Don Murray, I asked questions about his acting experiences with Marilyn Monroe in "Bus Stop." He answered with several marvelous visual anecdotes, any of which would have made a great lead to this profile. But, the story wasn't about a sex goddess, so I saved them for later in the piece. I was having difficulty writing the lead until I talked with Murray's wife, Elizabeth. She told me the story about her husband "selecting" her from photographs in fashion magazines.

"He picked me out of magazine," Elizabeth Murray says, her voice on the edge of laughter, her dusty-blue eyes dancing. "He picked six different pictures of models from magazines like Vogue, Mademoiselle, Bazaar—but..." she leans in close to my ear and says in a conspiratorial tone, almost a whisper: "What he didn't know was that five of those pictures were of one model—me!"

Actor Don Murray selected his wife from a magazine? A modern mail-order bride? What kind of a person *is* Don Murray?

"Shallow," Elizabeth says quickly. Then, "No! No. Joking. Just joking." She is having fun.

"Is he shy?" I ask.

"Uh uh...smart."

Elizabeth Murray, actor Don Murray's wife of the last twenty-two years, is sitting at the dining room table of their Spanish-styled Montecito home. She is tall, and blond, and slender—sleek might fit her better—with the chiseled cheekbones of a high-fashion model.

"But why was he looking for models in a magazine? How..." my question is interrupted when Don Murray walks into the room. He is also tall, and dark, and slim—lanky might fit *him* better—and he is dressed in a blue-denim shirt, levis and tennis shoes. With boots he would still look like that same exuberant cowboy who chased Marilyn Monroe in the 1956 hit movie, "Bus Stop."

"Bus Stop," which was based on the successful Broadway stage play by William Inge, was Don Murray's first movie. Since then he has starred in such critically acclaimed films as "Hatful of Rain," and "Shake Hands With The Devil." He says his most satisfying movie was "The Hoodlum Priest," which he wrote, produced and starred in. On Broadway, where his acting career began, he has been featured in such stage classics as, "The Hasty Heart," "The Rose Tattoo," and "Same Time, Next Year."

Because he feels that television movies are now dealing with important social concepts, such as teenage alcoholism ("License to Kill"), he made five television movies in 1983-84, including "Somebody Knows" with Angie Dickenson. For two and a half years he was also the star of the hit series, "Knott's Landing."

Don Murray motions me to the couch in front of the fireplace, while Elizabeth glides out of the room. "I'll get you something refreshing to sip on while you talk," she says, disappearing around the kitchen door like a curl of smoke.

I make a mental note to ask her—and him—how they came to meet in a magazine, then slip my mini-tape recorder on a table beside Murray. The red record light glows reassuringly.

I can't help but notice the huge painted wood cutout of Murray's dog that hangs over the fireplace in front of us. "That's Samantha," he says. "We call her, 'Sam.' A Heinz variety." There is a piano in one corner near the fireplace, on which rest several framed family portraits. There is also a dresser and a glass cabinet with more family pictures, and a wood screen, with cutouts from magazines, decorates a wall. Everything in the room seems to have been gathered from various places, a self-styled "homey" decor that would give an interior decorator an Excedrin headache. "Early eclectic," Elizabeth had called it.

Elizabeth walks back into the room and sets two bright pink drinks on the coffee table in front of us. "Cranberry juice, soda, a little lemon and orange, and a sprig of mint. Our favorite refresher." And she vanishes again.

I turn my attention to Don Murray and the interview, and say: "You don't seem to be like the wild and crazy cowboy you portrayed in 'Bus Stop.'"

"Nope, that wasn't me. Fact is, that was the opposite of me." He runs his fingers through his gray-streaked hair. It falls haphazardly back in place.

"When Josh Logan, the director, called me in to screen test for the film, I thought, 'Wow!' this wild, extroverted cowboy was not what I had played on stage. My Broadway roles had all been introverted characters. Besides, when I read for the part, I was very skinny. I mean real skinny. A real scrawny kid. I didn't look like I came off a ranch, I looked like I came out of a concentration camp.

"I have to give Josh Logan complete credit for my getting the role," he continues, relaxing a little as he begins focusing on images from the past. "For the screen test, Logan put me into this big sheepskin jacket. It was hot under the lights, I mean real hot, and I started to take it off, and Logan yelled 'Don't take the jacket off!'

"You must be a sadist, I thought.

"Just keep the jacket on," he said. I had to admit the jacket made me look huge, like rubber man in a Michelin tire ad. I was 6' 2" plus cowboy boots and that helped."

Murray got the part, and Logan took him aside and said: "Don, everybody who has played this part on the stage has tried to do it with sensitivity. Forget that. You're a bull in a china closet. I want you to come on that screen like Attila the Hun. I want you to be the biggest, the loudest, and the wildest cowboy ever." The part as Logan visualized it, called for total energy, and no inhibitions. "I just played any wild impulse that came to mind," Murray remembers. "I'd let Logan decide if it was too much. I'd come up with nine crazy things for a scene and he'd throw out eight of them, but with the ninth one he'd say, 'Yeah, do that.'"

Because of this unrestrained characterization, Murray was almost kicked off the film. After two weeks, the studio brass called Logan and told him to replace Murray. "This is Cinemascope! The wide screen!" they argued. "Murray is too *big*, he's too *loud*, he's too *everything*." Logan replied that Murray was playing the role exactly the way he wanted. Fortunately, the head of the studio, Buddy Adler, agreed. Murray stayed on.

Then there was Marilyn Monroe. The part of Cheri in *Bus Stop* was Marilyn's comeback role. She had quit the movies the year before and had gone to New York to study in the Actors Studio. *Bus Stop* became her shining moment.

Don Murray agrees. "I think she was one of the screen's best comediennes and *Bus Stop* proved it. But, you have to keep in mind that a movie is the only entertainment medium where you can take little pieces and put them together again like a puzzle. Marilyn needed editing. Not in a million years could she have become an effective stage actress. I think she would have continued as a marvelous film comedienne, and a great character actress, even into her sixties or seventies. The big question—and we'll never know the answer—was whether she could have emotionally handled that she was no longer a glamour queen."

He pauses for a moment, then says: "She had this aura..." And the images begin to flicker across his mind, impressions from the past. "I was in her dressing room, and she was stretched out on this white couch...She had just come from the shower wrapped in a white terry-cloth robe, and she had that marvelous platinum hair. No makeup on, just a little baby oil on her face, that smooth lineless face...It was an impressive picture, totally breathtaking." He pauses.

"That was the second time I met her. That aura wasn't apparent the first time. It was a few weeks before we started filming, and I was briefly introduced to her in front of her dressing room on the studio lot. The press agents had gotten us together for publicity photos. It was all a big rush." Murray starts talking rapidly, acting out all the parts: Marilyn, the press agents, himself:

" 'Marilyn, this is Don.'

" 'Don, this is Marilyn.'

" 'Howdy do, Don.'

" 'Howdy do, Marilyn.'

" 'Hey Don, throw her over your shoulder. Good. Great! Click, click, click, click.'

" 'Okay, Marilyn, we gotta go.'

" 'Bye Don.'

" 'Bye Marilyn.'

"And that was it." He claps his hands. "Boom, boom, boom—over."

"Was she heavy?" I ask.

He grins. "Never had time to notice."

"Was she difficult to work with?"

"Very difficult," he says, taking a sip of his drink. "Oh, not in the sense of being deliberately difficult. She wasn't temperamental. Actually she was very likeable. But, she was a child woman, it was like working with a child. The reason was her upbringing. She had had very little education, no emotional stability—her mother went to an insane asylum and her father denied her all her life. She was very insecure, and that insecurity made the filming of *Bus Stop* difficult from two aspects.

"First, she was always late. I don't mean fifteen minutes late, I mean three hours late!" Murray shakes his head. "Our call would be for 8:00a.m. and she wouldn't be ready until 10:00 or 11:00. She would come to the studio on time, then dilly dally around in her dressing room, fussing with her costume, her makeup. Basically, she was putting off getting in front of the camera. She was terrified of the camera."

Murray leans forward, elbows on his knees. "It was also very difficult for me as an actor. I had come from the theater where there is continuity; you get up in front of an audience for two hours, but in a movie, you go for ten seconds, then cut, then start again for another ten seconds." He leans back in the couch. "Frankly, I didn't think it was going to work.

"Oh, I could see Marilyn had marvelous moments, but these were followed by emotional outbreaks, writhing around, stumbling over lines. I couldn't envision the total impact of her performance, but it turned out to be brilliant. That's where the magic of the director comes into play.

"Josh Logan had given orders never to stop a scene. No matter what went wrong, the cameraman, or the soundman, or the actor, could not stop the scene. We had to keep going to save the precious little bits and pieces that worked for Marilyn. Logan handled her beautifully, and everyone said it was her best-behaved film." He throws up his hands. "Best behaved? Wow! All I knew, I was totally exhausted when it was over."

Exhausted or not, Murray had discovered something unique about acting. On the stage, or in the movies his acting caused an emotional catharsis. He explains it this way: "As you go through life you have feelings and frustrations bottled up inside that you cannot fully express. They can be positive feelings like love, or negative feelings like anger. Instead of expressing these feelings, we censor ourselves. We don't want to be embarrassed by showing a full range of emotions. So, we cut them off unsaid, or unfinished, and seldom realize the cathartic effect—the release that comes from full expression.

"Now, an actor can achieve this full range of emotion in full view of an audience. He can achieve an emotional involvement that has a beginning and an end. When it is over there is a feeling of exhaustion, but there is also a kind of spiritual uplift, a cleansing. That is the catharsis of acting.

"You know, I always knew I was going to be an actor. My mother was a Ziegfeld girl, and my father was a dance director for Fox Studios. When the Depression came along in 1929 they moved to Long Island. The whole family took it for granted I would be an actor, although they wouldn't let me be a child actor because they wanted me to have a normal childhood."

Murray graduated from high school at age sixteen and immediately enrolled in the American Academy of Dramatic Arts in New York. He also toured with a summer stock company to perfect his acting techniques. (The company included two other new faces: Jason Robards and Tom Poston.) A year after he graduated from the Academy he auditioned for a part in the movie, *Lights Out,* which starred a young actress named, Anne Francis. "It's funny," he says, "but I was Anne's first date in Long Island. We were neighbors then, both thirteen years old, and we went to a Halloween party and bobbed for apples. Now she lives in Santa Barbara too, just a few doors from my house."

Murray didn't get the movie part opposite Anne Francis, but he was offered a seven-year studio contract at $150.00 a week. That was ten times what he was making at odd jobs. Yet, he turned it down.

"I wanted to work in the theatre until I perfected my acting craft," Murray says. "The agent who made the offer was in shock. He pulled out a couple of other contracts, wagged them at me, and said he had just signed two young actors and was going to make big stars out of them. (Their names were, Tony Curtis and Piper Laurie.)" Still Murray turned the offer down, convinced he could succeed on his own terms.

It took two years before he got his next chance.

"I finally read for Tennessee Williams' 'The Rose Tattoo' and got a feature part," he remembers with relief. "The play was a huge success and won the Tony Award.

He was offered another, more lucrative, movie contract. Again, he turned it down. "They said, 'Who do you think you are, Marlon Brando?' I said, 'No, but I am going back to Broadway and practice my craft until I *am* Marlon Brando.' "

It would be another two years before he got to act again.

Because of his deep conviction about the brutality of war and killing, Murray had registered as a Conscientious Objector. When the Korean War broke out, he tried unsuccessfully to get to Korea as an ambulance driver or a Red Cross paramedic. He then applied through the Brethren Service Church as a kind of peace corps worker. He was accepted and sent to Europe.

"I worked with refugees in temporary barbed-wire encampments in Naples, Italy," Murray says. "They were homeless and destitute and the most I could do was try to get them re-established, and help them with food and clothing. I'd go down to the Navy kitchen with huge garbage pails—clean ones—and dump in the left overs. It was all very nutritious, but the chicken-ala-king would be glued to the pie-ala-mode. The one thing I couldn't give them was what they wanted the most——freedom."

(Murray later got the chance to provide that freedom, when he instituted a refugee resettlement project on the island of Sardinia in the Mediterranean in 1958. He established the project with the well-known social worker, Beldon Paulson, and used the money he and his first wife, Hope Lange, earned from the movie, *Bus Stop*.)

Emotionally involved with the plight of the refugees, and tormented by their anguish, he decided to extend his service for another six months. During that time he suffered two serious bouts with hepatitis. With regret, he decided to return to America.

He arrived back on Broadway looking more like a skeleton than an actor. Yet, it took him only five days to land one of the leads in "The Skin of Our Teeth," a play starring Mary Martin and Helen Hayes. From there it was only a few years until *Bus Stop*—and stardom.

He also married actress Hope Lange. "I had met Hope right out of high school on Long Island," Murray says. "We were engaged before we were both cast separately for *Bus Stop*. Even Logan didn't know. We were married during the filming.

"I still have a very good relationship with Hop," he says. "We recently starred together in the Broadway play 'Same Time, Next Year.' And we played a man and wife in a 1983 movied titled 'I am The Cheese.' Betty also has a good relationship with Hope, and she and one of my daughters recently stayed in Hope's New York apartment."

Murray has two children from his marriage with Hope Lange: a boy, Christopher, an actor who performed in the NBC production of "Mr. Roberts," and a daughter, Patricia, who is an actress in Los Angeles. He and Elizabeth have three children; a daughter, Connie, who, like her mother, is a model with the Ford Agency in New York and is also a singer; a son, Sean, a musician and composer who wrote the original music for the second season of "Knott's Landing;" and their youngest son, Michael, still in high school, who has acting aspirations. One has the feeling an acting dynasty is developing in a very gifted family.

"I wrote a television pilot of a series about a family of unusually gifted children," he says, draining the last of the cranberry juice from his glass. "It was called, 'City Lights, Country Road,' and was based on the musical talents of my own family. It was bought by CBS, then they decided they weren't doing family dramas." He sighs and shrugs.

For a brief moment, I can see the disappointment in his eyes, then it is gone, replaced by the light of some new dream. And he says quietly, "I'm having a fulfilling career. It can only keep getting better."

Elizabeth walks back into the room. "How about another cranberry juice?" she says.

"I think we're about wound down here," I say looking at the tape in the recorder. "But, I have one burning question left: How, and why, did your husband pick you from a magazine?"

She smiles and the blue eyes light up again. "Well, Don was working on "The Hoodlum Priest," and was recovering from his divorce. He was very unhappy. His partner, who knew every model in New York, jokingly threw him a bunch of magazines and told him to pick out six models. Five of the six were me."

"He didn't recognize you as the same person?"

"I was wearing different hats, clothes, even different hair colors. We didn't meet for six months, but I think he knew what he was looking for."

I had to know: "What happened to the one model he didn't pick. The sixth one?"

She grins at her husband. "We were on our honeymoon in Venice, when I saw her walking down the street. I pointed her out to Don."

"She was gorgeous," Murray says. Big smile.

"He laughed about trading me in for a new model." She winks at him. "But he didn't."

Monte Hale today.

Monte Hale

"Shoot low, they might be crawlin'"

Monte Hale looks like a cowboy legend. When I first met him, he wore a white hat, snakeskin boots, a gold belt buckle that looked like it came from a heavyweight fight, and a dazzling white cowboy outfit. (Not the dime store Roy Rogers kind with fringe.) He looked impressive, and he radiated a real down-home warmth. When I mentioned I'd like to interview him, he grinned real big and said, "Why sure, pardner. You just come on over to my place for chili!" I did.

They rode tall in the saddle, tracking down yellow-bellied varmints and double-dealing desperadoes in an unending series of shoot-'em-ups and showdowns. They didn't cotton to cuss words, or drink red-eye whiskey, or kiss cowgirls, but they always stood tall for the underdog. These movieland myths on horseback were known as the Hollywood singing cowboys, and one of the last of the breed was a tall, lanky cowboy who rode out of Texas with a guitar on his back.

"Pardner! Come on over for chili!" Monte Hale says in that aw-shucks, hot-dang-gol-darn-you'all Texas drawl that is as mellow as a dripping honeycomb. "I make chili *good*. That's why they won't let me *near* a chili-making contest." The lines on his face wrinkle into a winsome grin, the same grin he so often used on celluloid outlaws just before he duked them out.

He hands me a picture postcard of a youthful Monte Hale taken in the mid-1940s when he was making "horse operas" for Republic Picture Studios. He also slips me a silver and blue metallic looking sticker with the words: *SHOOT LOW! They might be crawlin'.*

"I pass out these stickers, kind of a calling card, must have given away a hundred thousand of them." He takes off his pearl-grey cowboy hat and brushes his hand through his thick white hair.

"I think the original joke was, 'Shoot low, sheriff, they're ridin' shetlands.' " A great rumbling laugh shakes his six-foot-four frame all the way down to his catfish-skin cowboy boots. "I was acting in one of my westerns and we had just dismounted and pulled out our guns, and I said to my partners: 'Shoot low, they might be crawlin.' The script girl thumbed pages looking for the dialogue, but the director liked it and left it in." He puts his cowboy hat back on his head. "Remember now—come on over to our spread for chili."

Monte Hale's "spread" is a Montecito beach house over-looking the Pacific surf where he lives with his wife, Joanne. I rap the bulls-head knocker and the door swings open and my hand is engulfed in a warm handshake. "Come on in!" Monte Hale says leading me into a brilliantly lit living room with wide picture windows overlooking the ocean. The room itself, as well as the adjoining rooms, contain an amazing museum of western memorabilia. "Everything here is Western, either cowboy or Indian." He pats the head of a life-size plaster figure of an Indian dressed in a plaid shirt, Levis and a cowboy hat. A holster and gun hang over the Indian's shoulder and a fifth of whiskey rests in the crook of one arm as he sits realistically in a rocking chair by the picture window. "I call him the Guardian of the Night," Monte drawls. "You should see him with a rifle in his lap. Folks looking up at this second-story window get quite a shock."

The walls are filled with paintings of western scenes. Huge bronze statuary, including a scaled-down, gold-plated model of a champion brahma bull, sit on coffee tables and cabinets. High on one wall are the movie posters of the nineteen films he starred in during his seven-year tenure with Republic. The movies have names like, *California Firebrand, The Missourian,* and *Home on the Range.* Below the posters hang a row of six-guns, including one Colt .45 that was used by Al Jennings, a real-life train robber.

And in the den are wall-to-wall autographed photos of Hollywood's famous: Mae West, John Wayne, Elizabeth Taylor, Jonathan Winters—the names go on and on. There are two autographed pictures of Ronald Reagan, one of a youthful "Ronnie" in a cowboy outfit, and then a "Presidential" portrait autographed to Monte and Joanne. "I sent him a signed picture of me inscribed, 'From one old marshal to another,' and he sent those back."

Monte pulls a Buntline Colt .45 out of a beautifully leather-tooled holster and twirls the gun on his finger before deftly slipping it back in an imaginary holster at his side. He grins that disarming grin he used in the movies, and for a fleeting moment, the six-guns blazing, Monte Hale of the Saturday western shines through. Like all cowboy heroes he had the ability to project a disarming niceness while at the same time suggesting that crossing him would be dangerous.

"Naw, I never could put it across very well that I was dangerous," he says putting the gun back in the leather holster. "I was just an easy-going cowboy. 'Course I could get pretty nasty—not mean like the villain—but nasty enough to put on a good screen fight. At the same time I was laughing and smiling inside. I also sang in every movie I made, pretty little songs that we'd throw in just before I had to shoot up an outlaw, or knock him out in a barroom brawl."

Monte raises his fists in a wide-armed fighting stance. "I was taught to movie fight by a cowboy named Yakima Canutt who was the world champion bronc rider in 1919." He motions to an imaginary camera, demonstrating. "You see, the camera is behind me— here, stand in front of me and throw a punch." I hesitate, but he nods to go ahead, so I throw a looping right at his chin which he quickly blocks with his left forearm, then counters with a right hand that whizzes by my chin. The doubled-up fist looks like a bowling pin as it goes past. "Hey, you're supposed to duck," he says.

Maybe Yakima Canutt was a better teacher, I think.

"Now, suppose the camera is at your side, in profile..."

"Suppose I sit down," I say.

"Naw, I won't hurt you. Just swing easy...com'on, throw a punch."

Reluctantly, I smolder another shot on his forearm and he slides a freight car past my nose, but this time I bob my head to the left as the express passes.

"Hey, that's better, a whole lot better, pardner."

"Just a survival instinct," I say. "Did you ever accidently punch someone out?" I ask as I settle down into the security of an overstuffed couch.

"Nope, never did," he says plopping into an armchair. "Had my nose broken once. Good friend did it in a wagon fight in the studio. The stage hands were rocking the coach and my friend missed his footing and caught me square in the nose and broke it. The director liked all the bleedin' and spurtin' and left it in the movie."

There was little blood, either real or of the ketchup variety, in the rough-riding, six-gun blazing, shoot-'em-ups that Monte starred in. The action, along with the dialogue was totally predictable.

"Now, in every cowboy movie you see, the hero comes into town on his horse," Monte says leaning forward in his chair. "He's riding down the street just a bird-doggin' and lookin' around kinda quiet like, and there's a couple of guys over on the old board sidewalk, and they start jabbin' each other with their elbows and one says, 'I think that's him,' and the other keeps noddin' kinda bug-eyed."

Monte made his movies at the end of the era of "B" ("stands for budget," he says) Westerns that spanned almost fifty years. It all began with William Farnum who starred in 1903 in the original western, *The Great Train Robbery*. William S. Hart, the first "Robin Hood of the West" stereotype, quickly followed, then came the legendary Tom Mix who became the prototype for the non-smoking, non-cussing, non-drinking, white-hatted hero. Buck Jones and Hoot Gibson followed in his hoofprints, both steely-eyed and silent, their guns blazing white smoke.

The great days of the westerns arrived with the advent of sound, for, after all, westerns thrived on dialogue. The talkies also gave birth to the singing cowboy who not only knew how to use a six-gun but who could sing some of the humdinginist, spur-jangling melodies that ever wafted over western skies. Gene Autry started the genre followed by Roy Rogers and Dale Evans. Then came Rex Allen and a fresh new face—Monte Hale.

He sinks lower in his chair and adds, "My contract called for $100 a week with a $25 raise every six months. After six years I wasn't making $350 a week. But I did right well with personal appearances at rodeos and fairs and I did make some good investments."

One lucrative endeavor was Monte Hale comic books. On the wall of his den are two framed comic books with a color photo of Monte adorning the cover. Every month six million copies in twenty-seven languages were printed. "All I did was pose for the picture on the cover and they gave me a royalty on each copy sold. So, I guess if you add it all up I did right well with those nineteen movies."

After Monte left Republic in 1950, he worked on several television shows including a few episodes of "Gunsmoke." "Gene Autry also offered me a television series with his horse, Champion, and a role playing opposite Gail Davis in the successful 'Anne Oakley' show. I have always regretted turning those shows down as I have always admired Gene."

Monte looks at a picture of himself with James Dean taken for the movie, *Giant.* "I worked for six months with Rock Hudson and Elizabeth Taylor in *Giant,*" Monte remembers. "That was some movie. The last film I did was in 1965. It was called *The Chase* and starred Marlon Brando. It was also Robert Redford's first movie." He pauses for a moment. "I guess what I needed was the right management and the guts to go on. I really didn't hit the long ball in the movies..." He shakes his head. "But, you know, I feel darn lucky to have been able to do anything at all. Like the old cowboy says, 'I really believe I was born to plow.' And that's the truth. My goals weren't much beyond plowing when I was growing up."

When young Monty Ely Hale was nine years old his major goal was to get lucky enough to earn a dime so he could go to the Saturday matinee cowboy movie. "I had to hustle to get a dime," he remembers. "Never had enough for popcorn, but I sure could go into the lobby and smell it." He grins.

What Ely Hale really wanted was to play the guitar. "One day an old man who I'd heard play the guitar invited me into his house and said, 'Son, pick up that guitar over there,' and I did. It felt like a million dollars holding that guitar in my arms. Then the old man showed me how to make a G chord." Monte clamps his thumb and forefinger around the throat of an imaginary guitar. "I strummed it. It sounded a little tinny. But in a little over a month I had memorized four more chords, eyes closed. So, I saved everything I could scrape up and finally bought myself a guitar from Sears & Roebuck for $8.50."

Monte taught himself to play that guitar and when he was nineteen he got an opportunity to sing and play in a Galveston vaudeville theater. "I was so proud, and I can remember after the first show I was sitting around in the lobby of the Jean Laffite Hotel with my guitar in my lap saying 'Howdy' to folks when a gentleman stopped by me and said, 'I'm Phil Isley.'

"I said, 'Yes sir.'

"He said, 'I've got a troupe of movie stars coming in on an army bus to take part in a War Bond drive and I need a guitar player. Can you do it?'

" 'I think you're at the right window,' I said, 'and if you're waitin' on me you're backing up.' And pretty soon this load of movie stars file into the hotel including one of my heroes—cowboy star Johnny Mack Brown. I just stood there with my mouth open."

Monte Hale toured with the group for thirty-five days. "I was just like a kid catching his first bass," he says. "I just loved mingling with them stars. And during the tour we sold sixty million dollars worth of war bonds, and I was glad to be just a pinpoint part of it. Besides, here I was riding on the same bus with Johnny Mack Brown, just sitting right next to him. One day he said to me—'Son, always remember that *what* you are speaks so loudly I can't hear what you say,' and I said right back, 'Mr. Mack Brown, you are *so right!*' I imagine it took me an hour and a half to figure out what he had said."

Phil Isley, who had hired Monte, liked his young guitarist so much that he wired the boss of Republic Pictures, Herbert Yates, recommending Monte for a screen test. "Mr. Yates sent back a telegram," Monte says. "He wrote that if I wanted to take a gamble and make the trip to Hollywood, I might get a chance to work in the movies."

Monte was able to borrow enough money from a friend to make the trip, and when he stepped off the plane the only luggage he carried was his guitar, and in the guitar case was a toothbrush and a shirt. "My grandmother had made me an old cowboy shirt several years before. She cut the tassels off a bathrobe belt and sewed them on the shoulders for fringe. It was a two-tone dirty color like early fungus, but it was my first cowboy shirt." The next day he went to see Herbert Yates.

"I was as nervous as a prostitute in a prayer meeting when I got to the studio," Monte remembers. "When I got there Mr. Yates was sittin' in one of those director chairs directing a picture and chewing tobacco, looking for a place to spit. And he had six guys around him with spitoons so you *knew* he was important. I walked up to him kinda scared and said, 'Mr. Yates, I'm Monte Hale and I got a telegram from you. It's a little wrinkly now—but you can read it...' "

Yates looked at the tall cowboy and at the dog-earred telegram. He spit, then took Monte to the set of a western he was filming called *The Big Bonanza.* He stood him up against a bar in a saloon set and said, "Sing."

"I sang four verses of 'The Old Chisom Trail,' " Monte says. "They filmed it and liked it so well it was left in the movie and I got a screen credit. That's how it all started. After that I did *Home on the Range,* the first cowboy film in color." He stretches his arms over his head. "I'll tell you, pardner, I been pretty lucky." He looks at the tape recorder and says, "That thing about out of tape? Chili must be simmering good."

I tell him I have a few more questions, and he settles back down. "Shoot, pardner."

"Why Santa Barbara," I ask.

"Well, Joanne and I lived in Santa Monica until two years ago, but the traffic was always bumper to bumper, and we were always coming or going. I like a town where the dentist, durgstore and the groceries are right next to one another."

Joanne, Monte's attractive wife, walks into the room from the kitchen. The spicy aroma of chili follows her. She is tall and slender with vibrant red hair. Monte looks at her affectionately. "You see, Joanne and I can build a life here, just the two of us."

Joanne sits down next to her husband and says, 'This way we're building new friends together. Before we were married five years ago, I had my friends and Monte had his friends. Santa Barbara is the right place to meet new friends together."

"I met Joanne on a golf driving range," Monte says, "I was leaning back on a bench, eyes closed, getting a little sun, and I heard someone trying to hit a golf ball, and I squinted one eye open and there was this pretty red-haired lady standing there trying to hit a golf ball, and she's hitting it about four feet. I said kinda quiet like, 'Pardon me, but you're not hitting that ball too good so why don't you sit down for a while, and we'll visit a bit.' And she did. 'Why don't you fly down to Memphis with me?' I kidded her. 'I'm going there for a film festival.' And she said, 'Why, I couldn't do that.' I said, 'Don't worry about it, we'll take separate airplanes.' She started laughing and has been laughing ever since."

"I had never seen his kind of life before," Joanne adds. "I told him I wanted to see everything that he has ever set eyes upon."

Monte grins. 'I told her that's a pretty tall order, but we'll just give it a try. And we have. She goes everywhere with me, to rodeos, fairs, parades, all sorts of guest appearances. She even goes with me visiting hospitals.

"You know, I have been in every Shriners Hospital in the country and most every childrens hospital. If I see a kid that will never walk again or someone with a terminal illness, and if I can meet them or talk to them, or even lay a hand on them—even if they don't know me from Adam—well I can't tell you how good that makes me feel. Sure, I've cried walking out of hospitals, tears running off my chin, but I've never turned down a visit. It makes me feel good to help. God, I hope I live another thirty or forty years just so I can keep on doing this."

Monte Hale is silent for a moment. Joanne sits next to him and touches her hand to his arm. Then he leans forward, his fingers intermeshed tightly together and he recalls a poem he wrote many years ago:

"Life is like a journey taken on a train,
With a pair of travelers at each window-pane,
I may sit beside you the whole journey through,
Or I may sit elsewhere, never knowing you.
But if fate should mark all of us,
To sit here side by side,
Then let's be pleasant travellers,
Because it's such a short old ride."

He presses folded fingers to his lips and his eyes are misty. Then he leans back and claps his hands.

"Pardner, let's have that chili!" he says rising, taking Joanne's hand.

And so we do. Sitting there overlooking the foaming surf and the brilliant western sky, we had chili.

And let me tell you one thing for sure "pardners," that chili—it was *good!*

Karl Malden on the television show "Streets of San Francisco."

Karl Malden

Everyman

An interview with Karl Malden is not a question and answer session, nor is it a conversation. It's a dialogue. Malden's intensity, his nose to nose responses to my questions, made me feel like I was on stage playing a part opposite a great entertainer. As a sometime community theater actor, I was able to live out a performing fantasy. I didn't win an academy award, but Karl Malden did.

Karl Malden pads toward me in stocking feet. He looks just as I expected: tall, with the face of Everyman. He could pass for the owner of the Mom & Pop grocery store on the corner, your favorite bank teller, a country doctor, a minister....

"A walrus," the Academy Award-winning actor says.

"What?"

"A walrus," he repeats, smiling, leading you away from the open front door to the living room of his Santa Barbara home. "I just agreed to play a walrus in the new TV production of *Alice in Wonderland* for CBS."

Surprisingly, that seems to fit. Not only are his facial features—including his distinctive bulbous nose—seemingly able to change instantly with any mood, but his versatility is legendary. His acting talent makes even a walrus take on new possibilities.

The recipient of the Drama Critics Circle Award, the Donaldson Award, and the Critics Award for his outstanding work in Broadway plays, the seventy-one year old actor also won an Academy Award for best supporting actor in the classic film *A Streetcar Named Desire* and a best actor nomination for his portrayal of the feisty yet sensitive priest in *On the Waterfront.*

Critics and fellow actors acclaim him for an intensity of characterization seldom matched. An actor for nearly five decades, he has performed in an array of roles that stretches from the brutal villain in the *Hanging Tree* to the compassionate Omar Bradley in *Patton.* Yet it took the role of Mike Stone in the long-running 1970s television series "Streets of San Francisco" to make his face a household image. And then came even more recognition with his popular commercials for American Express Travelers Cheques.

"Ah," he says. "Never leave home without it."

Impressed by his remarkable accomplishments, I follow him as he shuffles along in his sweat sox across the hardwood floor of his spacious, sunny living room to a smaller room. This room seems a bit spartan in its furnishings: there are no rugs or window drapes, just a couple of straight-back wooden chairs, a coffee table, a television set, and an overstuffed sofa. I look down and notice a pair of worn tennis shoes on the floor next to the couch. "Just finished a little gardening," he says noticing my stare.

Malden motions me to one of the hardwood maple chairs. He plops on the couch, and lifts his stocking feet onto the coffee table. He immediately strikes me as being warm, friendly, comfortable—and at home. I turn the mini-tape recorder on and and watch the red record light blink on. He smiles and waits for my first question:

"Was your face recognizable to movie fans before you started doing the American Express ad?"

"People would occasionally walk up to me, look kind of hard, then say, "Aren't you from Kalamazoo, Michigan? Or, 'Do you work in the First National Bank?' "

"People recognize you now."

"Young kids see me on the street, do a double take as they walk by, then I can hear them behind me..." he lowers his voice into a hushed whisper, '*Don't leave home without it.*' "

"That must feel good."

"I love it."

So does American Express. Malden's catch phrase, "Don't leave home without it," has become part of the American pop vocabulary.

Malden's appeal as a spokesman centers around his ability to make a mass audience feel as if it is one person. He appears to speak to each viewer on a one-to-one personal level.

"I guess the American Express people wanted an actor who also projected sincerity and honesty," Malden says.

"A face people could trust?"

"Trust. Ah, yes..." He nods his head, and thrusts his chin forward. "Yes, Trust..."

A father image.

"Trust me..."

A priest's image.

"Trust me..." He stretches his arms outward, eyes to the ceiling and says in a pontifical tone, "*Trust* me my friends!" Then he laughs. That was fun.

It was also vintage Karl Malden, the consummate character actor practicing his craft. Malden has been a character actor all his life. "I knew I was never going to be a leading man," he says. When a director has a particularly difficult part, he calls on Karl Malden. When a producer wants recognizable talent, he calls on Karl Malden.

"If I may say—and this may sound a little egotistical—when the chips are down, *I produce!*" He tightens his lips, and his eyes suddenly become alive. "You gotta produce! You see what I mean? No matter how small the part, you gotta produce. Don't say it's a nothing part—produce!"

He swings his feet to the floor, and leans in close to my face, and for a moment he is Father Barry from *On The Waterfront* nose to nose with Marlon Brando, telling *him* what he has to do.

"You've got to work! I don't care if the part has four lines, or four pages, or forty, you've got to *work* on it. I always worked hard on a part. I figured it out. I figured out what I could do with it." He waves his arms around. "Sure, I was not always right, but I presented SOMETHING!"

He sighs, and leans back in the couch, letting the tension melt a bit. I relax too, feeling like I've just been a character opposite Malden in a short but very intense movie scene. Finally, Malden says: "To this day, after almost fifty years as an actor, the greatest pleasure I get is figuring it all out. I love the creating part."

"You have a certain...ah...intensity."

"Yes, that's me. That's me! I have that same intensity about life too." His feet go back to the coffee table, one sock crossed over the other. "When I talk to some people, they back away and tell me—'Hey, wait a minute, don't get mad.' I'm not *mad!* It's just...it's just the way I was trained as an actor. It was the training I had with the great director, Elia Kazan.

"Kazan's theory was that you work to *grab* the audience," Malden continues dropping his feet to the floor again. "Once you have *grabbed* them, never let them go." He clenches both fists together, his body hunched forward. "You grab and grab, until they can't take it anymore—then you *squeeze!*"

I look at his fists and ask if he can *feel* when he has an audience in his hands.

"You're damned right I can."

"How? A stage actor can't see the theater audience, except, perhaps the first rows in the glow of the stage lights."

"Ah...(long pause) by certain signs. When you hear the theater seats squeaking, and hear rustling and coughing, then you know you have lost them. But, if you hear silence...and it's black out there—by 'black' I mean there is nothing out there, no

44

sound—then you know you have them." He presses his lips together and is quiet for a moment, then says in a whisper, remembering a second, or a minute from the past. "Ahhh...the 'blackness'...the silence....those are the moments that last forever."

Karl Malden has had many such moments. In a career that has led him from the Broadway stage to the movies and television to spokesperson for American Express, Karl Malden has been "on stage" almost from the moment he graduated from high school in 1931.

Malden grew up in the steel town, Gary, Indiana, during the deepest part of the Depression. "When I got out of high school there was nothing to do," he remembers. "I didn't have enough money to go to college so I bummed around for eight months, stood on street corners watching the girls go by. My dad was lucky enough to hold his job as a milkman, made $14.00 a week. I finally got hired at the steel mills and worked for three years, but I realized I was getting nowhere fast. I needed a real career, a profession. I decided to be an actor."

"From a steel mill worker to an actor?"

"Genes had something to do with it," Malden replies. "I think my dad was a frustrated actor. The family dinner converstion was always about music or the theater. We were not far from Chicago and I used to go the the Goodman Theatre in the Art Institute and watch the students act. Finally, I went to the head of the school, and said, 'I'd like to be an actor, but I don't know whether I belong, and I don't have much money.' "

Malden stretches his legs across the length of the couch and continues, "He asked me if I was a gambler, and I said, 'No, I'm not.' He said: 'Would you gamble on *yourself?*' I nodded, and he told me that if I would pay for the first three-month term, he would evaluate my abilities and see if I was good enough to have a full scholarship. It was a good gamble. I stayed the whole three years and finished the acting program."

While enrolled in the acting school, Malden met a playwright named, Robert Ardrey. He told Malden he liked his acting style and if his new play was produced in New York he would give Malden a call. Three months after Malden finished school the call came, and the aspiring young actor was off to Broadway. After he arrived he was told the play was cancelled; the producer had backed out.

Malden had $350.00 in his pocket and decided to stick it out. A week later he went to work as the assistant manager in the play "Golden Boy." The job didn't pay a lot but it did include a small stage part. Even more important he met Elia Kazan who would play a great part in his career.

"The first seven years, I worked on anything," Malden remembers. "I didn't ask how much the money was, or how big the part was. They'd say, 'We've got something for you,' and I'd say, 'When do I go to work! I was in fourteen plays, one flop after another."

It was during these "lean years" that Malden fell in love with actress Mona Graham whom he had met at the Goodman Theatre. "I married Mona in 1938," Malden says, "and we're still together." The Malden's have two daughters, Mila, and Carla, who now have families of their own.

"Look, I'll tell you a story you can write," Malden says, sitting up straight in the couch. "It's a sad story, a *really sad* story. My wife and I were married on December 18th, when I was working on a play called *Gentle People,* and on December 25th after rehearsal we decided to go out and get something to eat. I asked her how much money she had. 'Forty cents,' she told me. I dug in my pocket and found sixty cents, so we walked to a place called Chock Full of Nuts and ordered a hot dog and a donut apiece. That was our first Christmas dinner. Sad, huh?" and he grins as he remembers that far away day.

In 1943 Malden joined the Army Air Corps and ended up in a military review called, "Winged Victory." After being discharged in 1945, Malden returned to Broadway and got a part in Arthur Miller's *All My Sons*. Then he did *Streetcar Named Desire,* which was directed by Elia Kazan. In 1945 Kazan hired him for a Hollywood film, the first of many. For the next decade Malden commuted between Hollywood and his home in New York, performing in first a play, then a movie, then another play.

"This was the period when I thought I didn't want to bastardize myself by becoming a movie actor," Malden says. "The theater was *the* place, the only place for actors, and Broadway had always been good to me from a career standpoint. The only problem was I hated New York.

"There was always a fight to get on a subway, then to get off; a fight to get a cab...you fought to put your quarter in the automat! Finally, in 1960 we gave it up and moved to Los Angeles, then later bought a weekend home in Santa Barbara.

"We bought this home to have a place to get away, a place of our own, not a hotel or resort. We never went to the movies in Los Angeles, but here my wife will say, 'Let's go to the three o'clock movie,' and we're off. I also like to do a little gardening—that's what I was doing before you arrived. I guess I'm just a small-town guy."

"Getting back to New York..."

"We really left New York because I was doing mostly movie work, and that was in Los Angeles." He was playing supporting roles in exceptional movies such as *Ruby Gentry* and *Fear Strikes Out* opposite exceptional actors and actresses: Vivian Leigh, Rod Steiger, Lee J. Cobb, Eva Marie Saint, Marlon Brando...

Ah, Marlon Brando. "How was he to work with?"

"Don't you think he's been talked about enough?" Malden shrugs. "What more can you say about him?"

I persist: "After all, Brando won't talk about himself."

"Okay, here's my version of Brando—he's a genius." Malden pauses, purses his lips, then continues. "Brando is without a doubt the most brilliant actor I have ever worked with. But...like a lot of geniuses, they go haywire. Look at another genius—Orson Wells. Marlon is brilliant, perhaps to the point that he feels he can't trust the abilities of any director. He's so talented, it's reached the point where he doesn't even work anymore."

"What does the word "talent" mean?"

"I don't know...(a long pause) It's a mystery to me. I know that an actor must have some basic natural talent. And luck. I have been lucky with my acting career. Luck had a lot to do with my going to the Goodman Theatre, with my talking to the playwright that got me to New York, then meeting Elia Kazan who kept using me in plays and movies."

He leans forward, more intense now. "I have taught acting in colleges and I don't know whether I am a good teacher or not, but I do have one quality"... He closes both fists and brings them up to his face. "I can *excite* young actors and actresses about the theater...Yes, I can excite them. I know that, I have done that, but whether I can teach them how to act...!

"The problem as to why young actors aren't more successful is that they don't have staying power. They don't have the desire, the perseverance, the discipline. They don't know how to be knocked down and get up again." He opens his fists and spreads his hands wide. "This generation of actors want it all handed to them. They literally want you to give them a job, and when they get a small part, they say, 'Ooohh, it's nothing, it's terrible.' " Malden sighs and relaxes back in the couch. "They have to learn it takes time.

"I have a theory, and I tell it to young people—the only way to hit a home run is to get up to bat. If they sit down and wait for a home run it will never happen. Go! Do! Get up to bat, and maybe the ball will take off for you."

"How did you 'get up to bat' for the television show, "Streets of San Francisco?"

"For a while I guess I didn't consider television legitimate theater. I had been called several times to do a show, but I always said no. I wasn't interested in TV. Then I was called to play this detective. I said I didn't want to play this detective role. I thought it would be a year's work, but the show was successful and lasted five years."

Then came American Express.

"While I was doing the detective show I was asked if I wanted to do a commercial. I had never done a commercial in my life. I said...'well, I don't know...a commercial...' " He wrinkles his nose distastefullly. "Then a friend reminded me that Laurence Olivier had done a commercial, so I said I'd look at the idea. They wanted Mike Stone, the detective from 'Streets' with the black coat and hat posing in front of a police station. I have always tried to keep away from being typecast, so I said, 'I'll compromise—no coat, no shots in front of the police station, but I'll wear the hat.' They bought it."

"The commercial has been, well...lucrative?"

Malden smiles, big. "It's been a wonderful association,and I've been happily doing it for over twelve years now. I've never worked for a better group of people."

"What's next for Karl Malden?"

"I'd love to do a situation television comedy," he says.

"Would you take anything that came along?"

"Well, being old and 'square' I wouldn't take any sex films, which seems to be all they're doing right now. But a good comedy show, no crazy gags, but a situation story that is funny, that I'd really like to do."

And will Karl Malden ever retire from show business?

He puts his stockinged feet on the floor, and slaps his knees. "No! I'll never quit. I would be absolutely bored. I wouldn't know what to do with myself. Even doing a little gardening can't keep me occupied."

He smiles that irresistible Karl Malden grin—EVERYMAN again.

"I'm the luckiest guy in the world." He stands up on the smooth hardwood floor and wiggles his toes. "Yeah, the luckiest guy in the world."

Fess Parker—from Davy Crockett to today's real estate developer.

Fess Parker

American Traditions

It took three years to get the Fess Parker interview. That's how long it took to have his convention center project on Cabrillo Boulevard approved by the city council and a voter referendum. He didn't want to talk before the issue was settled, and I agreed it would be best to wait. As soon as the convention center project was approved and the celebration over, I called for the interview. He said, "Let's do it. Now!"

"Dear Fess,
"Sorry I'm so long in answering..."
Fess Parker looks up from the bevel-edged card with the White House seal and says in his soft Texas drawl, "Uh...little hard to read her handwriting..." He turns the card toward you, showing the jumble of words, half printed, half in script. "Let's see..." and he continues.

"I've been a little busy here..." Parker stops reading again and peers over his granny glasses. "She is one fine, busy lady," he says, then goes back to the card.

"Thank you for helping..." he stumbles over the words again. "Uh...*helping with the tennis tournament. Couldn't have done it without you...* Well," He reads silently for a moment, then turns the card over showing the signature on the back—*Nancy.*

"The note goes on," Parker says, tapping the card on his thumbnail. "About her war on drugs. I guess we raised over $400,000 at that White House charity tournament, all of the money benefiting Nancy Reagan's Drug Abuse Fund." He glances at the signature on the card again. "She's a lovely lady, and we're so lucky to have her. Clearly, I'm not too objective, but I admire her for so many things."

Parker drops the card on one of the piles of paper that clutter his desk. Behind him is a bookcase with another disorderly heap of papers. Perched on one stack is a large color photograph of Parker chatting with Nancy Reagan. There is another half-hidden picture of Parker rejoicing with a friend the night Santa Barbara voters decided by a landslide margin to approve his Park Plaza Hotel project. Above the papers and photos the office wall is bare.

"This office is for a little corporation I formed," Parker says, noticing my stare. "I call it *American Traditions,* and I guess it represents how much this country has offered to previous generations—and to me. And to my children. It means you can start with nothing, pursue your dreams and achieve—anything."

Fess Parker's "persona," that outer personality that he presents to the public, has been nurtured over the last thirty years by the two character parts he has portrayed on the screen, Daniel Boone, and, most notably, Davy Crockett. Both are historical idols, solid, down-to-earth American folk heroes. Their honesty, loyalty and trustworthiness read like the Boy Scout Creed. It's an image that most politicians would give up half their campaign funds for.

The Fess Parker of today is not as lean as the Davy Crockett he portrayed thirty years ago, and his head of hair, although it is still a thick, shaggy mop, is gray. Chances are you would not recognize him walking down the street. But, if you stopped and talked to him—if you got him to say, "Howdy"—that slow, soft, butter and honey drawl would have you saying—"Why, it's Fess Parker!"

"I imagine it's a shock for people who have only seen me on reruns of my television shows," Parker says. "They tend to view me as fixed in time, and when they see this head of gray hair they wonder who that old guy is. They finally begin to realize I'm not Davy Crockett anymore."

"I remember the day when Disneyland opened in 1955, I was there at the ceremonies as Davy Crockett and Ronald Reagan was the announcer, out there with a microphone commenting on the parade and interviewing Walt Disney and others. I talked to Reagan several times after that. When he ran for governor, I went on a few trips and spoke for him. Seems like I have seen him more since he's been President.

"Recently I went to Australia as the President's U.S. representative for an American Friendship Week, and it was one of the most interesting experiences of my life."

While in Sydney, Parker had to answer some serious questions by Australian reporters about his friendship with Ronald Reagan. "I had been briefed by the State Department to expect that." Parker says. "But one question came as a surprise. I was asked if the President was going to appoint me as U.S. Ambassador to Australia?"

Parker answered that he hadn't been asked. But the question got him to thinking, and began to spark his interest in public service.

"I really don't know if I'll ever get appointed to, or elected to anything," Parker says. "I look at it this way—life unfolds in a certain way and there is a rhythm and an ebb and flow to it. "

"Chance" to Fess Parker is something that comes to the prepared mind. It was in the summer of 1950 that he went to Hollywood to take a chance on the movies.

"I had seen a film crew make a movie when I was in the Navy in World War II," Parker remembers, "and I thought it would be great to be an actor. After I got out of the military in 1946, I decided I'd better go back to the University of Texas and get a degree first. After that I would give myself three years in Hollywood to see if I had any future in the acting business."

Parker leans back in his chair. "Well. . .about two years and nine months after I arrived in Hollywood, I got this bit part in a picture called *Them,* a science fiction feature about ants which had mutated into huge creatures after an atomic explosion. I had a very good scene in the picture, but James Arness was the star."

James Arness was that "chance" Parker needed.

"Walt Disney came to see the movie," Parker says. "He had the idea of casting James Arness in a new live action film he was planning about Davy Crockett. They tell me Disney saw my little scene and said, 'Who's that!' "

As chance would have it, Walt Disney was just finishing his plans for Disneyland. He needed cash for the project, and took ABC as a partner. Disney got his fantasy park and ABC got what would become one of the hottest television shows of the decade, "The

Wonderful World of Disney." The program opened with a three week series called, "Davy Crockett, King of the Wild Frontier." The show catapulted the new actor with a Texas drawl right from mutated ants to instant stardom.

"I know how Elvis Presley and the Beatles felt," Parker says with a shrug. "Within three weeks after the Davy Crockett show premiered I couldn't leave my hotel room without a swarm of fans around me."

"For the most part I guess I handled it okay. After all, I wasn't seventeen. I was thirty, been in the service, college degree, and had even done graduate work at the University of California. But it still wasn't easy." He smiles, and points at his teeth. "I had thirteen cavities at the end of the first year. I don't know why. There have been studies that say stress produces a certain enzyme. My food habits changed, maybe my dental hygiene wasn't the best. Anyway, I now have more gold in my mouth than King Solomon ever had."

Fess Parker's other gold mine, the Davy Crockett television series, was filmed as three one-hour Technicolor episodes. Since television wasn't broadcast in color, the shows were seen in black and white. The three hours of film was edited to less than two hours and released in Technicolor to movie theaters. The film was a phenomenal success, and soon every kid in the world seemed to be wearing a coonskin cap. Parker got ten percent of the merchandizing.

After two years, the Davy Crockett mania began to ebb, and Parker was cast by Disney in several more films: *Old Yeller*—"That one turned out to be pretty good," Parker says, and *The Great Locomotive Chase*—"That one was duller than sin," he adds.

Parker leans forward, his arms crossed on top of a pile of papers. "In those days I wanted to be the best actor I could, but the films weren't much good. Eventually NBC tried to get me for a series about the further adventures of Davy Crockett, but Disney objected."

It was then that some bright studio executive came up with the idea that if Fess Parker could play a frontier hero like Davy Crockett, why couldn't he do equally as well as another coonskin-capped legend—Daniel Boone?

"That was a very difficult and personal decision for me," Parker says. "My identification with Davy Crockett was pretty complete, and the Daniel Boone character was very close. Could I call myself Amos instead of Andy?"

He could, and did. For the next six years Parker filmed 165 episodes of Daniel Boone for television, an undertaking that can be compared to making eighty feature films.

In 1958 Parker bought a weekend home in Santa Barbara and two years later married Marcy Rinehart, a band vocalist who he had met in Hollywood. The Parkers have a son, Fess Elisha Parker and a daughter, Ashley.

By the late 1960s Parker was getting bored with the movie and television industry. "I could have gone on with television," Parker says leaning back in his swivel chair. "I turned down the 'McCloud' series that Dennis Weaver did so beautifully. I guess, I kind of made an appraisal of what was happening in the film business and after twenty years felt like I had become a component of a process that turned out cans of tomatoes. I had become disillusioned with the prospects of improving myself as a performer. I wasn't growing. It was time to change."

Parker looks at a large rectangular map on the wall, an aerial photograph of the beach on East Cabrillo Boulevard. "That's when I got interested in developing real estate."

The result of that interest was Parker's Park Plaza Hotel/Conference Center. The area where Park Plaza is presently being built was originally a 32.35 acre eyesore.

"I had been living in Santa Barbara for sixteen years and wondered why that property hadn't been developed," Parker says shaking his head. "In 1976 I asked about it and was told eight and half acres were available, so I optioned it with the idea of building a tennis club." He looks at the aerial wall map. "Hyatt Hotels had an option on the rest of the property, but gave up developing it, deciding the land might become a controversial political issue. They sure were right!"

So, where angels and the Hyatt Hotel's top brass feared to tread, Parker walked in. In 1979 he bought the property, all 32.35 acres of it. Now all he needed to do was to convince a hotel chain to build on the land.

"I talked to everybody," Parker says. "The Marriott people, Hilton...finally I called the Chairman of the Board at Red Lion Inns, and they got interested." He pauses and grins sardonically. "Six years later, after appearing before a multitude of councils and commissions, overcoming a dispute with Red Lion Inns, and a voter referendum, ground was finally broken on the project." He shakes his head, then adds, "If I ever told the whole story it would make a fabulous book."

The approval of all the committees, commissions and the voters of Santa Barbara has been gratifying, but Parker has the strange feeling he was given his cake—but can't eat it. He feels the convention center concept—a good one and a needed one—was scaled down too much.

Parker's original proposal included a 500-room hotel, a 1500 seat conference center, 10 tennis courts and 200 condominiums. The much reduced plan that is now being built on a 23.5 acre strip along Cabrillo Boulevard, will be big enough for 360 hotel rooms, a large banquet room, meeting rooms, restaurants, bars, a health club, swimming pools, and enough parking spaces to accommodate 1,000 conventioneers.

"I don't believe the city approved the conference center size that was needed," Parker says with a sigh. "One of the big stumbling blocks was the concept of traffic congestion." He leans forward, hands clasped together. "Look, there are 2,000 seats at the Arlington Theater on State Street, and at the height of traffic there is no problem. I just feel that to put only 360 rooms on 23 acres is a misuse of the city's waterfront resources.

"Anyway, the project is going forward, and I have a deep and sincere interest in seeing Park Plaza built the way I represented it." He looks at a artist's drawing of the project that leans against the office wall. "Shortly after the project was approved, Red Lion Inns sold their company. It was bought by what I call the 'Entity,' an executive hiearchy made up of bankers and buy-out specialists. They will execute the project plans." He pauses. "The problem is, *I don't know what their goals are.*"

"I mean, a lot of time has been spent making this a first class project—and that could change. The basic design will be the same, but it could be built with the quality of a Motel 6. I have done everything I can to make sure the quality remains—more like a Biltmore. I only hope these 'bankers' will take the same pride in the Plaza that the people of the community have."

You can see in Parker's eyes that he is concerned, not only about the project that has his name on it, but about the future of Santa Barbara.

"You know," he says. "We tell everybody to come to our city and have a great old barbeque, to use our beaches, and to have a lot of fun. We like to think of our city as another Carmel or La Jolla. But we're not. We allow tourists on our beaches in droves, but *we don't merchandise ourselves.* That's like riding a hot and lathered horse home, and putting him away in the barn wet. The horse sure isn't going to be any better for it."

"Let's face it, shopping in this community is very limited. I don't believe the prospective plans for a department store in the 700 to 800 block of State Street is the complete answer. It's just a start. As we all know, things happen extremely slowly in Santa Barbara, and it is time to plan for something more in the future.

Parker stares across the room at a poster-size, framed picture. It's a picture of a lean, strong-looking man in his early forties.

"My father," Parker explains. "He was in public service, a county supervisor. My grandfather was also extremely active in his community. I think we all respond to what's going on through some kind of...well, let's call it 'generational preconditioning.' That may be stretching it. Anyway, I call it my 'roots for involvement.' "

He picks up the thank you card from Nancy Reagan, turns it over and smiles at the signature. Finally, he says in a soft voice that sounds like—well, Davy Crockett: "Just like this here lovely lady, I reckon I'll always be involved in ideas and dreams."

"Why shucks, that's the American tradition."

Jonathan Winters at home in Montecito with his wife, Eileen. (Cork Millner photo)

Jonathan Winters

No Foolin'

Jonathan Winters was my first celebrity interview. I met him at a Montecito patio party, and quickly asked him if he would sit for an interview. Just as quickly, he answered, "No." I bumped into him at another party several weeks later and asked again. He said, "No." Frustrated, I asked a friend of Winters' how I could get the interview. He said "Let's take him to lunch." We did, and after an hour of pleasant, and usually hilarious conversation, I asked Jonathan for the interview. He grinned that wicked little grin of his and replied, "I thought you'd never ask."

Jonathan Winters squints his face into a shriveled lemon look-alike. His mouth purses open and out comes the creaky voice of Maude Frickert, the world's oldest living airline stewardess.

"My older brother, Lamar Gene, he always wanted to fly. He kept jumpin' off roofs—broke ever' bone in his body. Then one day he stepped into the stone quarry—he'd scotch-taped 156 pigeons to his arms—and he said, 'I'm gonna fly!' And with those little birds on his arms a rip-roaring', all 156 of them, he got off to a running start. He was airborne for ever' bit of five seconds when this kid threw a box of popcorn in his path..."Jonathan Winters' face relaxes into soft lines and he slouches deep into the sofa of his Montecito home. He closes his eyes for a moment and remembers, "That was the longest laugh I ever got in my life. It was a funny picture—156 pigeons..." Jonathan brushes an imaginary speck from the front of the Cincinnati Reds baseball uniform he is wearing (he has an uncanny resemblance to Babe Ruth) and adds, "I guess it was the funniest picture I ever painted verbally."

Winters paints thousands of funny verbal pictures, and he does it instantly. A genius of improvisation, he can loose lightning bolts of his own wacky brand of humor at the drop of a straight line. "It's a matter of instantly picturing the situation in your mind then reacting to it," Jonathan says. "I have to believe in my warped little mind that the audience out there will see the same picture and laugh."

Jonathan Winters is an intense man with an incredible arsenal of voices, characters, and sound effects that spring from the fertile and evidently bottomless well of his mind. He seems to love to transform himself instantly into a fantasy character and then for one brief moment to live their dream lives. Perhaps it is the Walter Mitty within him struggling to get out.

Yet not everything is funny to Jonathan Winters. He is much more than a lifesize cardboard cutout grinning like a court jester. He is an enormously complex man with little tolerance for convention, and beneath much of his humor is the hard cutting edge of satire and a strong social statement. Like all great comedians he is deadly serious about being

55

funny and in sudden moments of oconoclastic fervor he will fearlessly smash any idol in his path.

It takes very little to get Jonathan's impulsive mind working. A verbal challenge such as, "Jonathan, you're in Kentucky, a hillbilly setting on a porch..." and his voice quickly dissolves into a backwoods drawl and he says:

"Jest cast yore eyes down there among those plum trees and those apple trees, fruit all over the ground, wrinkled and shriveled—my face is jest like 'em. You see those cows down there? Made of tin. And the horses? Made of wood. Jest too much of a chore to go down thar and feed them. Look at that cat, her eye all shriveled too. Some kid poked her. But that eye will roll back before winter, just like a pinball machine. Right now the eye is white, so we call her Little Orphan Annie."

Images, images, images. Yet when asked to dream up a visual image of himself he has to think hard for a moment twisting and changing the images in his mind until he says, "I'm sitting in front of a full-length mirror, nude, painting a suit on myself, putting the little white collar on, the tie...I'd have to shave my chest and probably my legs. I'd have to paint on boots, cowboy boots..." He laughs for a moment, liking the picture.

Jonathan is obsessed with entertaining; compelled to be funny; he can't walk into a restaurant or a hotel, or arrive at a party without feeling the desire to be "on."

Some people may not laugh at everything Jonathan says, but then he can't be funny to everyone. What he fears the most is the person who never laughs—the person without a sense of humor. "A sense of humor is essential," he says. "It will see you through almost any kind of tragedy; it will see you through life. What's frightening to me is the guy who says when asked: "What is funny to you?"

"Nothing."

"That's scary," says Jonathan.

At the other end of the spectrum are meetings and moments that Jonathan will cherish forever. One such moment came when he shook the hand of Neil Armstrong. At that meeting the comedian said simply, "Dayton, Ohio." And Armstrong said, "Boy, do I know you! I'm from Wapakoneta!" And Jonathan thought, "My God, this man who came from a town near Dayton about the size of this room—we didn't even play them in football—is the first man to step on the moon!" Meeting Neil Armstrong was doubly important to Jonathan because forty years earlier he shook the hand of the man who had climbed the first rung of the ladder into space, Orville Wright. Jonathan Winters was born in Dayton on November 11, 1925. When people ask him what sign he was born under he replies, "Slippery when wet." He had no brothers or sisters which he says, "Was a great break. There was very little in the will. I got the table."

He lived with his mother, who worked in radio for thirty-five years ("Kind of a watered down Arlene Francis," Jonathan says), his grandmother, and a stepfather. He listened to these older people. "I was like a gigantic sponge, absorbing everything I heard," Jonathan remembers. "I felt like I had this fantastic movie camera on my shoulder with two lenses taking pictures and recording the sounds of people, factories, ships, cars. All I had to do was go in the darkroom and develop what I had seen and heard."

Later he used the people he knew and lived with in his childhood as part of his comedy routines. The grandma character, Maude Frickert, was something like his aunt Lou Perks. "My aunt was a big lady with snow-white hair," Jonathan says. "She had a great sense of humor. Like Grandma Frickert she wasn't exactly a dirty old lady; maybe 'blue' old lady would be a better word." To prove his point Jonathan's face turns lemon-like again and the creaky voice of Maude Frickert begins to speak:

"I'm eighty-seven years old and I've had seven husbands. But Tom, the hired boy—he's thirty—is built like a Belgian horse. He's so strong he carried me to bed every night. We play pretend; what we call 'rescue.' He carries me up there to my room and puts me on the old quilt...he's a joy to have around. I just look at him. He's a bronzed god. In the winter months he'll get white, but I have some stain. I keep him stained."

Jonathan learned by listening but he says he didn't listen well in school, although he did have a love for art, and "recess." He finally quit school and joined the Marine Corps. "My Mother said it would be just like a big summer camp," Jonathan recalls. He was a Marine corporal stationed on the aircraft carrier Bon Homme Richard. After three years of "camp" he went back to school to study art. There he met Eileen, a slim, attractive girl with sparkling blue eyes. They were married in 1948. Not long after their marriage Jonathan asked her why she married him. She replied, "Because I thought you were the funniest man in my life."

To develop this natural ability to be funny, Jonatahn took a job as a disc jockey at the local radio station in Dayton, WING. Since he had no one to interview on the air he started to make up his own characters. In the next two and a half years he developed the routines that he would use so successfully later as a stand-up comedian.

In 1953 Jonathan headed for New York with fifty-six dollars and forty-three cents stuffed in his pocket. He told Eileen that if he couldn't make it with comedy routines in a year he would return home. He made it in seven months. The Winters' family including a son, Jonathan (Jay), born in Dayton, and a daughter, Lucinda, born in Bronxville, lived in New York for the next eleven years.

Jonathan played the night clubs, made TV guest appearances on Steve Allen's "Tonight Show," Jack Parr's "Tonight Show" and the "Gary Moore Show." He even took a one-time shot at the theater in John Murray Anderson's *Almanac*. But his fondest memory of those days came when Alistair Cooke asked him to be a guest on "Omnibus"; Jonathan was the first comedian ever asked on that show.

The comedy scene of the mid-50s was the perfect place for Jonathan's satirical, nonconformist style of humor to be born. The Eisenhower presidential years had begun to dull the senses and the American people were suffering from a lack of energy. Jonathan and his generation of comedy rebels were trying to shake people awake.

"Mort Sahl, Lenny Bruce, all of us wanted to turn this attitude around somehow," Jonathan says. "We wanted them to listen. Lenny gave them a pretty good shock. He had this cattle prod that he turned on the public and—wow—they either went with it or jumped. My only criticism of Lenny—and I knew him very well—was that he wanted to get them up in their seats twisting and turning, almost in agony. It worked; there were a lot of people picking up on the shock value, but I kept thinking of the families with kids and how they were worried that this stuff's getting pretty raunchy. I mean, I don't think of myself as a cardboard cutout of Pat Boone, but I always argue that you *can* be funny without being filthy."

"Mort Sahl was and is one of the brightest guys around for what he does—political satire. I've always liked Mort, and I have a great respect for him. He and I were similar except he went political, while I tried to cover the general subjects. We were both trying to tell the truth though, and it can be awfully hard to tell the truth through jokes."

"You know," Jonathan sighs, "a comedian *says* funny things. A comic *does* funny things. Laurel and Hardy were the greatest comics. No one has replaced them, not Rowan and Martin, not Martin and Lewis, nobody. Abbott and Costello didn't even come close. Thank God, every once in a while someone like Laurel and Hardy comes along. They were never dirty, never told a joke, but they did funny things." Suddenly Jonathan changes his face and voice into that of the skinny Stan Laurel and mimics:

"Laurel— 'What was that Ollie?' "

Then he's the patronizing Hardy: "That is a tarantula. *Touch* it and it will *bite* you."

"No it *won't* bite me. I know a tarantula when I see one." Jonathan reaches down, then quickly pulls his hand back. "Ouch! it *did* bite me!"

"You can make anybody funny,' Jonathan says, back in his own voice. "There are a lot of raised eyebrows about that, but you can. You can put funny clothes on them, or you can give them funny things to do or say, but the one thing you can't do is make them *think* funny. Thinking funny is, I believe, a God-given talent."

Jonathan has been using *his* talent to "think funny" for over some fifty years and he has finally decided to write some of his thoughts down on paper. His autobiography is titled, *I Couldn't Wait For Success, So I went On Ahead Without It*. The book is not a typical Hollywood diary of who did what with whom and when. Rather, it is a time capsule report about what a man thinks of the world and the people around him. It is an autobiography of thought.

"I just sat down one day in 1975 and started to write," Jonathan says. "Not with the idea of putting it on all the bookshelves in America. I just thought it was time for me to write down all the things I thought were important to me. I believe I had said a lot in my comedy, but maybe I hadn't said enough. So I took my time and wrote it all down, by hand, some 500 pages in a large artist's sketch book.

"One publisher looked at the manuscript and the first thing he asked me was, 'What about your affairs?' I said, 'They're all in order.' Besides what kind of guy runs down the roadway yelling, 'Hey, I just made it with Alma!' "

It's a book in which I tell the truth; my feeling about doctors, lawyers, dentists leaving you in the chair with fifty-five tools in your mouth saying, 'Sorry, Jon, I want to watch the World Series.' I talk about the toys I had as a kid, and what it might feel like to be a seagull, and what heroes are like. I try to say what I feel about laughter, and sorrow and pain."

"I dedicated the book to all people who are overly sensitive. They should never be ashamed of it—it beats being overly bitter. The overly senstive are on a different frequency, and they can turn their antennas a little different and pick up signals that are incredible. Sure, they take a lot of blows, but they live a richer life."

Jonathan wrote one other book, a little book with his own drawings called *Mousebreath, Non-conformity And Other Social Ills*. "It sold fifty-one copies," he says, "to small institutions. The patients threw them at each other. One guy ate my book. That's all right. I've done the same thing. *National Geographic* on a Sunday afternoon is delicious— just stay away from the color photos of the turtle cemetery on the Galapagos Islands."

Jonathan sinks deeper in the couch and pats his stomach, perhaps thinking about lunch only an hour away. Around him on the walls of his private studio hang some personal memorabilia: photos of himself in baseball uniforms; a framed set of marine gunnery sergeant stripes; a small painting by Walter Lantz showing Woody Woodpecker swimming through the surf to escape a shark; and one painting by Jonathan Winters titled *Conductor In Space,* a surrealistic fantasy image that might be compared to the paintings of artist Paul Klee. Jonathan paints extemporaneously, the same way he breaks loose his comedy routines. The paintings are of motion and whimsey, a happy array of colors that sparkle joyfully against one another.

"I started out to be an artist," he says. "Why did I quit? Starvation was a factor. But the truth is I didn't have a style." It took twenty-five years before he discovered his own style in art, and then he started painting again. Then in 1975 his paintings were featured in a show at the Ankrum gallery in Los Angeles. Jonathan designed the brochure for the show which includes color representations of five of his paintings. "I sold about ninety-five percent of my canvases at that show," Jonathan says. "I also got a good write-up from the Los Angeles Times Art Critic. To me painting is therapy. I enjoy the privacy of art. It's fun to come down here and relax. I consider it one of the rare times in one's life when you can be your own man."

"In painting I also think it's important to see something on the canvas that you can recognize," Jonathan continues, his eyes very serious. "I feel there is too much of modern art that is a cop-out for people who can't draw or paint. I can't believe that you can take cobalt blue acrylic paint and throw it against a fifty-five by sixty-foot canvas and say it belongs in a museum. First of all you have to learn how to draw. Learn anatomy, and if you can't—go to chickens, quick. But to do this?" Jonathan throws an imaginary glob of paint against the wall and assumes a prissy voice:

"Oh exciting. I'll call it 'Santa Barbara at Dawn.' "

"I don't understand," he continues in a deep voice, "where are the buildings, where are the mountains."

"That's it, that's the way I felt," says the prissy artist.

"That's the way you felt, huh? Right out of the old acrylic tube. Use any turpentine?"

"Yeah. Whole gallon of turpentine. It makes that runny look."

"Oh? What's that running there? Are those animals?"

"Oh my no, that's just turpentine. I'll call it 'Turpentine Running.' "

Jonathan Winters: painter, writer, comedian—what's next? Is there some last illusive piece of a master jigsaw? The answer is yes—one last piece.

"I want desperately to perform in a good dramatic film." Jonathan says, leaning forward on his elbows. "I'm not trying to prove anything, it's just something I want to do. I think I am capable of it. I've come close a couple of times. Once with a Rod Serling "Twilight Zone", and I did the movie *The Loved One* which was more of a comedy satire. Of course my first big movie break was *It's A Mad Mad Mad Mad World.* I may never do one bigger than that."

"I've seen some of my contemporaries turn the corner and go dramatic. Alec Guinness went from being a comedian all the way around to being a dramatic actor of great force. I've seen Red Buttons, Ed Wynn—God, the people—Jackie Gleason. Peter Sellers waited thirteen years to do the movie *Being There.* I don't know of any actor who wouldn't have given his right loafer to do that movie. Sellers did a brilliant piece of work. He was one of the most talented men of his time because of his 'ear.' He could literally leave his body as an Englishman and become a Frenchman, a German, and an American with a hundred dialects. He could become anything!"

Jonathan looks blankly out the closed screen door past the oak trees, then finally says,

"It was fascinating the short time I knew Peter. He was terribly shy. He felt in the *Pink Panther* series playing Inspector Clouseau, that he had sold out. Peter would argue that the only time he came to life was when he had a good script, and that he really didn't have much to say. I told him I didn't believe that. Maybe it was true of a lot of other actors, but I didn't believe it was true of him. Peter Sellers was a special guy."

"I think of myself as a survivor," Winter says seriously for a moment, then quickly changes to comedy and continues. "I want to be buried in a baseball uniform with a parking meter above me. You slip a nickel or a dime in and you can talk to me through the grass. No, I think it would be better to be cremated. I see no reason to water something that isn't going to come up. I just don't want to take up any space. I have taken up a lot of time and space in my life." He stands up, stretches, then winds up with an imaginary baseball and throws it through the screen door. Yep, Babe Ruth.

There are a lot of Walter Mitty's walking around out there, dreaming their secret fantasies, pretending they are Superman, Bluebeard the Pirate or Robin Hood—or maybe even Babe Ruth. Jonathan Winters is only one of them.

He just happens to be the funniest.

John Ireland in the award-winning movie "All the King's Men," with Irene Dunne.

John Ireland

Ireland's Way

Prior to this interview with John Ireland, I had chatted with him at several social functions. Like most actors, he was outgoing and talkative, and at ease in mentioning his early relationships with such actresses as Joan Crawford, Shelley Winters and Kim Novak. At the time, he told me he wouldn't talk about these affairs during an interview. He was saving them for a book. Because of his close family ties with his wife, Daphne, and his children, the book may never be written.

The driveway to actor John Ireland's Montecito home curves steeply upward like a huge question mark. Halfway to the crest of the hill the two story Mediterranean-styled house bursts into view.

The sandstone-hued home doesn't look like an actor's residence. Not really. It would better fit a dowager or a duchess. It looks too imposing, too formal, too classically Italian, more like a miniature version of the Pitti Palace in Florence, Italy.

The asphalt road continues its questioning curve around one end of the house until it abruptly ends in a large gravel courtyard. The hill behind the house continues to rise, shaded by oak and eucalyptus trees.

I park my car, grab my note pad and mini-tape recorder, then check my watch. Right on time—2:30 p.m. The gravel seems to protest my arrival as I crunch to the front door and ring the bell. No answer. I ring again. It is very quiet.

I push the button once more, and cock my ear to the door, assured by the faint buzzing sound inside. I look at my watch—2:35. Then, behind me, I hear the grinding of gravel as a car comes into the courtyard. Actor John Ireland has just made his entrance behind the wheel of his car.

"Sorry," he says in his deep, sonorous voice as he gets out of the car. He sheds his rumpled sport jacket—"Too hot for this."

I take the chance to look at this tall, slim (although balding), yet still easily recognizable actor. He has performed in over two hundred films, most of them—by his own definition—"B" movies. ("'Garbage' would be the best way to describe them," he says.) Yet, it wasn't all second-rate stuff. Early in his Hollywood career, Ireland performed in a series of superior movies, such as *Red River,* with John Wayne and Montgomery Cliff, and most notably the classic film, *All the King's Men,* for which he received an Academy Award nomination for best supporting actor in 1950.

He has also played Shakespeare on Broadway. His acting career was launched in New York in 1941 when he appeared in Macbeth, a drama for which he has a deep feeling. "I really want to do "Macbeth," he says. "I mean *play* Macbeth. I've been in five bloody productions of it and have performed almost every part, except Lady Macbeth—*and Macbeth.*"

I am still pondering how an Irish actor named Ireland, who has played mostly cowboy roles in the movies, and who was born in Canada and raised in Harlem, got his first part in a Shakespearian tragedy called "Macbeth" when I hear the front door opening. "Come on inside," Ireland says.

I walk inside the house—and almost walk *outside*. I can see right through the house to the front patio which is separated from the main entry door by a ten foot wide hallway. For a moment I feel like I have walked through the Hollywood facade of a movie-set mansion that has been skillfully created by studio carpenters.

We step into a large, formal dining room complete with a fireplace, then into the kitchen. It is a square room with modern white appliances: I count two refrigerators and a freezer standing in a line.

"The kitchen is the only room my wife, Daphne, and I had to remodel when we bought the place in 1975," Ireland says. "The house was built in 1914 by the owners of a steel company, and there is enough metal in the structure to outfit a battleship. It's solid. Look at the roof and walls, not one hairline crack from earthquakes."

Ireland leads me back down the hallway to the other end of the house. I follow watching him for some hint of the slow, defiant walk he used in so many western movie shootouts. We continue past the moderately-sized living room decorated with white and beige sofas.

We pass a wall-to-ceiling bookcase, which is opposite the staircase that leads to the upstairs bedrooms. Daphne Ireland, John's attractive wife is just coming down the stairs and says hello. I mention the uniqueness of the house.

"I adore this house," she says with exhuberance. "It has a personality of it's own. It appears big, but it is very uncomplicated. Still, I call it my big old family home." She laughs, a bright, happy sound. "I don't think a house can be too big. You need room to grow, room for children, grandchildren, in-laws. I don't want to discard anyone. I would like to have a castle in Ireland, a really huge one, where everyone in the family could have their own turret."

She starts down the hallway, then turns, "You know, people have a tendency to capsulize themselves, and as they get older move into a smaller place. It's lke getting closer to that final box they'll be in." She smiles and says, "I'll leave you two alone."

Ireland leads me into a small sun-swept study. Here again the decor is in light tones that intensify the brightness of the room. There are only a few decorations: on one wall is a drawing of John Ireland, and on one end table a few framed family photographs.

"This okay?" he says, sitting on a couch. I nod, pull up a chair, click on the tape recorder and begin:

"Tell me how a kid from Harlem with an Irish family ends up doing Shakespeare?"

He laughs. "I may have been a kid from Harlem, but I loved the movies. My mother worked, and I'd be left alone all day, so I played hooky and went to the movies instead of school.

"I was fascinated with movie stars. I'd watch Henry Fonda and notice his strange walk, like he was walking down cornfields, so I'd walk home on the pavement in Harlem like I was loping through a cornfield. People thought I was crazy."

Ireland settles back into the cushions, and crosses his legs. He doesn't wear sox. "I hadn't really thought about becoming an actor, until one day in 1940 when I was eighteen, and I saw this ad in the paper that said, 'Free Theater.' I thought, Wow! movies for nothing. I went and was shocked to find that the 'movies' was *real theater,* a legitimate play. I had never seen one before. And I was hooked—I wanted to be an actor."

"Why? What was the impulse?" I asked. "An inherent talent waiting to get out?"

"Sure, there was something," he says, "a spark, an unknown desire. It wasn't hereditary. My parents weren't involved in the theater."

I thought of Ireland's children, a girl, and two boys. "How about your children? Any of them have a desire to act?"

"My daughter, Daphne. . ." he begins, then hears footsteps coming down the stairs. Daphne, the Ireland's fifteen-year-old daughter walks into the room.She is a slender girl with delicate features and lustrous blue eyes.

"May I listen in?" she says brightly.

"Okay with me," Ireland says and introduces us: "My daughter, Daphne."

"Named after your mother," I say as we shake hands.

"Yes." Her voice is soft, but not frail.

"I have two sons, John and Peter from my first marriage," Ireland says. My wife, Daphne, also has a son, Cameron."

"Did you tell him how you and mother met?" Daphne says. "It's funny."

"Well, it hapened at a mutual friend's house," Ireland says, leaning forward, "One day Daphne—looking gorgeous— visited with her son. I said, 'Who is that lovely girl with her younger brother?' It must have been the right thing to say. 'We've been married twenty years."

Daphne smiles at the story she has heard many times before. "Your father and I were talking abut talent, and love for the theater," I say. "Do you share the same love?"

"Oh yes, more than anything," she responds eagerly.

"I did a theatre tour two years ago," Ireland says. "It was an eight week run with eight performances a week. Daphne came along and saw every performance."

"I love watching the theater," she says. "But, more than anything I want to be on stage. I want to be a serious actress."

"She has the right instincts," Ireland says. "She wants to go to London's Old Vic Theater. She'll get more acting experience there than anywhere else." He looks at his daughter. "You'll also paint scenery."

"Like you." She smiles.

"I did that the first year. After I saw my first play, I asked the theater owner for a job, and he gave me one—painting. Later I worked with a touring company for six months doing Shakespeare," he says. "Then I did a special audition for the famous Broadway acting team, Alfred Lunt and Lynn Fontaine. It was a contest and I won in the men's category. The Lunt's matched me up with the winning girl, hired a director and produced an audition sequence for their "special friends." The night the new actress and I performed, Noel Coward, Joan Crawford and other members of the Theatre Guild were in the audience. I guess I was okay, the next play I did was on Broadway. It was *Macbeth.*

"To get the part I had written Lynn Fontaine a letter asking if she could get me an audition for *Macbeth.* But, in the letter, I spelled it, 'Mcbeth.' She wrote back, 'never, never, *never,* spell *Macbeth,* Mcbeth!' She still got me the audition.

"I remember after the show opened one of the critics wrote: 'When John Ireland learns to speak English, he will make a helluva Shakespearian actor.' "

He leans forward in the couch. ' 'I used to go up to the roof of the theater and read Shakespeare out loud. I mean really *loud*. I figured it would not only help me develop vocally—and get rid of my Harlem accent—but through practice I could learn the *quality of the words*. I memorized most of the lines in *Macbeth*." He pauses. "I still have them memorized.

"To learn more I used to watch John Gielgud do *Hamlet*, then, just down Broadway, I'd go and see Leslie Howard. Gielgud had an amazing vocal quality, and I'd listen to the words. Leslie Howard had a delicate, ethereal quality, so much so that I would cry listening to him. '

"I know an actor, a big star, and *he* can't get parts. I asked him—'Whatta ya do?' He said: 'I play golf, I walk, I read.' Even when you get something it doesn't mean it'll work out. A couple years ago I was cast in a television series called, 'Cassie and Company.' Angie Dickinson starred and played a private eye. I was her helper. It bombed."

"Why?"

"The writing was trash! One writer had only done children's television, the other had written some 'Kojak' stuff. You'd find yourself reading lines that went out with Bogart, like, 'Who's the old shamus?' then the next bit of dialogue would be, 'I'll tell you my darling...' Finally Angie said to me: 'John, *I can't say these lines!*' " He sighs. "They were enough to make any actor cringe.

"I used to give my son, John, some of my 'B' movie scripts to read. He'd say, 'Dad. This is terrible.' Then he'd see the film and exclaim: 'Gee, the way you read the line makes it sound much better.' " He pauses. "But nobody can make a lousy line sound *great*."

When John Ireland was first called to Hollywood, he was cast in excellent films. Two weeks after he arrived he was on his first movie set filming, *A Walk in the Sun*, with Dana Andrews. "I didn't even have to read for the part," Ireland says. After that he did *Red River*—and married his lovely leading lady, Joanne Dru, in 1949. Next came his stunning performance in *All the King's Men* and the academy award nomination.

Darryl Zanuch bought Ireland's contract and put him in an excellent movie called, *My Darling Clementine*, which starred Henry Fonda. After watching Ireland's performance in that movie, Zanuck got the idea of starring his new actor in a fantasy comedy. "He can do comedy," Zanuck said. "Ireland's funny."

"I did the next movie Zanuck scheduled for me against my better judgement," Ireland says. "It was a semi-musical called, *Give Me the Simple Life*. The script was the worst piece of writing I had ever seen. I even had to sing the title song. *I can't sing*. I was awful. The movie was worse."

Ireland tried to avoid second-rate scripts, even to the point of demanding better parts. "I got antagonistic." Ireland shakes his head and his mouth takes on a hard line. "I said I wouldn't make anymore rotten movies. So they *told* me to take a part in something titled, *It Shouldn't Happen to a Dog*. That was apropos, it was a real dog. So, I rebelled. They said: 'Okay, do *this* dog,' and they gave me a script, *Behind Green Lights*. 'Do it or don't get paid.'

"You have to remember in those days everyone was under stuido contract. I was getting paid a salary every week to perform." He shrugs. "I didn't have much choice. So, I did a lot of rotten movies.

"It became a game, and I'd try to manipulate them back. I remember doing spaghetti westerns in Italy—I did about ten of them—and to get paid was a real trick. In a strange way, I enjoyed all of it. Still do."

"I think you thrive on it," Daphne says.

Ireland laughs. "That's what your mother says."

"Do you feel cheated?" I ask.

"No. No, any cheating was done by myself in accepting all the movies. I guess I was young, and they dangled all that money in front of me...you *can* be swayed by cash and the good life, and I was having a great time. With all the glitter, you forget about quality. Soon you're accepting garbage and then there is no room left for flowers."

"Some of the movies weren't so bad. I liked doing, *I Shot Jessie James*. It only took eight days to shoot, but it was good. I also liked doing *Little Big Horn* with Lloyd Bridges." He stops and thinks for a moment. "That movie had a new actress named, Marilyn Monroe. She had a bit part playing an Indian squaw and only had one line. I was asked later why I never paid any attention to her. I said 'you should have seen her.' She wore this black wig and a dirty, greasy buckskin. Not very sexy."

I ask him what female stars he liked to work with.

"Vanessa Redgrave is a great actress," he replies. "So was Joan Crawford. I worked with her in two films. She had a kind of magic..."

"What about Shelley Winters," I ask looking at my notes. In her book, *Shelley,* Shelley Winters referred to her affair with Ireland, and described him as being "...very handsome, tall and sexy..."

"What was she like?" I ask.

He pauses, a little reluctant to answer. "Well, I met her when she first came to Hollywood, about the same time I did my first movie. I remember her as being very ambitious, with not a lot of talent. Just a personality. But she sure did well."

One final question: "What are you doing now?"

"Some stage acting and a little writing. I have just finished three half hour scripts for a television trilogy called, 'The Cheaters.' I also recently played in a revival of the old drawing-room comedy, *Pleasure of His Company,* with Cyd Charisse. I'd like to bring that show to the Lobero theater here in Santa Barbara. Of course, I would *really* like to do *Macbeth* at the Lobero."

I look at Daphne. She nods in agreement.

"Yeah," Ireland continues almost to himself, *Macbeth.* "That's the one part I want to play before I shovel off."

He stands up and stretches. I look at my watch. We have been talking for almost an hour and a half. I click off the tape recorder. He shakes my hand, and I shake Daphne's, and they walk me down the wide hallway.

Driving down the curving driveway, I turn back to look at the house. No. A dowager really wouldn't be happy there. Perhaps it is the right place for an actor. Or even a king.

Like Macbeth.

Jane Russell, age 64, in her studio home. (Bill Boyd photo)

Jane Russell

Just One of The Boys

Jane Russell is a real homebody. After her autobiography was published, she had to go on an intensive book promotion tour. I happened to see her on a television talk show toward the end of the tour, and she was obviously tired and homesick. When the talk show hostess asked her what her future plans were, Russell replied, "I just want to end this tour—and go home." When I talked to her at her new Montecito home, she was still in the proces of redesigning and redecorating it. Yet she was "home"—and happy.

"Jane Russell is an authentic original. She is pragmatic in her faith and fanatic in her loyalties. She disdains the weakness of vanity, and guards the truth with moral zeal. She tells it like it is."
                                    —Robert Mitchum on Russell's autobiography

"I wanted a nice classy portrait on the jacket of the book," Jane Russell says holding up a copy of her recently released autobiography—*My Path & My Detours*. "My publishers convinced me that this *thing* in the haystack my first movie, *The Outlaw,* was *the* Jane Russell people wanted to read about."

She drops the book onto the coffee table in front of her and sighs, "I'm sick of the picture."

I pick up the book and spread open the dust jacket. On the full-color wrap-around cover, Jane Russell is shown reclining seductively on a stack of hay with her skirt lifted high on her thigh. Her peasant blouse is pulled tightly across her ample bosom, and her mouth is pouting sensuously. "I always looked like I was wrapping gum around my teeth," she says.

I look up from the once scandalous photograph, and look at the real Jane Russell, now 64 years old. She is wearing a baggy lavender and gray jogging outfit and gray leather tennis shoes. She looks comfortable, not seductive.

However, forty years ago, with the release of *The Outlaw,* Jane Russell became the most famous sex-symbol in America. The five-year publicity campaign that preceded the movie's release had made her face and figure synonymous with lust and desire, and everything good boys of the 1940s were not supposed to think about.

"They were selling Jane Russell," she says, running her hand through her long auburn hair. "It was like slapping a label on a can of tomateos."

Jane Russell is sitting on a couch in the living room of her Santa Barbara home. The room, which was once an artist's studio, is bright and airy. Three large studio windows angle upward to the sky, and another wall of windows overlooks a new redwood deck. There is the smell of fresh paint and newly-cut wood. Inside the room, one wall is dominated by a black and gold Japanese folding screen, the other by an old Franklin stove. Strangely, there are not any photographs of actress Jane Russell.

I had hoped for a museum of Jane Russell memorabilia; a few 8 X 10 glossies from *the Outlaw,* perhaps a couple of color enlargements from her most successful movie, *Gentlemen Prefer Blondes,* in which she starred with Marilyn Monroe, and maybe a theater poster from the Broadway musical, *Company.* I looked around the room again. Not so much as a polaroid. Where were the photographs of her with Clark Gable in *Tall Men,* or Robert Mitchum in *Macao,* or even Bob Hope in *Paleface?* At least I expected a cutout from one of her Playtex bra ads?

Nothing.

I asked her why.

"Oh, I 've done all that," she says with a shrug. "I've been in the movies, and it's all fantasy. That sexy broad on the screen really wasn't me."

To the movie goer of the '40s and '50s, Jane Russell was a long-legged, lushly proportioned sensual fantasy. In real life she was a teenage tomboy who loved to climb trees and slide down haystacks with her four younger brothers. She was the girl next door, the girl who married her high school sweetheart, football legend Robert Waterfield, and lived happily married for 23 years. She was also the mother of three adopted children, Tracy, Thomas and Buck.

Early in her marriage, her deep love for children led her to found the national adoption organization, WAIF. Working with Eleanor Roosevelt, Russell was able to get the Orphan Adoption Amendment of the Special Migration Act of 1953 passed. Because of it, children who had been accepted for adoption could enter the United States without being restricted by emigration quotas. In 1977 WAIF started concentrating its efforts in locating parents for orphan children in the United States. In a little over 30 years WAIF has placed 36,000 children.

Jane Russell's primary goals were never her movie career and stardom. She preferred her close relationships with friends, and her family, and, most of all—her personal faith in "the Lord." "The Lord is a living doll,' she once said and was widely quoted in the press.

Jane's personal references to "The Lord" are a bit disconcerting, and far from her publicity office image of a "bad girl." I asked her if she had difficulty selling her autobiography to a publisher because of her beliefs.

"Sure," she answers quickly. "I had to go from publisher to publisher, until I found someone who would leave in most of the stuff about the Lord. The book was my life story, and there was no way anyone could take the Lord out of my life. It was the main cornerstone."

"What are your religious beliefs?" I ask.

"I hate the word religious," she says. "To me it means there is too much formailty in the church. I like the story where Jesus is walking along and he sees a little black boy sitting on the steps of a massive, silver-domed cathedral, and he says, 'What's the matter, sonny?' And the kid is crying, and answers, 'They won't let me in there.' And Jesus nods, 'Well, don't feel bad, they won't let me in either.' "

She laughs, then says, "You see, my belief is based on the Bible. That sounds like fundamentalism, but it isn't. I don't preach to anyone. If someone asks me, I'll just say, 'Know the Lord.' That's what I tried to show in the book."

"Then you're satisfied with your autobiography," I say.

"Sure, except for the 200 pages they cut out," she says. "After the editor at Franklin

Watts read the book, he told me, 'Okay, you've covered the Lord, your family and three marriages, and your career, but we just can't go into all these friends!"

She sighs, and picks a cigarette out of a pack on the coffee table. "They took a lot of fun out of the book, and I think it became too serious. My first marriage with Robert Waterfield lasted twenty-three years. Twenty of those years were very happy, but the book was edited to focus on the three bad years. Those were the most dramatic years. After all, how often can you describe a perfectly nice day? I was lucky to get in one page about the normal days in our marriage."

She takes a drag on the cigarette, looks at it in disgust and says, "The Lord's going to get me over these things one of these days."

She laughs, then runs her long fingers over the cover of her book. "All in all, I'm pleased with the book. It was the long book tour I hated. After two months of saying the same thing over and over until I could scream, all I wanted to do was finish the tour and *go home.*"

Although Jane Russell claims to prefer a quiet homelife over the glamour of being a movie star, she admits she is not very domestic.

"I can't cook!" she says. "Robert, my first husband and I, had a perfect arrangement;: he did the cooking, I did the dishes. I sat on the sink while he prepared the food and we'd talk over what he did with the Rams football team that day—he was the team's star quarterback and eventually the coach—and I'd tell him what I did at the studio."

"The first thing I ask a man is if he can cook. It works too—I married three great cooks." (Russell was divorced from Waterfield in 1967. In 1969 she married actor Roger Barrett who died tragically only three months after the wedding ceremony. In 1974 she married John Peoples, a Santa Barbara real estate investor.)

"Not long ago a publisher wanted to do a photo layout with me in the kitchen," she continues. "My husband, John, told them that would be the biggest joke in the world. 'Get her out of the kitchen!' he said."

"You mean you've never cooked a Thanksgiving turkey," I ask?

"Oh, no!"

"Spaghetti?"

"Never!"

"Boil water?"

"I made Eggs Benedict once, but I got the hollandaise sauce out of a can." She throws her arms up and cries, "I don't want to cook!"

"Would you rather be in motion pictures again," I ask?

"In the movies—today?" she says wide-eyed. "There is too much sex and nudity. I would have never done a nude scene. I even refused to wear a bikini that Howard Hughes had designed for me in *The French Line.* Too embarrasing."

"Have you tried television?"

"I did an episode for the action drama series, 'Hunter' recently. It was terrible. They are in such a hurry grinding it out. There is no time for caring, just slap, slash. The last shot they did of me was a close up when I was tired. When I saw it on the screen it was the worst thing I have ever seen. I looked awful."

"Did you like yourself in your first movie, *The Outlaw?"*

A long pause, then a deep breath. "I thought I was...slow. I looked wooden. Look, I'm not the hysterical type. I don't move quickly. I take things easy." She sighs, then throws her arms up. "Okay! *I'm lazy.* I had a marvelous Russian drama teacher who once told me, 'You know, Jen, you could be a very good acktress, but you haff no energy.' It's true! On the screen I seemed to be moving in slow motion."

She absently picks another cigarette from the pack and lights it. "In *The Outlaw* I was terrible. but, I have to blame a lot of it on the direction. We had to do each scene over and over again, maybe ninety takes, until it got to the point where I wasn't allowed to raise my eyebrow, or lift my shoulder. There wasn't anything natural about my movements. That wouldn't have happened if Howard Hawks had stayed on as director. It would have been a wonderful picture."

"That must have been very disappointing," I say.

Another pause, "Yes...very. But...Howard Hughes was the producer. It was his picture, and he kept interfering with Hawk's directing, telling him what to do, what he liked, what he didn't. Finally Hawks blew up and said, 'Okay, Howard, direct it yourself!' and left. Unfortunately, Howard decided he would do exactly that—direct *The Outlaw.*"

"Did you know Hughes was going to make a superstar out of you?" I ask.

"No. He just said he was going to make a picture. I said, 'Well, okay, I'll give it a try."

How did a nineteen-year-old girl with no acting experience get selected for the starring role in a Howard Hughes movie? Like many movieland success stories it began with a photograph. A Hollywood photographer happened to see Jane, thought she had potential, and took some photos. Through an agent, the pictures ended up on Howard Hughes' desk, and he just happened to be searching for a new face to star in his picture *The Outlaw.* Jane Russell, with four other girls, was selected as a finalist for the role.

"For that final screen test, we were all dressed alike in the peasant blouses," Russell remembers, "and were all brunettes and we were all nervous...Then it was my turn. Honestly, the camera didn't bother me, and the lights were so intense that the people standing around just faded away...I knew my lines and said them. That's all."

Howard Hughes had not been present at the screen tests, and it was two days before Jane got a call that the director Howard Hawks wanted to see her along with a new actor, Jack Buetel, who had auditioned for the male lead.

"At first Hawks didn't say a word," Jane says. "He just sat behind his desk looking at Jack and me. Then in his slow quiet way, he said, 'Well, you two kids have the parts. Mr. Hughes has looked at all the tests over and over and you're our decision.' "

Once Hughes' new star was signed to a contract, he went about making her the publicity event of the decade.

"Oh yeah," Jane says. "I was supposed to be a poor Cinderella who had been lifted out of poverty to become a movie star and was helping to support her mother and four brothers. Little did the public know that I could barely make my car payments and eat on my salary of fifty dollars a week, let alone support anyone."

During the publicity campaign, the shooting of *The Outlaw* continued under Hughes' plodding directon. There was one major problem. His star's bosom. A custom made bra would have to be constructed to best show off Jane's bustline under the peasant blouse. Hughes decided it wouldn't be any harder to design a bra than it would be to design an airplane. He would design it himself.

"A Mr. Playtex he wasn't" Jane says. "He was trying to design a seamless bra, which was way ahead of its time, but when I tried it on I found it uncomfortable and ridiculous. I wasn't going to do 103 takes with it on, so I put on my own bra, covered the seams with tissue, pulled the straps over to one side, and went out to do the scene. Everyone behind the camera stared. Howard looked closely, then finally nodded okay. I never wore his bra."

Howard Hughes' relationship with his new sex symbol was platonic. Whether he wanted it to continue that way is doubtful, however, his shy overtures were met with stoic resistance from his married star.

"I was later told that Howard had confided to a writer that I 'terrified him.' Howard said he wasn't going to fool around with a married woman, especially one married to a football star, Robert Waterfield. That's a laugh! Imagine that poor, darling man afraid of me!" She rolls her eyes. "Sorry folks, another legend shot down.

"One thing..." she quickly adds, "he wasn't a weirdo. He was kind and considerate, with a childlike sense of humor." It is obvious that Jane Russell had a great deal of affection for Howard Hughes. I asked her if she was disturbed by his macabre death.

"I think there was..." her voice lowers to a whisper, "I think there was some dirty pool going on. Those men that were keeping him didn't help him when he needed it. And all the people who *did* care about him, were not allowed to see him. How could that beautiful, strong-willed man have allowed it to happen? Unless..." She pauses, "unless they got him on drugs..."

She is quiet and there is genuine concern in her eyes. Howard Hughes had been too much a part of her life and her career to be forgotten. Hughes kept her under contract for most of that career, loaning her out to other studios for special movies. One of those movies was called *Gentlemen Prefer Blondes,* and co-starred the Blond bombshell, Marilyn Monroe.

"The press tried their best to work up a feud beteween us," Russell remembers, "but they were sniffing up the wrong tree. When the movie was released, the reviews were great. They called us the "Haystack Brunette versus the Blowtorch Blonde" and said how well we worked together. I had a ball on that picture.

"Marilyn was very sweet, and shy, and very serious, and would stay for hours after the day's shooting working with her drama coach. On the set, I was usually made up and ready to go before she was. I'd drop by her dressing room and say, 'Come on, blondy, let's go,' and she'd say, 'Oh, okay,' in her whispery voice, and we'd go on together. She didn't show any temperament at that time."

"How was working with Robert Mitchum," I ask?

"I did two movies with Mitch," she says, *"Macao,* and *His Kind of Woman,* and he was great to work with. He never made a mistake, and was totally a professional. I know he has the image of Peck's Bad Boy, but that's just devilment. When visitors would come on the set he would do something to shock them. He said they had come to look at the clowns and he wasn't going to let them leave disappointed."

"And Clark Gable?" I ask, mentioning her co-star in *The Tall Men."*

"He was a doll to work with, and a terrible tease. I loved him. You know, I never had any clashes with my leading men. I guess I really love working with people, that's why I liked doing the Broadway musical, *Company."*

Company, which opened in 1970, with Russell in the lead role, achieved the critical success that had eluded her in her movies. One reviewer wrote: "This debut may well mark the beginning of a whole new career for an actress whose celebrated attributes up to now seem to have been only her cleavage."

"I had never been so happy with my self as I was then," Russell says. "Thirty years after my debut as an actress in *The Outlaw*, I had opened on Broadway and received rave reviews. As my Mom would say, 'Praise the Lord.' "

Performing in *Company* also led to a contract with Playtex Company. "While I was doing *Company*, the Playtex people asked me to be their spokesperson for their company's bras. They thought I would be a natural. I knew Betty Grable had done a girdle commercial for them, and it was done in very good taste. Besides, the product was something I've always believed in—bras!

"I did that first commercial in 1971 and have been doing them ever since. Once a year I go to New York and they get tickets to the shows, provide a limousine, a driver, and a suite in a hotel."

"And they pay you for this?"

"Yeah, can you imagine? Half a day in front of the camera. It's like stealing."

She plucks another cigarette out of the pack on the coffee table and lights it. She looks at the smoke curling from the end. "The Lord is little by little sluffing off my bad habits. The booze went a few years back. This..." she waves the cigarette around making circles of smoke, "...this is next."

I pick up her autobiography and ask one last question: "You've written your life story in 300 pages," I say. "How would you sum it all up in one sentence?"

She thinks for a moment. "You know, I was always a tomboy, and I've mentioned climbing trees with my four brothers, sliding down haystacks, and riding horses. But, at six years of age, I also found the Lord...I guess you could say that I was just—'One of the boys who found the Lord.' "

Dame Judith Anderson as Minx Lockridge in NBC's soap, "Santa Barbara."

Dame Judith Anderson

The Sound of Silence

Dame Judith Anderson, a diminutive woman ("I'm still shrinking," she says), opened the door of her cottage when I arrived. Behind her legs, her two dachshund's barked insanely. I stepped through the doorway—and squished into a fresh pile of dog-do. I groaned, "Oh, shit. I stepped into dog-do!" After scolding both dogs with a wag of her finger, Dame Judith gave me a couple paper towels to clean off my shoe. The odor permeated our ensuing conversation.

"A diminutive woman, burning with passion, she gave heroic performances."
—Brooks Atkinson, Drama Critic.

"The silence," she says.

"The silence from the audience is the wonderful part. That's when you have them, when you have grasped their minds totally." She stops for a moment, remembering. "The greatest audience I ever had was at a USO show for our soldiers in World War II. There were three other actresses and a pianist and we read from the classics like Shakespeare. When we were through, a voice from deep within the audience of 10,000 called out, 'Could you say the 21st Psalm for me?'

"And I could remember...'Yea, though I walk through the valley of the shadow of death....'"

Then Dame Judith Anderson is very quiet as if listening to the past. "Even to this day I can hear the silence. There was not a sound. And it was wonderful...wonderful."

The lady is charming and gracious and as she speaks her voice rings with the resonance and electricity that poet Robinson Jeffers once referred to as "liquid fire." Dressed warmly in a sweater and slacks, Dame Judith Anderson presses herself tightly against the arm rest of her living room couch. "It's my spot, I always sit here," she says. She is tiny. But her presence is commanding. And the words that come from her lips have the richness that made her one of the most successful dramatic stage actresses of this century.

The couch she sits on is patterned in blue and white circles that look like tiny spoked wheels and mirror the design from a large collection of Delftware plates that hang on the wall behind her. The sun struggles to shine through the early morning fog and through the French windows opposite of the couch. Beyond the window the mountains can be seen through the haze. Her Montecito home suggests an English cottage set in a secluded grove of oak trees.

Dame Judith's dachshund, Heidi, jumps on the couch and tries to climb on her mistress's lap. "No...no, I don't want you there," she says and the dog looks balefully at her, then touches a cold nose to the side of her leg and remains, unmoving and contented, through the next hour and a half as Dame Judith Anderson talks about herself, her family, her love of theater, the passion she feels for her art, acting, and her unique ability to mezmerize the audience—into silence.

It's been decades since she stunned theatergoers with her performances as a tormented Medea or a pensive Hamlet or the evil housekeeper in the movie *Rebecca*. At age 86 she thought she was through with acting. That's when she got a call to play the Vulcan high priestess in *Star Trek III,* which was soon followed by an offer to star on the television soap, "Santa Barbara."

Seeing Dame Judith on a "soap opera" is sort of like finding Princess Di slumming on Hollywood and Vine. But there she is each afternoon playing Minx Lockridge, a feisty, haughty grande dame trying to maintain her television family's fortunes.

"I don't see any conflict in doing a soap," Dame Judith says. And I certainly don't see any comedown." To friends, neighbors and critics who say, "How could you?" she replies, arching a well-used eyebrow: "What would you want me to do? Sit here and rot?"

Dame Judith has experienced a multitude of memorable moments in her acting career. The first happened on the day she was born.

"I started acting the moment I got out of my mother's womb," she says. "You see, I died when I was born. The heart stopped. I don't know for how long, but I was dead. That was my first big scene. It was my defiant way of saying, 'I can do this! and there will be a lot more to come!'"

Her magnificent portrayal of the barbarian queen in the classic Greek tragedy, *Medea,* won her the accolades of audiences and critics the world over, including the Queen of England.

Broadway drama critic Brooks Atkinson wrote of her performance: "Hell hath no fury like Medea scorned when Miss Anderson played that ruthless part with an evil grandeur that snatched Euripide's tragic drama out of the textbooks and poured it into the bloodstream of the audience. If Medea did not understand the temperamental convulsions of her own character, she would have done well to consult Miss Anderson."

A little over a decade after Atkinson penned those words, "Miss Anderson" was knighted by Queen Elizabeth as "*Dame* Judith Anderson."

"When Queen Elizabeth stopped in front of me, she said, 'Did you come all the way over here just for this?'"

(Over 20 years later on a wet and dreary day in 1983 the Queen and Prince Phillip visited Santa Barbara. Dame Judith waited in the receiving line in the deep, wet grass of the Court House's Sunken Garden. The queen said to her, "Ah, you're living over here now?" Right behind, Prince Phillip looked at Dame Judith's soaking shoes and smiled, "If you stand in the wet grass too much longer, you'll begin to sprout leaves.")

Dame Judith once said she attributed her success to her ability to clothe herself in the genius of great authors. She waves her arms in the air as if brushing away a swarm of flies. "Oh that! 'Clothe myself in the genius of great authors!' That's the only clever thing I ever said. I use it a lot. I can't make speeches; and when I am called in front of a group, I read from a great writer like Shakespeare, or O'Neill, or my favorite, Robinson Jeffers."

It was poet-playwright Jeffers who first "clothed" actress Judith Anderson in the words that created a legend. "Here again it was tinged with luck," Dame Judith says. "That was in 1947 and I was starring in a Broadway drama that was quite fulfilling, and I really didn't want to think about another play. But the producer, Jed Harris, asked me if I would consider doing a new adaptation of *Medea.* He gave me a couple of outlines to read. They were awful. I told him if he wanted it done right, he would have to call up Robinson Jeffers who I had worked with on an earlier play, *Tower Beyond Tragedy.* Harris said, 'Why don't *you* call up Jeffers?' And I did, and on the phone I said, 'Robin, I'm going to ask you something and I want you to answer, 'No!' Will you do an adaptation of *Medea?* He immediately said, 'Yes!'

"I discovered many years later he had written a poem called *Solstice,* and when I read it I finally understood. It was *Medea* in a modern setting at Big Sur. No wonder he said yes so quickly and emphatically. He loved the story." She pauses, then adds, "Thank God!"

In 1983, over twenty-five years after the opening night performance of *Medea,* Dame Judith was instrumental in getting the play taped at the John F. Kennedy Center for Performing Arts and aired on the Public Broadcast System. Dame Judith relinquished her cherished part to Zoe Caldwell, and she played the part of the Nurse. It was a bit of a role reversal as the two actresses had performed in the original New York opening. Dame Judith as Medea, of course, and Caldwell in the Greek chorus. "Zoe Caldwell is a wonderful actress, and she was perfect for Medea. The Nurse was the natural part for me as I was much too old to do the lead.

"One thing I don't want to talk about is old age," she says, crossing her arms across her chest. "I have lived a long time and age is a very tender subject to me." Her voice rises as if she is reaching for the last row of the Met. "Everybody should have a twenty-first birthday, splash bang! then no more birthdays. I think this business of plastering your age all over a magazine like an obituary column is offensive!"

Dame Judith played with Laurence Olivier in the movie *Rebecca.* "With" isn't the right word according to Dame Judith. "You don't play *with* anybody in the movies," she says. "You just go in and play a little scene here and there. The movies were a total departure from the stage, and I didn't enjoy the experience at all. Mostly because I hate the mike which must become a part of you, and the lense that becomes another part of you. There is also no audience to feel and be felt by. Movies...it's simply a technique I don't understand.

"I was doing a film called *The Red House* and had just finished rehearsing a scene, and the director said, 'Watch your eyebrows.' I asked why, because I thought the scene had gone perfectly. The director agreed, but said: 'When you raise your eyebrows a quarter of an inch it will look like six feet on the screen.'" Dame Judith raises her arms over her head and sighs. "I'm not able to cut down like that. If I want to make a quick move—" she makes a slashing motion across her chest—"I do it. Or, if I want to shout—I SHOUT! The movies? No, I can't handle the movies.

"What I like about the theater is opening night," she continues. "Of course, I was always petrified, fearing that everything would go wrong. I was nervous, waiting and wanting to be *great.* I am like any stage actress or actor, I want to be great, and afterward I want to be told that I was great..." Dame Judith stops for just a moment, then hesitantly continues, as if the memories she is about to reawaken are ones best left untold. Finally, she says: "My mother would never praise me. It was always, 'You can do better'... better...."

She looks out the window, staring blankly as the sun begins to penetrate through the clouds. "My mother came to see me play Lady Macbeth in London. After the performance we were sitting in this beautiful dressing room—in silence. I had just acted my heart out knowing she had been out there. It was as if the Queen had been watching in her royal box. I asked, 'How was I Mum?' She just looked around this gorgeous room and said, 'What's that over there...and that over there?'" Dame Judith pauses and there is electricity in her voice. "Finally, I said, 'Mother. *How was I?*' she turned to me and said lightly, 'Oh, I've seen you do better.'"

Dame Judith closes her eyes for a moment then continues, "She loved me. Still, I will never forget when I was on the west coast acting in another drama, and I had taken too much of the work on my shoulders—I even chose the music—and I blew several lines during the performance. After the curtain I was at low ebb and in tears." Dame Judith touches her fingers to her lips before she speaks again. Then: "My mother said to me, quite simply, 'You were *great.*'" Dame Judith's mouth trembles, and she closes her eyes as the tears start to come, and she says in a tiny, almost child-like voice, "I remember, and it makes me cry..."

As a child Dame Judith Anderson went by the name of "Fannie." (Her real name was Francis Margaret Anderson.) She also tried, "Francie."

"I fiddled around with my name," she says. "As a young actress in Australia, I went by Francé, then an actor told me it was a silly name and if I wanted to be a dramatic actress I would have to take a dramatic name. So, I took Judith. I think it is a beautiful name."

When Francis Anderson was eight years old, she sang at recitals. A visiting musician saw her perform and advised her mother to send her to Europe to study. Unfortunately, the Anderson family was broke. Judith's father, who had once been called the "Silver King of Australia," was also a great gambler. "He once bet 30,000 pounds on a race horse," Dame Judith remembers. "He gambled everything away."

At age 19 she and her mother made the trip to California carrying a single letter of introduction to Cecil B. DeMille. "He took one look at me and just shook his head," Dame Judith remembers. "He looked at this little *joey,* this kangaroo in a pouch, and turned away. I had no look, I had no clothes, I had no chic. I was nothing at all. But..." and Dame Judith's eyes begin to glow white hot, "but, he didn't know I had something he couldn't see—a burning desire to be a great actress."

It was off to New York where newly christened Judith Anderson got a job with the 14th Street Stock Company. Her first step toward Broadway was in a touring company of a play called, *Dear Brutus.* Then, suddenly, she was offered the lead in a play by A.A. Milne—on Broadway! "My feet didn't touch the ground all the way home," Dame Judith remembers. "I screamed at my mother, 'I got the lead! On Broadway!'" She sighs. "The next day I lost it. I wasn't pretty enough." She pulls on a strand of gray-white hair. "I mean, look at my eyes, it never was a pretty face. But, losing that acting job was both destructful and wonderful. For a day I was on top, then in one instant plunged to the bottom. In the long run it helped me, you can't know the heights unless you have seen the depths.

When I first came to New York I had told my mother I wanted to live as close to the Belasco Theater as possible because that was where I was going to be a star. When the chance came for an interview with Davis Belasco, I went out and bought a new wardrobe, new underwear, new stockings, and then I went to see the great man.

"His manager told me to wait, then fussed around saying, 'The Gov'nor's coming down in a moment to see you.' Next he said, 'The Gov'nor is leaving his room upstairs.' Then: 'The Gov'nor's on the first step...' I really didn't get excited by all this silly hype. I just wanted him to get there and give me a job."

The job she got. A five year contract to star in Belasco productions. The egotistical director also got more than one bargained for in a diminutive fireball who would not cow to his wishes or bow to his presence. "On the original contract I wanted more money," Dame Judith says. "I was advised by his people not to worry about it. He would give me a house, a car, a chauffeur, everything. I said that no man was going to keep me. I was going to act, and I was going to get paid for it." She got the contract she wanted.

Belasco starred her in many productions but was always concerned that his "naughty little girl," his tempermental star, would not succumb to his authority. He finally realized he could not control his actress the night Charlie Chaplin saw her perform. Chaplin came backstage after the performance and told her, "I am going to make you a famous star. I'll have a play written for you. No! *I'll* write the play. I'll build a theater for you!" The press got hold of Chaplin's musings and headlined: CHAPLIN TO BUILD THEATER FOR ANDERSON. Belasco, who was out of town, read about it and was furious.

"I got a five page telegram from Belasco calling Chaplin a pie-slinging, no-good comedian. He also referred to me as his little slut." Dame Judith shrugs. "I never worked for him again."

It is not that Dame Judith Anderson is a tempermental actress, but she is coldly aware of her craft. "I suppose I can be tough and cold to work with," she says. "But I will fight for what I think is right. If I have an idea that is in opposition to the director's, I will fight it out until I can be convinced I am either right or wrong. I have found myself wrong— happily wrong—on many occasions. I don't think I'm hard to get along with, but I am a perfectionist. To me the play *really is* the thing. Yes, the play—I love it."

She pauses, the sun is shining through the window now, and it lights up her face like a spotlight. Finally, she says softly, "The play...it is my life."

Perhaps Brooks Atkinson summed up this amazing actress best when he wrote: "She can only be compared to herself."

Dame Judith in the 1947 Broadway production of "Medea."

Bo Derek. (John Derek photo)

Bo Derek

Bo! A Portrait

I first met Bo Derek at the 1986 Humane Society's celebrity charity show. She had brought along one of her horses and its trainer to demonstrate trick riding. Watching her horse go through its paces, she reminded me of a child at a circus, clinging to the edge of her chair, wide-eyed, pink-cheeked, and laughing. I was as enraptured watching Bo as she was watching her horse.

"Isn't he magnificent!" Bo Derek says leaning farther over the rough rail fence of the corral. "He's a Spanish horse, an Andalusian breed. Look how fast he's going, he's flying!" She claps her hands ecstatically. "See the fire in him! *I love him.*" She continues to watch as the spirited animal kicks up plumes of sand, and tosses its head arrogantly in response to the trainer's silent demands.

I turn from the horse's performance and focus my gaze on Bo Derek. Her cheeks are a bright pink from the crisp Santa Ynez Valley air, and she has on a head scarf, a felt hat, a heavy sweater, jeans and boots, and a bulky nylon jacket. She looks like a bundled-up Peanuts character ready for an outing on an icy pond.

Still, she *is* beautiful.

"I don't consider myself a '10' in any way," she had told me earlier. "But everyone involved in the movie tried to create an *illusion* of absolute beauty. Nobody can be a perfect '10' because everybody's standards are different."

It was the movie *"10"* that turned Bo Derek into an American icon of beauty. After the movie's phenomenal success, she entered an orbit of her own where she could grasp anything she wanted. She was immediately offered a five million dollar two-picture deal. She turned it down. "John and I felt we wanted control of ourselves," she says. "We decided to make *Tarzan, the Ape Man*—together."

In that jungle movie Bo appeared as a nude, sexually assertive woman opposite a Tarzan who critics refererred to as "nothing more than a spear carrier." Because of her nude scenes, Bo was dubbed, "Little Bo Peek," and "PeekaBo."

John Derek's critics accused him of exploiting his wife's spectacular figure. He answered matter-of-factly, "God assembled her brilliantly. It's what she feels and thinks and does *without* her clothes that makes her exciting and attractive."

In person, without makeup, bundled up against the cold, and animated from observing her favorite horse, Bo Derek, twenty-nine, is considerably more beautiful, softer looking than she was in *"10"* or *Tarzan,* or *Bolero.* She has the aura of an angel, wide-eyed, excited, and a bit astonished with her first trip to earth.

"He's dragging his hind legs," John Derek says, edging next to his wife at the corral's rail. He stares intently at the horse being maneuvered in tight circles. "Look at him kicking up the sand. He's being lazy." John Derek, an expert horseman, brushes a strand of gray-white hair from his deeply-tanned face. At fifty-nine, with his graying beard and penetrating stare he is beginning to look more and more like a Hemingway character. Formidable, with a sharp cutting edge to his personality which he tries—usually unsuccessfully—to blunt, Derek is constantly besieged by a hostile press.

Shoulder to shoulder, John and Bo watch their prized stallion for a few more minutes then Bo shivers and says, "It's really getting cold. I'm a beach girl and not used to this." The temperature, unseasonably brisk for the Santa Ynez Valley, is forty-seven degrees.

As she and John walk toward their Spanish-styled ranch house, John bends down and picks a purple wild flower, then pulls Bo toward him and puts the flower in the headband of her hat. It is a warm, affectionate moment, one of the many they have shared in their ten year marriage. "I'll go in and put a couple logs on the fireplace," he says, turning toward the house.

Continuing with Bo on a tour of the stables, I ask how she and John have managed a marriage which a critical press predicted would fail.

"We have the same likes and dislikes," she says with a grin that heightens her high cheekbones. "Neither of us smoke or drink, I've never been one for parties, neither has John. He has lived his life much longer than I have, and very fully, and I enjoy learning from him."

She pauses, then answers my unasked question. "The age difference starts getting smaller. People ask me what I will do when I get old, and I tell them I don't care what I look like. As for John..." she smiles a cute, wicked little smile, "I'll just take away his glasses."

In front of the stables, she pauses for a moment to hug the neck of a white mare, purring into the animal's ear, "Ummm...pretty baby."

She continues: "John and I have a good support system. He worries about me, I help him." She laughs. "When I fuss or talk back too much, he says he's going down to the local high school and find another. It's all a joke and we both understand it."

John Derek's first marriage was to French actress Patti Behrs, by whom he had two children, Russ, thirty-five and Shawn thirty-one. His second marriage was to actress, Ursula Andress, who was followed by Linda Evans, both of whom bear a striking physical similarity to Bo. All three have square shoulders, a tiny waist, identical rib cages, a generous bosom, high cheekbones and delicate features. Because of these similiarites, John Derek has been accused of being a self-styled Pygmalian, molding his "cardboard cutout" wives to his own emotional, physical and intellectual specifications.

"Oh, the press has been insisting since we were married that John is my Svengali," Bo says. "I wish he were. I wish he did make all the choices for me. It would be a lot easier. But he won't. He says: 'It's up to you; it's your decision.' "

To thumb their noses at the incessant Svengali criticism, the Dereks named their production Company, SVENGALI INC., and listed Bo Derek as president. Then they asked artist Frank Frazetta to design special stationary. Lying on her stomach across the top of the full-color letterhead is a flesh-toned drawing of a nude Bo Derek manipulating puppet strings from which dangles the limp form of John Derek.

Bo stops at a corral next to the stables and calls to a white, and very pregnant Andalusian mare. "She's Spanish, with such a pretty head," Bo says, kissing the horse's neck. "Look at her big black eyes." The mare turns away satisfied with the attention. Bo whistles softly after her. "She's going to have a baby in April. She gets bigger every day."

A wild assortment of dogs, eight of them, bark and tumble playfully with each other on

Bo Derek riding at her Santa Ynez Valley ranch. (John Derek photo)

the grassy hillside near the Dereks' house, 'Why did you decide to move to the Santa Ynez Valley?" I ask as we walk toward the side door.

"Funny, but we used to visit the area in our van and we'd stop at a Solvang parking lot to sleep. We both thought we'd live in this valley someday." She looks at the two-story white house with its typically red-tiled Spanish roof. "When we first drove up here, we knew without looking at each other that this was the place."

She turns and looks across the rolling hills of their forty-eight acre ranch, past the stables and the corral where the trainer is still guiding the stallion through its paces to the gray layers of clouds beyond. "I could just stay here all the time," she says wistfully. "I love it here."

We step inside the house which isn't any warmer than the outside. "Don't you have central heating?" I joke, remembering the houses that I had been inside in Spain which were like icy tombs in the winter.

"Sure," Bo says. "But we don't use it."

John walks in with a firewood log the size of a sequoia tree trunk and dumps it in the fireplace on top of several smaller burning logs. "We do burn the fireplace every day," Bo adds.

We're in an open kitchen area with counters covered in colored Mexican tiles. On one end of the kitchen is a large family room with comfortable overstuffed couches in pink and mauve. Eating from a bowl on a tile countertop is a beautiful cat with powder-puff fur that matches the sofa coverings. "We call her 'She,' " Bo says as I pet the animal's soft, warm coat.

At the other end of the open kitchen is another room with a long rough-hewn table next to the fireplace. Just outside the window a curtain of water falls from the red-tile roof into a black solar swimming pool. "We recycle the water from the pool to the roof," John says, poking at the blazing logs. "Makes a unique waterfall."

Bo sets a pot of tea and cookies on the table. As I sit down, she pours the tea, then pulls out a leather-bound photo album and opens it. Inside are color photographs of the *rejoneador* (fighting on horseback) bullfight sequence from the movie, *Bolero*.

"This was the most exciting horse to ride," Bo says, pointing at a black stallion. "He was the wildest of all."

Looking at the bull in the photos (actually a large calf), I asked how she learned to ride like a Spaniard in the *rejoneador* fight sequences.

"John," she says. "He taught me how to have a light hand and a good seat, to ride like a Spaniard as if I was part of the horse." She looks at another photo of her riding an agitated palomino past the horns of the calf. "For the fight sequences we used some of the most famous horses in Spain, which we got from the Peralta brothers, the great *rejoneadors*."

"Was filming the fight terrifying?" I asked. The calf looked big, and it did have leather-covered horns.

"No, I was too excited," she says turning a page of the album. "We went to Spain six weeks early to train so I could get accustomed to the horses before going into the ring with the calf. Unfortunately, I only had three days to train. Then I watched the Peraltas in actual bullfights. When it was time to film, I went in the ring and did it—the first time!" She laughs. "Everybody was shocked, me, John—the Peraltas most of all. They told me I did ride like a Spaniard."

That's quite a compliment.

"Oh, it was," she says, eyes bright and proud.

John moves away from the fireplace and says, "We were going to take three days to shoot the sequence, but we only had half a day. When Bo got in the ring she was high as a kite with excitement.

"You like bullfights?" I ask John.

"He studied to be a bullfighter for three years," Bo says quickly.

"You have to be involved with the macho," says John. "It was something I was at the time. I hated acting, thought it was very sissified." (Because of his boyish good looks Derek was condemned to playing pretty-boy romantic leads in such movies of the '50s as *Rogues of Sherwood Forest.* His best known acting success was as an accused killer opposite Humphrey Bogart in *Knock on Any Door.*)

"Bullfighting does not have to be dangerous," John continues. "It's when your ego gets in the way; that makes it dangerous. The crowd starts pushing you and because you are sick of them, you say fuck it and get your ass clobbered."

"Lucky you didn't get into bullfighting," I say.

Bo laughs. "His ego would have gotten him killed."

"Ego is a terrible thing," Derek admits.

No one speaks for a moment. I look at the bullfighting photographs. "Did you fake any of the fight sequences?" I finally ask. "Did you use a bull's head mounted on wheels?"

"No, not in the movie," John says. 'Just for some of the still photos." He goes back to the fireplace, pokes the logs a couple of times then leaves Bo and me alone to finish the interview.

"Do you plan on breeding Andalusian horses?"

"Yes. They are fabulous horses. Spanish horses have so much—nobility. There are only a limited number in the United States, perhaps 1,000, and I would like to promote the breed. It's the kind of horse you have fun with."

"Were you the typical sixteen-year-old girl who fell in love with horses?"

"Kind of. My father always knew I wanted a horse, and he finally bought a twelve-year old rental horse with bones that stuck out. But, it was my first horse, and I loved him. When John and I got together, he wanted horses. They had almost been his whole life. He's a great horseman."

"When you're not training and breeding horses, what do you do?" I ask.

"We travel a lot," she says. "John and I just came back from Indonesia and Hong Kong."

Looking for movie locations? I ask, noting that the Derek's have not filmed anything since *Bolero,* a 1984 release. Other than her nude exposure, she has been far from overexposed by the few movies she has acted in.

"We have two projects we are thinking about filming in the Orient. We may be wrong, but we're not in any hurry," she continues, crossing her legs under her in the chair, curling like a cat into a feline position. "We don't have to leave home to work. We don't have an entourage of agents, managers and lawyers. We do it all ourselves, and produce our own movies. The Tarzan movie was commercially very successful, as was *Bolero.*

"Unfortunately, *Bolero* was completely misunderstood by the critics and most of the audience. The ad campaign by the movie company portrayed the film as a *serious picture.* We were making an erotic, sensual, silly, *fun* picture. It was camp, a corny romance."

She leans forward and her angelic features strive for a harder line. "I haven't done anything in any of my movies that I *feel bad* about. Besides, I would rather use myself as a commodity and exploit myself rather than have someone else do it. What most producers don't realize is they are not exploiting a product, they are exploiting a person. That's dangerous."

"And you felt you would have been exploited had you made movies for other producers?"

"Oh yes! Absolutely. I am a very strong person, but I was not so strong in the beginning of my career that I couldn't have been used. Believe me, the movie industry can be rotten and miserable and you meet rotten people."

"You have taken a lot of severe criticism from the press and movie critics," I say. "Does it hurt?"

"When I walk down the street people are really friendly," she says slowly, "and I wonder how they can be so nice with all the horrible things that have been written about us. We have done several television interviews here at the ranch to show people *us,* how we really are."

"Why has the press treated you this way?"

"There is always someone they are attacking, someone they have put on their 'hit' list."

"How did you make the list?"

She curls herself tighter in the chair. "It began with Life magazine. Life was looking for a new girl to discover, like they had done with Marilyn Monroe. Producers, as a matter of habit, send movies of their new actresses to Life for consideration. Orion Pictures, who had just made *10*, but hadn't released it, sent it in. Life picked me as their new discovery."

She unfolds herself and stands up. "Life wanted me on the cover coming out of a burlap sack, naked, with a bow in my hair!" She raises her arms over her head illustrating the "popping out of a sack" idea. "Inside the magazine I was supposed to pose for look-alike pictures of Rita Hayworth and Farrah Fawcett. I was to be 'Life's Gift to America.' I didn't think of myself as Life's discovery or as their personal present to America, so I said no thank you."

She plops down into the chair. "That made Life furious. I got an immediate call to meet with five of Orion Picture's top *honchos.* They couldn't understand why I wouldn't pose for the cover. You would have thought these guys had better things to do than badger one little girl for an hour and a half on the phone. They kept using the old cliche: 'You'll never work in this town again,' but that didn't bother me. I wouldn't be in the movie business or any business and do things against my will. That they couldn't understand.

"I had already signed to do my second movie, *A Change of Season* with Shirley MacLaine and Anthony Hopkins. Well, the Orion people called the movie's producer, Marty Ransohoff, and tried to get him to take me off the film. Marty was also a rebel and wouldn't do it, so the editor of Life called him and tried to get me canned. Imagine, *the editor of Life!*"

"They weren't used to anyone, especially a young actress, saying no," I offered.

She giggles happily, a little girl giggle, bright and vibrant. "It was so strange to them. Once you say no, that makes them even more determined to get you to say yes. Life magazine called me again and said they'd take whatever photos I wanted. I said I'd do beach shots, so they sent over a photographer. *He came with the burlap sack* and an order to shoot the look-alike poses. Again I said no." She sighs. "That's how I got on the 'hit' list."

Even without the cover of Life magazine, Bo Derek became a cinema sensation. The press clamored for information about this new girl who had made the number ten synonymous with beauty. Orion Pictures, who hadn't dreamed of the impact the movie would make, didn't have a personal biography on Bo. To have something to write about, editors dug out information on John Derek.

"It was all so silly," Bo says. "They found stuff about John being a Svengali, and how he had made Ursula and Linda famous. That press stuff just wasn't true. Ursula and Linda made it on their own. But the writers figured that John was a pygmalion and that I was his next creation. They termed him a hypnotist, a black magician, a sinister Svengali."

"Yet, you wouldn't be where you are today without John," I comment.

"That's true," she answers. "I'd still be a beach bum named Mary Cathleen."

Mary Cathleen Collins met John Derek when she was a sixteen-year-old fledgling actress auditioning for a film Derek was directing called, *And Once upon a Time.* (The picture has never been released.)

"I never did feel like Mary Cathleen," Bo says. "I wasn't a 'Cathy.' John started throwing names at me, and I responded to 'Bo'. I knew it was right. John, along with his wife, Linda (Evans), discouraged my phony smiles, scrubbed my face clean from the awful makeup I was wearing—I thought it was sophisticated—then took some photographs."

When Bo saw the photographs, she saw someone else, someone not just pretty—which she had been told she was—but someone beautiful, which she didn't realize. John Derek had introduced Bo to herself.

Bo had not seriously thought about being an actress until she met John. She had no theatrical training, and her only link to the movies was from her mother who was a Hollywood hairdresser with clients such as Ann-Margret. (Bo is the oldest of four children. She has a brother, Collin and two "very beautiful" sisters, Kerry and Kelly. Kerry works as the Derek's secretary.) One day while Bo was backstage with her mother in Las Vegas an agent spotted her and said, "You should be in pictures." Then John Derek came along.

"Soon after we first met, we hated each other," Bo says. "He kept picking on me saying I was lazy. I thought he was mean. But he was right, I was terribly lazy, which was hurting the film. I wanted to be on the beach."

"On a scale of one to ten, how do you rate John as a husband?" I ask.

"For me he's great," she answers.

"Any faults?"

"No. . . ." Bo pauses. "Well, he is very opinionated. And. . .sometimes he's hard to live with. He wants things done now, he has no patience. Most of all he can't understand carelessness. I can be careless and do silly things and that doesn't compute in his brain."

"Children?"

"I love children," she says, then adds quickly, ". . .the *nice* ones. John wants a guarantee that it will be a girl, but what if we got stuck with a little monster?" she shakes her head. "We're really on the move too much for children, perhaps if we ever really settle down. . . .Then I'd have to have a nanny. I don't want to be tied down and resent having children."

"You evidently feel you have your head screwed on right," I say.

She giggles and her dimples deepen. "One of the things that bothers John is that I never contemplate who I am. For me to think about myself is a waste of time. I'm not interested in wondering about the future or why we were placed on earth."

"Too bad," I say with a smile. "I was going to ask you to define civilization."

She laughs and gets up from her chair. "Ask John. He'll have a ball with that one!" She walks to the window and silently looks out at the rolling hills beyond. Then she says, "I don't need to know what will happen. I've got it all here."

She turns to me. "And I *love* it."

Cher

Just You and Me, Babe

"Cher gave me this Christmas card last year. She wrote: 'Merry Christmas Mother—You're old, but you're still a sex goddess...Love—ME!'"   Georgia Holt, Cher's Mother

Cher's Mother, Georgia, is standing in front of the sound studio microphone belting out a rhythm and blues song:

"I sure don' wanna love you..."

Cher's sitting in the glassed-in sound booth, watching and listening to her mother. Her lips move soundlessly with the music, and her body sways instinctively with the beat. She whispers, "Okay, Mom...good...very good...terrific!"

In the studio, Georgia presses the "Mickey Mouse" headphones tightly against her ears and squeezes her eyes shut, listening to the taped musical beat.

"I don' wanna call you baby..."

Suddenly she stops: "God, I'm so *flat* on so *many* notes! I sound like the chorus from *Rosemary's Baby*."

Cher presses the mike button on the console in front of her, and her voice echos out into the studio. "Look, Mom," she says reassuringly, "Pick up that last line—just do it—you *know how*."

And Cher continues to listen to her mother's voice, singing "Good. Yeah, really special..."

Today *is* special. For the first time, Georgia Holt, who lives in a modest home in Montecito, has asked her daughter, Cher, who lives in a massive new Egyptian-styled mansion in Beverly Hills, dubbed "Queen Tut's Tomb", to help her do a musical recording; to "Kinda be her producer."

Sure Mom.

Then Georgia asked her to stick around for a TV taped interview. "I'll ask the questions."

Sure Mom.

Ian Bernard, Montecito writer, musician and musical director, agreed to produce the half hour "special" and Cox Cable would film it. So, here Cher and Georgia are, in the Santa Barbara Sound Studios (where folks like Kenny Loggins, Burl Ives and Neal Hefti record their songs), having a special day together. But, it hasn't always been like this between Cher and Georgia.

Uh uh...not even close.

"Good God, no," Georgia Holt recalls later, relaxing in an overstuffed chair in her Montecito home. "Cher and I had some very bad periods of estrangement. We wouldn't speak to each other for two, sometimes three years at a stretch."

"I sure don' wanna love you . . ."

Cher, still listening intently to her mother's singing, smiles. A thin gold retainer, almost like a piece of jewelry, is fitted across her teeth. Her raven-black hair is a marvelously calculated mop, immaculately coifed to appear casual. A loose fitting cotton sweat shirt falls off one shoulder showing a perpetual California tan.

"I called her 'Poke' when she was little. For Pocahontas. Everyone said she looked like a little Indian. Her father was Armenian, and she took his dark coloring. She hated the skin color and hair because the California golden girl was in style. She finally had to set her own style.

To achieve her own "style" Cher made herself into a kind of trash *objet d'art.* She became known as the "First Lady of Flash" and the "Queen of Glitz." During the hip-hugging decade of frenzied pop music, when Sonny and Cher's "I Got you, Babe" zoomed to the top of the charts, Cher was the pig-tailed princess in love beads and chains, in fringed blouses and mini skirts. She was the Pocahontas hippie princess incarnate.

"Cher invented herself." Georgia says. "She is her own creation."

Cher also created her own publicity. In 1969, when Sonny & Cher were getting started, they wore fur vests and jeans into the London Hilton—and were promptly thrown out. Cameras flashed. In the '70s Cher's navel appeared on television; her right nipple made it on the cover of *TIME* in 1975. In the same decade she introduced a clothing style that was quickly gobbled up by a generation looking for anything new—bell-bottoms.

"I remember she used to stare at pictures of old movie stars when she was a child. Like Greta Garbo and Jean Harlow. She loved a photo of Jean Harlow in loose silk pajamas with wide legs . . ."

Cher has always had an incurable disease for clothes. A clothesaholic. She once told a rude sales girl who wouldn't wait on her, that she "wanted to buy *that* dress in every color" they had. She knew it was an original Rudi Gernreich and very expensive. But, that's the Cher who loves clothes, who loves money (one of her fears is losing it all), and who loves to be famous.

"She knew she was going to be famous when she was a little girl. I remember seeing her practice signing her autograph when she was only 12."

Cher didn't start out to be a star, even though she says she always knew she *would* be famous. The problem was she didn't know *how* to be famous. She didn't know *how* to do *anything* that a famous person should. She *did* sing around the house. She learned that from her mother, Georgia, who was a sometime actress and model on the "I Love Lucy" show, and who had also appeared as a vocalist in night clubs.

"I was singing at the 'Swing Club' in Fresno when I was three months pregnant with Cher," Georgia remembers. "Cher was born when I was nineteen."

What talent Georgia had rubbed off on Cher in a big way. It had to as Cher had no skills. She was also terribly shy.

"She wouldn't even call information to ask a question."

Yet, Cher wanted to be famous.

"I kept telling her she was something special. She had a luminous quality, a 'presence.' "

Cher wanted *something* desperately, but she didn't know what. The strain led to serious mother/daughter confrontations. Finally, when she was sixteen, she left home and moved in with a girlfriend who had a boyfriend named Sonny Bono. *The* Sonny Bono. The one who's new songs were being recorded. *The* Sonny Bono who was playing background music in a band. "When I first saw him everything else just faded away,' Cher remembers.

Sonny said he didn't "find her particularly attractive," but offered her his house as a roosting place. No questions asked. She lied to her mother, saying she was moving in with a stewardess. (She also lied to Sonny, telling him she was nineteen.) Georgia found out about the arrangement and forced her daughter to move out.

"That wasn't our best year."

A week later, Sonny called Cher and said: "Don't you think it's about time you asked me to marry you?" They didn't marry for several years, but they quickly gave birth to the singing duo of *Sonny & Cher*.

It all happened by accident.

Cher was standing around in a recording studio watching Sonny play, when—get this—a guy comes running up and asks her if she can sing. It seems one of the background singers hadn't shown up and they needed someone fast. Can you sing?

"I dunno," Cher shrugged.

"God, she had been singing around the house since she could talk!"

So, the guy asked her if she could carry a tune. "Yeah," she replied. And he said: "Get out there and make some noise."

Cher made a lot of "noise" in the next two years. "I Got You Babe" sold over four million copies and knocked the Beatles out of first spot on the charts. Little Cherilyn Sarkisian was finally famous—at age eighteen.

"Cherilyn...that's what I named her. Cheril Lynn was Lana Turner's daughter's name and I loved it. I just kind of combined the two names."

Eighteen and an overnight success. Cher was in shock. She wasn't mentally prepared to make it that big, that quick.

"She wouldn't go on stage if Sonny wasn't with her. She was shy, and held her head down, the hair hanging in her face. Everyone thought it was 'cool.' She was terrified. Like a baby."

"I don' wanna call you baby."

Georgia finishes the song, takes off the headphones and walks into the glassed-in sound booth. Cher applauds.

Georgia grins and sits beside her daughter.

"You're ready for an opening night in Vegas," Cher says.

"I remember your first opening night in Las Vegas, you had on those sexy black high heels and that gorgeous black outfit, and you did a turn and the shoe went flying off. You had to do the number in one shoe."

"People will forgive anything if you put your *best foot* forward." Cher shrugs at her little joke. "I'm not a letter perfect performer, but I do try and reach an emotional level. Now television..." She grimaces and looks past the lights at the cameramen. "No offense, guys." Everyone laughs. "Television is a mediocre medium. You don't have to be good, just personable."

"Yet TV was the training ground for your opening on Broadway," Georgia says.

"Television taught me a lot," Cher agrees. "When I went to Broadway I was shocked to see all the girls throwing up before they went on stage. I mean, they were great stage actresses, but they weren't used to being on stage the way I was—alone. Once you have been on stage by yourself, you learn there is nothing to hide behind."

Cher had been hiding behind her music for over a decade, yet, she really wanted to be an actress. She feared becoming the Dinah Shore of her generation. To break from the *Cher* mold, she went to every major movie studio in Tinseltown, but producers said no one watching a movie would ever believe she was anybody but *Cher*. "My career had cooled down to an ice cube," she recalls. "The only offer I got was to do movies like, *The Fish Who Saved Cleveland*. She was beginning to worry if there was life after flash.

That's when Georgia, quite by accident (she had dialed the wrong number), called the movie director Robert Altman. Altman politely asked what Cher was up to.

Georgia said that Cher was in New York studying acting with Lee Strasberg. Altman, who just happened to be directing his first play in New York, remembers he had a "vague thought." The thought matured enough to send Cher a script of his play, *Come Back to the Five & Dime, Jimmy Dean, Jimmy Dean*.

"Now don't hold out too much hope," Altman told Cher, "You're in fast company with actresses like Karen Black and Sandy Dennis." Cher read for the part—and got it. When the play opened she got better reviews than anyone else.

"When I saw her on the stage in New York, I started to cry," Georgia remembers. "I was so nervous. I had the same feeling I have when I fly. I hate to fly! I don't move, I don't breathe, I don't go to the bathroom. I think Mike Nichols must have felt the same way when he came by to see Cher in a matinee."

Enter Mike Nichols, the director with the golden touch.

"Mike Nichols surrounds people with love," Georgia says. "When I first met him, I said, 'It's a good thing you're married, or I might try for number seven.' "

(Georgia has been married six times, three of them before she was twenty-one. "I haven't married for twenty years now," she says emphatically.)

In the sound booth, Georgia asks Cher: "When Mike Nichols came in for the matinee performance, did you know he was there?"

"No, thank God. Fortunately, matinees were where I did my best performance. There was no real pressure to be good. Nichols came backstage afterward and said..."

"He told her she was brilliant," Georgia interjects.

"He asked me if I wanted to do a movie with Meryl Streep. I was kinda flippant and said, 'Yeah, why not.' I really didn't believe he had offered me a part in a movie. Then the next day my manager called and said Nichols had asked for me in a movie called, *Silkwood*. I was thrilled, and scared half to death. I said to myself, "I can't do this."

In *Silkwood* Cher portrayed a character that is the antithesis of *Cher*, a dumpy middle-class female in threadbare jeans, polyester men's shirt, flat shoes, and no make-up. "I looked like a corpse." Cher says. When Nichols called her after she acepted the part (sight unseen), he said, "By the way, the character is a lesbian. But, you'll love her."

She did.

"When I first saw Silkwood, on that huge screen, I was terrified for Cher. It was in a private screening room and all Cher had told me was that she was playing a lesbian and not to let it upset me. I was sitting there and I started to sweat, not perspire, but sweat! Yet, the movie held me spellbound. I thought she—my daughter—was brilliant."

Georgia pauses, then looks over at Cher. "I guess I have one more serious question—If you could do anything over again, would you change anything?"

Cher shrieks in a little mouse-like voice and says, "Don't ask that..." Then, she shrugs, "Sure, I probably would have chosen to do a lot of things differently, but when you're going through life, you can't sit back and watch, then make your decisions. You have to make the choices that are available." She pauses, and breathes out heavily, as if it's time she got something off her mind. "I have made some dumb choices. The only thing I would have done, differently, is to do everything quicker. I wish I had only been married to Sonny three years. And, I wish I had never been married to Gregory Allman. I wish I had never seen Gregg except for that one required night that gave me Elijah Blue, my son. I just wish I had gotten through things faster so I would have more time. I have a lot of things to do—and time is running out."

Cher picks it up: "How about the day you beat up the Swedish masseuse."

Georgia: (She giggles.) "God, she was built like a wrestler."

Cher: "She called the dog pound to come get my dog, remember?"

Georgia: "She hit me and pushed me down the steps."

Cher: (Starting to laugh.) "But Mother, quick thinking, grabbed her by the hair and swung her around the yard."

Georgia: (Laughing, almost in tears.) "She made me mad."

Cher: (Pause, looking deeply at her mother.) "That was one of my first recollections of my Mother."

Georgia's giggles subside, and she looks back at her daughter for a moment and the eyes tell it all. After all of the rough days, after all of the harsh, meaningless words, all of the years apart, after all of that, they can still touch each other.

Then Georgia says, "I guess we finally got our act together."

Yeah.

"Just You and Me Babe."

Cher and her mother, Georgia Holt, at the recording session. (Cork Millner)

Anne Francis today in her Montecito home. (Hara)

Anne Francis

Ex-Sex Goddess

Since this profile was written, Anne Francis has moved from her beloved castle-like home, La Bergerie, *into a smaller house in Montecito only a few doors away from actor Don Murray. Amazingly enough, when they were both teenagers, Anne and Don lived near each other in Long Island, New York. Don Murray was Anne Francis' first date.*

"There is something new in Hollywood and 20th Century-Fox has her—a blond Mona Lisa who never allows her strikingly beautiful face to reveal her thoughts and feelings. Her name is ANNE FRANCIS and she is a tall self-assured youngster who in repose is a perfect prototype of the classical Leonardo da Vinci portrait."   —1950 Hollywood press release

Anne Francis is standing on the wide stone porch of her Santa Barbara home looking like a windswept heroine from a gothic novel. Behind her, her home, *La Bergerie,* rises like a medieval castle, a huge stone structure that seems to be trying to lift its turreted mass into the sky.

"Welcome to *La Bergerie,*" she says in a deep—almost Bette Davis-deep—voice. She smiles, not the Mona Lisa smile touted by Hollywood hype so many years before, but a warm "how have you been" kind of smile. She is tall and trim, her hair still palomino blond, but bobbed rather than hanging to her shoulders. And the mole—her trademark—is still there at the corner of her mouth.

Anne Francis is no longer the "sex-goddess" that Darryl Zanuck, boss of 20th Century-Fox studios, tried so desperately to groom her for in the early '50s. She never quite fit the Mona Lisa mold he had envisioned for her. The problem was that Anne Francis never wanted to be a sex goddess. It just wasn't her style. When she finally told Zanuck she wanted out of her contract he pouted, "But, I thought you were going to be a sexy starlet."

"Starlet!" Anne Francis says as if an electrical impulse had coursed through her. "How I hated that word—starlet. It sounds like something cute and snuggly, and has the connotation of a little fluff of an actress on a producer's arm; a hollow empty-headed image in a padded bra." She sighs heavily and steps through the doorway of her home. "But that was what I was, at least in Hollywood vernacular—a starlet. I was *in* the business, but I wasn't *of* the business!"

She walks down a hallway and into a large living room. "You see, at the studio they only groomed stars, not actresses, and I had begun to realize there is a lot more to life than being a big star. I needed to discover the real me—the *inner me.*"

The discovery was slow at first. She was kept busy playing in such movies as *Lydia Bailey, Bad Day at Black Rock* with Spencer Tracy, *Blackboard Jungle* with Glenn Ford and *The Rack* opposite Paul Newman. She also starred in a television series called *Honey West* in which she portrayed a female James Bond character. But her active mind kept searching for a deeper meaning to her existence, and her thoughts led her to an awareness of the impulses that moved her life in many different directions. Finally she traded her lipstick for a typewriter and wrote a book on her inner experiences and called it, *Voices From Home: An Inner Journey.*

"It is not the typical Hollywood autobiography," Anne Francis says, shaking her head. "But..." she shrugs, "since I am an actress the first response to the book was, 'Aha! Another Hollywood biographical expose.' And the next thought was, 'Who cares?'

"Well, I care! *Voices From Home* is not about hidden skeletons, social calendars and name revealing dalliances. It is about my experience with the essence of my being, the same essence that pervades us all."

The critics response to Anne Francis' book—kind of a new and personal look at "positive thinking"—has been favorable. Rex Reed called it an "extraordinary book on many levels." Earl Wilson wrote: "Anne Francis proves it can be done. An actress can write a book that is not a sex confessional but an adventure in the good life."

Yet the book is still an expose. A spiritual expose. An exhilirating pilgrimage into the actresses own personal "inner space."

The book is about the "essence of being," the inexplicable reality of mysticism, psychic phenomena and the inner workings of the mind and spirit. Anne Francis says she first became aware of the mind's power when she had a "near-death experience" at age four. "I nearly drowned. Suddenly I was immersed in water surrounded by glorious translucent green light, colors beyond human imagination came toward me. I was close to going to the 'other side' when I was pulled out. And I was angry. Angry at being taken away from all that beauty."

"You see each of us has an inner eye and an inner ear of spirit which are far greater and far more real than anything that exists on a physical plane. And that's what my book is—an inner journey. It is about the flashes and insights that happened along the way— the signposts in my growth."

Anne Francis touches a copy of her book which is resting on a small table in the living room of her home. She is sitting in a straight-backed chair next to a massive fireplace that is right out of Ivanhoe. Wide French windows open onto a wide expanse of lawn and through the pine trees the Pacific Ocean can be seen hazy in the distance.

"When I first saw this house in 1976 I felt like I was going back in history," she says, touching the arm of the chair with her fingers. "I felt that I had been whisked into a little Normandy Chateau. It was as if I was being transported back to France, but in another era. It was almost as if I had been here before in a previous existence. At the same time, I became aware of what seemed a 'gathering' around me and there was a message that said, 'this is the place.' "

She pauses and lets that sink in, then explains. "Reincarnation? I'm not one to dwell on that concept to the extent we are excusing the present." She smiles. "Besides, the problem with reincarnation is having to learn to tie your shoes again. Or tell time—the big hand is on the twelve—or learn to do math again. Ugh."

She makes a sweeping gesture around the living room. "Yet, there is a feeling of solidarity and tranquility here in this house, or what some have called a 'castle.' The name *La Bergerie* means the 'sheepfold' and it has a warmth and charm, even with fourteen rooms and five baths. And, of course, there are three of us here with my two daughters, Janey and Maggie.

Santa Barbara has the same charm. There is the feeling of the Mediterranean and Hawaii mixed together—mist on the mountains, palms along the beach and old Spanish and French architecture. Santa Barbara ground radiates peace to me."

Anne Francis' move to Santa Barbara and into her private castle was not an easy task. Most of the money she had made as a Hollywood star had vanished. "When I decided I had to have this house, I realized I was not a wealthy lady. I doubt I had a thousand dollars in savings. However, a few investments that seemed doomed to dormancy suddenly yielded profits and another house soared in value, so by 1978 I felt I could manage the purchase. Of course, I also had to go back to work as an actress.

"Starting again isn't easy," she says, brushing a blond curl away from her forehead. "I've had people come up to me and say, 'I know you! Now let me see, what's your name...don't tell me...it's, it's...' To which I finally reply, 'Anne Francis.' They look startled and say, 'No, that's not it.' Once in an elevator a most serious gentleman studied me very carefully, then asked, 'Whatever happened to you?' "

She laughs, a deep throaty rumble. "There is the story about the distinguished actress, Mildred Dunnock. A producer asked her, 'Now, Miss Dunnock, what have you done?' To which she replied, 'About what?' " Anne Francis grins at the story, then her eyes take on a burning intensity. "If anyone asks me what I have done they better be prepared to get their ears bent back like one of Uri Geller's spoons."

Like most actresses of her generation, Anne Francis watched her career change radically as she passed the age of forty. However, because she had constantly tried to cast off the image of a sex goddess she found that she was able to adapt to character roles more easily than svelte starlets. She has done television roles as varied as Patti Colson in *Born Again* and a roller-derby queen on *Fantasy Island*.

"I've turned down a lot of scripts," she says. "I love acting, but you wouldn't believe some of the things I have been sent to read. I had to turn down a very good role because of the violence in the script. I simply couldn't handle that. At least I didn't have to cope with the sex and violence when I began my career."

Anne Francis' career began during the Depression years when she was six years old. A New York friend suggested to Anne's mother that Anne would make a pretty child model. "We went to the Robert Powers modeling agency," Anne remembers. "While we were waiting in the lobby Mr. Powers stuck his head out of his office door, pointed to me and said, 'I'll take that one!' "

As a teenager she appeared in her first movie, cast in the role of a teenage prostitute, *So Young, So Bad*. The director insisted his young star wear falsies in a scene where she was doused with water. "He even had the wardrobe woman sew buttons on the tips so I would look sexier," Anne sighs. "That was my first taste of some of the indignities in the world of film-making."

Darryl Zanuck, the head of 20th Century-Fox, happened to see Anne in *So Young, So Bad* and offered her a contract with his studio. She went to Hollywood—"a frightening and alien place"—and became—a starlet.

Zanuck groomed his young glamour girl for stardom, and cast her in *Lydia Bailey*. In one color extravaganza little blond Anne Francis was remade into a celluloid goddess of the cinema. Eager publicity agents tacked on sobriquets such as the "Mona Lisa of Movieland," and "The Palomino Blonde."

"I was completely wrong for the part in *Lydia Bailey*" Anne says. "It should have been a flashy, dark-haired actress like Linda Darnell. I was much too blond and much too young for the character. But it was quite an experience for the first time out, and I learned what Hollywood was all about. I didn't like everything I saw and did, but that's what Hollywood and the studios wanted of me."

Hollywood kept their new star busy making films, casting her opposite established male stars such as James Cagney, Spencer Tracy, Glenn Ford, Paul Newman, and later with a new actor called Burt Reynolds. "When I worked in the movie *Impasse* in 1972 with Burt, I wondered why he wasn't the biggest star in the business," Anne says. "He had charisma and that marvelous sense of humor. But they kept giving him wooden characters to play. He used to call himself the 'wooden Indian.' Then he did the centerfold in Cosmopolitan and everybody wanted him."

She is interrupted when the front door opens and Janey, her oldest daughter, calls down the hallway, "Hi, I'm home!" Anne calls back "We'll have meat loaf—left over..." and her daughter's footsteps recede down the hallway. Anne pauses and says, "Where was I? Oh, yes, 'The successful sex goddess.' " She puts on a wry smile. "I suppose that, to the movie going public, I was very successful. What they didn't know was in those years my personal life was a mess." She stops, thinking back. "I was in my early twenties when I met a poetically frail, and darkly handsome UCLA film production student. The marriage lasted three years. It was the successful wife and the struggling husband plot all over again."

Not long after the divorce she met and fell in love again. She tells the story in her book: "He was a gentle man with kind authority and a warm humor. But as time wore on I began to realize that he did not love me as I loved him. The telephone became my lifeline to happiness."

It was during this period of emotional stress that she made the movie, *Forbidden Planet*, an early space thriller that has become a cult film for science ficton buffs. "I went to see the movie not long ago," Anne says. "It was being shown in an auditorium where I had been asked to speak. I sat there watching this pretty little blond actress on the screen, this cherubic creature wearing brief, flashy costumes, and I thought, You are such a sweet little girl and you have so much ahead of you to learn—so much to learn... It was a strange feeling to see that happy kid up there and remember the turmoil I was going through in my life at the time. Here I had been married once and was going through an unrequited love affair, and I was also terribly unsure of myself, my life and who I was. I kept staring at this pretty self-contained blond creature who appeared to have the world by the tail—but didn't."

It was not long after that a second marriage also failed. "We were both on rocky emotional ground," Anne says. "Ten months after the birth of our daughter, Janey, we were separated." She wrote in her book: "I had realized once and for all the emptiness of believing another to be the answer to one's inner yearnings."

Anne began to search for the inner meaning of her existence, a search that eventually culminated in her book, *Voices From Home*. At the same time she continued her acting career, working in comedies, science fiction and drama. Then in 1965, at the age of thirty-five, she starred in the television series, "Honey West." The show was all tongue in cheek," she says. "The violence wasn't real. I remember doing a lot of physical work, running and climbing; I even studied karate for six weeks."

The show was a smash success and thirty-two segments were made. Then it was abruptly cancelled. The producer was able to buy the British import, "The Avengers," starring Diana Riggs, for less than it took to film "Honey West."

"I was surprised and disappointed when it was cancelled," Anne says, "But there was a dichotomy within my feelings. Janey was only four and I had hardly been able to give any time to her. That's also when I decided to adopt my second daughter, Maggie." Anne relaxes in the chair and smiles. "Life has many treasures and miracles for all of us if we take the time to receive them. Janey and Maggie are my miracles."

She fluffs her blond hair with her fingers, then goes on, "You know, my life has been kind of a mixed tapestry. There has always been so much to learn and I seem to be falling short in my own development, but I'll keep on searching. I think it is important to search for that power within ourselves. We may not reach ultimate perfection, but at least we are reaching."

Eva Marie Saint and her husband, Jeffrey Hayden, at home.

Eva Marie Saint

On Stage — Together

I knocked on the door of Eva Marie Saint and her husband, Jeffrey Hayden's, seaside condominium five minutes early. Hayden answered my buzz, and led me into the living room. As I passed a closed bedroom door, I heard Eva Marie's voice: "You're early!" Hayden handed me a cup of coffee, and a few minutes later Eva Marie came in all smiles. As I reached out to shake her hand, I tipped the full coffee cup and dribbled all over my pants leg. There was an embarrassed silence as they must have thought, "What kind of fool is this?" Yet, the interview went smoothly, and, much to their amazament, the coffee stain dried and vanished.

It's like watching a scene from a television situation comedy. Or even better, a "slice of life" sequence from a play by Pirandello.

Eva Marie Saint, winner of the Academy Award for Best Supporting Actress in the classic movie *On The Waterfront,* and her husband, Jeffrey Hayden, who has directed such television shows as "Magnum, P.I.," "Quincy," and "Night Rider," are sitting in the living room of their Montecito beach condominium talking about their life together in the theater. As we enter the scene, the dialogue is centered around the genesis of their thirty-four-year-old marriage.

Jeffrey: "I was going home from the NBC radio studios one night on the New York subway..."

Eva Marie: "You could ride the subway at night then, that was the late 1940s."

Jeffrey: "I was looking at watches in the window of a subway arcade shop. I never owned a watch, and I told myself, 'Look, you're making $35 a week. Buy yourself one.' "

Eva Marie: (Turns to him, cocks her head, a quizzical look on her face.) "I never heard *this* story before." (Laughs happily, a nice ringing sound like wind chimes.)

Jeffrey: "I had a Mickey Mouse watch when I was a kid."

Eva Marie: "You should have saved it. Might be worth something now." (More laughter, bubbly, a cool stream.)

Jeffrey: (Serious) "And I looked into the reflecton of the store window and saw the most absolutely wonderful woman go by. She had this terrific walk, and I had read Stanislavsky about observing people, you know, their walk..."

Eva Marie: "Not my body?"

Jeffrey: (Still serious) "I couldn't see her face as she walked by, but I observed that she was carrying an actress' portfolio, and I read her name on the side—EVA MARIE SAINT."

Eva Marie: (Turns on the couch, arm on the back cushion and looks intently at her husband, amused and fascinated with the retelling of this chance meeting that happened so many years ago.)

Jeffrey: "A month later at the NBC actors' lounge I saw her again from the back, same blond hair, same portfolio, same name. Luckily, she was talking to an actor I knew, so I went up and said hello."

Eva Marie: "Ah...you saw my face for the first time?"

Jefrey: "It was a pretty face. So I said, 'How about coffee?' She said, 'No.' "

Eva Marie: "I was so busy beginning my acting career."

Jeffrey: "Another month. I saw her again. And I decided to ask again..." (He turns toward her, looks deeply in her brilliant blue eyes.) "How about lunch?"

Eva Marie: "No candlelight dinner?"

Jeffrey: "She remembers candlelight, linen table cloths, but it was just a primitive little French restaurant with wooden tables."

Eva Marie: "I thought he was a nice looking fellow and I loved the way he talked."

Jefrey: "Dissolve to three years later..."

Eva Marie: "We got married."

The Jeffrey Haydens were married in 1951. And, as the boy-meets-girl movie script goes, they've lived happily ever after. In a business not noted for long marital relationships, the Haydens have managed to compatibly meld their respective professional careers with marriage. They also raised two children, a son Darrell, and a daughter, Laurette.

"Our family is very important to us,' Eva Marie says. "We never allowed our professional careers to interfere with being a close family."

Eva Marie would never do more than one picture a year, so she could have enough time with the children," Jeffrey adds. "She was never really a stage mother. I think that's the secret of raising children in an acting atmosphere."

"One agent got very upset with me," Eva Marie remembers. 'He said, to be a superstar I had to go immediately from one film to the next." She shrugs. "I was at home with my children more than a 9 to 5 mother."

On several occasions Jeffrey has directed his wife in stage plays and television productions.

"Being married to someone in the business is so important," Eva Marie says. 'It's not like being married to a doctor or an English professor. We understand each other's needs in the theater. Jeffrey understands how I feel as an actress, and I know what he's thinking as a director. When we work together on stage or in a televison show, it's like putting icing on the cake."

"We have done a number of plays together," Jeffrey says running a hand through his graying hair. "Eva Marie acts and I direct. We even work on scenes at home after rehearsals are over. It's a real plus to have all that extra working time together."

"We have shared so much," Eva Marie says. "So many times."

DISSOLVE TO: 1954.

PLACE: New York.

EVENT: The Academy Awards. Eva Marie has been nominated for Best Supporting Actress in her first movie, *On The Waterfront*. She is also nine months pregnant.

Eva Marie: "There I was at the awards about to give birth, and Jeffrey was sitting next to me, and he looked at me all blown up and pregnant and whispered, 'If your name is called, honey, *relax*. Count to ten.'—Then the announcement came, 'And the winner for Best Supporting Actress is...' "

Jeffrey: "Eva Marie Saint!"

Eva Marie: "And I'm sitting there, smiling and counting, one, two, three...and Jeffrey has his hand on my knee and won't let me stand up until I've counted to ten."

Jeffrey: "Two days later she had the baby."

Eva Marie: "I could have had the baby right on stage."

After winning the Oscar in 1954, Eva Marie Saint's acting career blossomed and she went on to star in such movies as *Exodus* with Paul Newman, *North By Northwest* with Cary Grant, and *Raintree County* with Montgomery Clift ("I loved doing that one," she says.) She has remained active in the theater for the last three decades and most recently starred in a 1984 mini-series for television, "Fatal Vision," which also featured Karl Malden whom she had worked with in *On The Waterfront*.

The film also starred a young actor named Marlon Brando. "I usually tell groups I am speaking to that there is one question I won't answer: *What is Marlon Brando really like?* Everyone laughs, then I say, 'Confidentially, he was terrific!' " She pulls her legs up on the couch and curls them under her. "I think he was the finest actor I ever worked with. I knew him when he was finding joy in his work. He was a prince at that time, one of the most considerate actors I ever worked with. He was giving, both on and off stage, caring about whether I was cold or comfortable..." She pauses, then: "I haven't seen him since we worked together in "Waterfront" thirty years ago."

She leans her head to one side and the blonde hair drifts almost to her shoulder. "I remember auditioning for the part in *On The Waterfront*. They got me together in a room with Marlon and he started improvising a scene, kidding me a little, being fresh, and I got so involved I ended up crying and hitting him. It was a very emotional improvisation, but the director Could see we worked well together. Marlon made things happen so easily, he just kept pushing the right buttons."

Starring in an Academy Award-winning Movie was an auspicious start for the young actress. Yet, life in the theater is not all "highs." There have also been many lows. Eva Marie Saint's lowest moment started out as a wonderful, career-enhancing dream come true.

CUT TO: 1948.

PLACE: New York.

EVENT: Audition for the Broadway play, *Mr. Roberts*.

Eva Marie: "The first part I ever tried out for was as the Nurse in the stage production of *Mr. Roberts*. The play was directed by Josh Logan and starred Henry Fonda. When I was chosen for the part, I was elated! Then two weeks later I was *fired*."

Jeffrey: "Asked to *step down* might be a better way of saying it."

Eva Marie: "The producers thought they had a big hit on their hands, and must have become nervous about casting a new, untested actress, one who had never done a play before. I never really did know why I was *let go*. Years later "Hank" Fonda told me he figured they thought I looked too naive and innocent and virginal for the part." She smiles, and for a moment her face takes on a little-girl quality, a youthful happy aura that echos back to that day long ago. Then she adds: "Fonda also told me that when I left the stage I took the audience with me."

Jeffrey: "That was a nice thing to say."

Eva Marie: "Josh Logan, the director, who I admired and still admire very much, was the one who had to tell me I wasn't needed, but that I could stay on as understudy. I can remember thinking, 'I'm going to cry—but not in front of him.' So, I went downstairs in the dressing room and cried." Sitting there sobbing, I heard...(Taps her knuckles on the top of the coffee table in front of her—rap, rap, rap...) 'Eva Marie...can I come in?' and Henry Fonda walked into the dressing room. Then, one by one all the guys in the show— all thirty of them—came in. They told me they all had had their own disappointments and this could be one of the best things that happened to me, that I was young and this was my first theater cry..."

Jeffrey: "To cheer Eva Marie up they each told her their own tale of woe."

Eva Marie: (Pause.) "I still cried all the way home on the subway to Flushing Meadows. (Smiles miserably, still remembering that long-ago hurt.) I kept wondering what I was going to tell my mother and father. My Mom had hung a little gold star on my bedroom door, and on the subway I kept thinking, I'm going to have to take that gold star down. I sat there on the train thinking that if this was what acting was like, then it's not for me. *I didn't like this feeling.* I'll either get out or I'll continue to try, but I'll never allow myself to feel this way again. It was like a little voice telling me what to do, and I listened. And I have never felt like that again in my theater, televison or movie career."

Eva Marie Saint didn't start out to be an actress. When she left her home in Delmar, New York (near Albany), to enroll at Bowling Green College in Ohio, she had visions of being a teacher. "My mother was a teacher," she says, "and I knew how much she loved it. It just seemed a wonderful thing to train to be."

That's when a college friend "dared" her to try out for a play. She got the part and was hooked. She changed her major to speech and drama. "Perhaps the change wasn't all that sudden," Eva Marie says. "I had played the violin, sang in the chorus, was a cheerleader— I can still do my old high school cheer. . .I just loved being in groups. The theater filled a need at the time, and still does."

After graduation, Eva Marie went to New York and began to "beat the pavement" looking for work as an actress.

Also in New York was a young college graduate from the University of North Carolina at Chapel Hill named Jeffrey Hayden. Originally from the Bronx, Hayden had returned to the New York area with a strong desire to get into radio as a director. He got his first job with NBC in their studio research department. It was there, on a New York subway, that he saw Eva Marie Saint for the first time.

In the beginning they talked about their fledgling careers. Eva Marie had worked for eight months as the understudy in *Mr. Roberts* without getting the chance to go on stage. "One night the actress who played the part was very late and I was told to go on." Eva Marie says. "There I was in my nurse's outfit—I thought I looked so good in that little uniform—ready to go on stage, when the actress showed up. I was crushed."

"I told her to leave the show if she was unhappy," Jeffrey says. "Go! Get out in the world."

"That worked both ways," Eva Marie says. "Jeffrey wasn't happy either. His job at NBC radio wasn't creative. I told *him* to leave. Get into television."
Following each other's advice they left the security of their jobs and went into the new, rustic, untried theatrical medium of the 1950s—television.

"I went to work for ABC television in the late '40s," Jeffrey says. "I went from editing film to associate director for shows like 'Stop the Music' and the Julia Child cooking show, to becoming a director for live dramatic television.

"Both our careers were going in the directon of live television," Eva Marie says.

Jeffrey adds: "We were married in 1951 and worked in New York on such shows as Goodyear Playhouse, Philco, Kraft, Studio One. . ."

"It was like working in the theater," Eva Marie says.

"It was absolutely wonderful," Jeffrey says, a smile on his lips. "In those days you started with a beautifully written story; the writer had a vision. His story was about something, life and the human condition."

"Not car chases," Eva Marie says, nodding seriously.

"On television today you have to make certain compromises." Jeffrey explains. "The writers today are as good as they were in the first years of television, but now it's all a ratings game, and the way to get the highest ratings is to get someone like Tom Selleck, and add enough car chases to keep the action going. For instance, the show I am directing now is required by formula to have four major action scenes per hour. The writers have to write the way they are told."

"They are as frustrated as we are," Eva Marie says. "I can make bad writing *work*, I know I can as an actress, but sometimes I should fight harder for better dialogue."

"Eva Marie said she could make bad dialogue *work*. She didn't say she could make it *good*."

106

Both are silent for a moment, a little mentally exhausted from talking about the industry they have been so intensely active in for the last thirty years. Finally, Jeffrey says, "Whenever we've had too much television we go back to the theater."

"Live theater," Eva Marie clarifies. "We even produced the play, "Winesburg, Ohio", here in Santa Barbara about ten years ago." She looks out the window of their living room at the ocean. "We both love Santa Barbara. We also have a home in Los Angeles because we have to be close to our work, but we try to spend every weekend here. Santa Barbara is so beautiful, we can look out and see the mountains, the trees, the sand and the sea." She pauses and turns to her husband. "Did you know, Jeffrey even produced the pilot for the television soap, 'Santa Barbara.' "

"I loved doing it," he says. I know every part of the city, so I was glad I got the series launched. Soaps remind me of live television, and the theater and it was fun to do—for a while."

"I love the theater," Eva Marie says a bit wistfully. "I love those eight performances. I get excited at each one of them."

"That's because she loves to tell the audience the *story* of the play," Jeffrey says turning toward Eva Marie. "How about telling one last story?" Eva Marie smiles, a questioning look. "You know the time you got lost behind stage and missed your entrance."

FADE IN: A theater.

PLACE: Broadway.

EVENT: Dress rehearsal.

Jeffrey: "I was the director watching the final dress rehearsal and it came time for Eva Marie to make her entrance..."

Eva Marie: "I have this thing about always being early for my stage cue."

Jeffrey: "It was totally unbelievable. *She missed her cue.*"

Eva Marie: "I was lost. (Smiles weakly.) "The space behind stage at this theater was a maze of dressing rooms, prop rooms, and stairs, and I was lost in that maze."

Jefrey: "She finally struggled on stage, sobbing."

Eva Marie: (Acting the scene-crying, hands over her eyes.) "I'm sorry, I got lost..."

Jeffrey: "A director never stops the final dress rehearsal, but I had an hysterical actress on my hands..."

Eva Marie: "An hysterical *wife.*"

Jeffrey: "So I had to say, 'Let's take five.' "

They both laugh, remembering that moment, one of the hundreds they have shared in their thirty-seven years both on stage and off—together.

...And they lived happily ever after.

Fannie Flagg.

Fannie Flagg

Flagg Unfurled

What do I remember the most about my interview with comedienne Fannie Flagg? Her bathroom. It wasn't fancy—no gold faucets, or beveled mirrors. Not even an ivory throne. It was just a very long, narrow room with the usual amenities. But—on one solid wall, Fannie had framed and hung a wild assortment of photographs and drawings from her theatrical and television career. We chatted for quite some time, reviewing her life—as illustrated on a bathroom wall.

"Oh, hi there!" Fannie Flagg says, pushing open the screen door of her Montecito bungalow. A black cat jumps off the porch railing and darts through the open space.

"That's 'Roots,' " Fannie says glancing at the cat as it springs to the arm of a living room couch. "I thought about calling him Kunta Kinte but it was too hard to say."

She laughs and runs her fingers through her soft auburn hair and fluffs it a bit. Her silk blouse, in muted brown tones, picks up the color of her hair. "Come on in," she says in a voice that rings with a friendly, down-home kind of hospitality.

The early morning light shines brilliantly through the bare window by the front porch and reflects off several yellow and white polka dot cushions. Beyond the porch a twelve foot green hedge surrounds the small yard. The house itself has the warmth and appeal of an English cottage.

"I decorated it in a 1920s style to match its original character," she explains showing me through the old kitchen. "The house was originally built for English workmen who attended the adjoining estate. That has now been broken up into smaller lots like mine. They used to call this Gin Lane. The English always were big gin drinkers."

She leads me into a long bathroom which is more like a narrow hallway. On the wall opposite a two basin sink and a large mirror is a museum of Fannie Flagg memorabilia; framed photos from her childhood, and glossy mementos from her movie, television and stage career. There is one dazzling color poster of Fannie in a blue-sequined, tight-fitting gown with her arms outstretched, belting out a song. "That's when I played the lead on Broadway in *Best Little Whorehouse in Texas,*" she says. "I stole it from the theater lobby."

She walks back into the living room and settles on the couch in front of the fireplace. "C'mon, let's get comfy." Strangely, the lilt of her southern accent is soft and modulated. She seems out of character and far from the flamboyant, sometimes whimsical, oftentimes dizzy Southern belle that has become her trademark.

"When I first started doing talk shows I was really shy and introverted," she begins to explain. "That may seem like a contradiction of my character, but in front of the TV camera I was too embarrassed to be myself; to be this little girl from Alabama who didn't know nothin'. Finally one of the producers invented a character for me; jotted down an outline of a dipsy southerner and said: 'Play it.' And I did. I went out in front of the camera and played 'Fannie Flagg.' It worked. I learned I could hide my own personality behind Fannie Flagg's countrified skirts."

"My real name is Patricia Neal," she continues. "I had to change it twenty three years ago when Actor's Equity told me show biz already had a famous Patricia Neal. My grandfather advised me to take the name Fannie. He took it from Fannie Brice and said it was a lucky name. I was just a kid of seventeen, so I said okay. Then a friend called me up in the middle of the night and yelled over the phone: 'Fannie Flagg!' I asked him, where did he ever get a name like that, and he said, 'It's Muriel Dooley's grandmother's name!' So, I took it." She shakes her head. 'You know, to this day, I don't know who Muriel Dooley was."

She looks down at the gold rings spread over her fingers and absent-mindedly twirls one around. "It's a silly name. I'd like to change it."

But she can't. Not now. She can't separate herself from the caricature of Fannie Flagg, an image designed for it's theatricality. "Without that name," she muses, "I don't suppose I would have done as well in my acting career."

Fannie Flagg's acting career has unfurled in many directions, from stand-up comedy routines in night clubs, to television talk show appearances and situation comedies. She has also appeared in movies and Broadway musical comedies. More recently she has written her first novel, *Coming Attractions,* a widely acclaimed book that reviewers have compared to J.D. Salinger's *Catcher in the Rye.*

"The book is the most important thing I ever did," she says. 'Who would ever think this little old country girl could write a book? There is a tendency to think that comedians aren't..." she pauses, "exactly bright.

"I started writing the book right here in Santa Barbara. I moved here in 1976 and went to the Writers Conference, mostly to see one of my idols, Eudora Welty. As a student writer, I had an assignment to write this short story, so I sat down and wrote one out in long hand—and it won first prize!"

She decided to send the story to Harper & Row Publishers and a few weeks later received a phone call from the editor commissioning Fannie to do a novel based on the characters she had created in the short story. "I was scared to death," Fannie says, leaning forward on the couch. "I really didn't think I could do it.

"I was so scared of getting started with the writing that I spent the first five months researching. I went back to this little bitty Gulf Shores beach town in Alabama where I was raised, and started going through all the newspapers of the '50s era, checking the names of movies, the brands of cosmetics and cars—like Super Eight Buick Dynaflow. I wanted to make sure every page was correct. I was terrified someone would read it and say, 'Get back on your game show, you idiot!' "

Then she wrote the book, an unabashedly autobiographical account of the dreams, frustrations and growing pains of southern girlhood. "It's my life," Fannie confesses. "There is no way I could pretend otherwise."

In telling her often hilarious, yet sometimes poignant story, Fannie disguises herself as the heroine, Daisy Fay Harper. The book begins:

WHAT YOU ARE ABOUT TO READ...REALLY DID HAPPEN TO ME...OR MAYBE IT DIDN'T...I'M NOT SURE...BUT IT DOESN'T MATTER...BECAUSE IT'S TRUE...

DAISY FAY HARPER

What really happened to Daisy Fay Harper, alias Patricia Neal, alias Fannie Flagg, began forty four years ago in Birmingham, Alabama. "I guess I started out life as a twin," Fannie says. "My mother had a miscarriage in her third month, and my parents figured that was that. They sure were surprised when I arrived six months later."

As Fannie begins talking about her girlhood, a subtle change takes place. Like a movie werewolf bathed in the light of a full moon, she begins to slowly transform into the character of Fannie Flagg.

"When I was just a little bitty girl," she says, and the vowels begin to soften, "we moved to the gulf coast where my father bought an interest in a fast food shop. It was real great. I got to have a hamburger and a malted for breakfast every morning.

"My father was a dreamer. The stories I told about him in the book really did happen. He *did* invent the 'miracle machine,' which was a projector that shined an image of a plywood crucifix across the sky. He *did* put the microphone under the outhouse toilet seat, and half scared momma to death when he announced, "Lady, move over, we're working down here.' And he *did* want to be a taxidermist so he froze dead animals in the ice cream freezer then stuffed them when they thawed."

She is in full form now as she continues as the countrified Fannie Flagg. "My daddy may have lived in a fantasy world, but he taught me my sense of humor. I guess the greatest lesson I ever learned from him is that there is nothin' funnier than the truth."

Fannie's father spent most of his life working as a motion picture operator in a movie house, as did her grandfather. "I spent my entire life in theaters," she says. It wasn't exactly like being born in a trunk, but the lure of the stage was irresistible to Fannie.

When she was in the fifth grade in a Catholic school she wrote and starred in a play titled, "The Whoopie Girls." "The play was a fantasy about these two girls who move to New York," she says. "They have a maid, exotic clothes, and live in a penthouse on top of the Stork Club. During the play they drink twenty-seven martinis. That scene almost got me kicked out of school."

Fannie's first break came when her grandmother gave her fifteen dollars for her fourteenth birthday. She rushed down to Birmingham's Town & Gown theater to buy a season ticket for their stage plays. In the lobby she happened to bump into the show's director who was shouting, "We don't have anyone to run the spotlight for tonight's show!"

" 'Hey' " I said, " 'I can do that.' He looked at me and asked, 'Who are you?' " Fannie smiles with the memory. "I said, 'My name is Patsy Neal, and my granddaddy and my daddy work in the theater.' And that night I ran the spotlight and kept on a doin' it for the next three years."

Fannie graduated from the light board to the main stage in the play *Our Town*. The director cast her in the part of a seventy-year-old woman. "I was only seventeen years old," Fannie remembers, "but I did so well, he kept giving me character roles."

Her dream was to win a scholarship to a drama school. And to do that she figured she'd have to enter the Miss Alabama beauty contest. The judges passed out a drama scholarship each year to a runner-up.

"I wasn't concerned about winning the title," Fannie says. "I just wanted the scholarship. When I didn't win the first year, I just re-entered the next year." And the next, and the next—six times in all. Along the way she learned a few hard facts about the beauty-pageant business which she readily passes on to young hopefuls: "First, and foremost, never sit in a wicker chair before going on in the bathing suit competition. Never.

"Frankly," Fannie continues, "I never really wanted to win the bathing suit part. One night I came out dressed in a wet suit, wearing flippers and a face mask. Everyone cracked up." Eventually the judges, realizing her acting potential—or just wanting to rid themselves of this perennial joker—awarded her a scholarship to the Pittsburgh Playhouse.

After completing drama school, Fannie felt she was armed with enough professional weaponry to invade the theatrical ramparts of Broadway. As she was packing for New York, a local Birmingham television station, WBRC-TV, asked her to host a morning show. "I said, 'No way! I'm going to New York, lover! I'm going to be on the stage.' I was flip and obnoxious, and they thought it was hilarious, and wanted to sign me on quick. I wanted to get to Broadway quicker, but my mother thought I should do the TV show for a few weeks, for experience."

Three years later, Fannie—a seasoned television performer at age twenty—stuffed $175 in her purse, folded several comedy routines she had written in her pocket, and headed for New York. She immediately sold the skits to the Upstairs at the Downstairs night club for ten dollars apiece. When the comedian who was scheduled to perform the skits, became ill, Fannie was sent on stage. Allen Funt, of "Candid Camera" fame, happened to catch the act and hired her on as a writer/actress for his CBS television show. "He only had to pay one price for both," Fannie says.

After "Candid Camera," Fannie became a talk show regular on Johnny Carson's Tonight Show, and on the Merv Griffith and Mike Douglas shows. Her Southern-accented monologues on Lady Bird Johnson were just right for the times. She also became a daily performer on "The Match Game" quiz show, then turned to movies, such as *Five Easy Pieces* with Jack Nicholson. One of her later successes was starring with her friend, Barbara Eden, in the television series "Harper Valley PTA."

But Fannie's most gratifying theatrical experience came with her return to New York, playing the lead in the hit musical *Best Little Whorehouse in Texas*.

"I was in New York when the part in 'Whorehouse' came open," Fannie says. Her voice—now that her childhood story has been told—begins to soften, and the accent shifts gears to muted tones. "My agent thought I should try out for the part. But let's face it, I had never sung before. The Night before the audition I tried to learn the songs, and discovered they were not in any key I could sing. I was so terrified I stayed up all night drinking coffee and smoking cigarettes. By the time I got to the audition my voice had dropped into the right octave. I sang great!"

"You know, I never at any time in my life really felt like I was in show business," she says fluffing her red mane of hair again. "Isn't that weird! I never connect myself with being *in* show business. Maybe that's because I never really felt like I fit in. When I work in the theater I tell myself I am really a television personality, and if I am in a movie, I keep saying I'm really a writer. I guess there are just too many of me."

112

She stops for a moment, then continues, "One day my father told me, 'Honey, be a character woman. Do everything.' And I have. I just recently realized I have no fears in this business. I have versatility, a multi-level of creativity. And, best of all, I don't have to depend on my looks." She makes a funny face; pop-eyed and grinning. "After all, I'm not a Hollywood beauty."

She picks up a copy of her book, *Coming Attractions,* from the coffee table, and holds it tightly, as if for security. " Maybe what I really want to be is a writer. I have done a movie-of-the-week screenplay of my book, and I have been asked to write a second novel. Then I would like to do a theatrical play, a mystery comedy intrigues me. . . ." She gently sets the book back on the table.

"I guess the one thing I regret about the book is that my parents never got to read it. They both died just before it was published. I went through a bad year after that. I didn't want to work. Nothing. Now I'm getting my energies back. But I had to do a lot of reevaluation. I had to ask myself, have I been in this business for myself, or for them? I don't have to impress anyone anymore. Maybe my daddy achieved his fantasies through me, and if I made some of his dreams come true, then that made both of us happy.

"I guess you can sum up my life story as a little southern girl who, against all odds, got out of Alabama." Suddenly her eyes begin to glow, and I can see the transformation take place again, rapidly this time, and she automatically drops into a deep Alabama accent. "Why shoot, honey, that's the awful truth. The fact that ah'm not a little old hostess for a pancake restaurant still amazes me!"

And that folks, is the real Fannie Flagg.

Or is it?

Ollie Carey (at age 19) and her husband, silent-film western hero, Harry Carey.

Ollie Carey

The Emotion Pictures

Author Barnaby Conrad told me I should interview actor Harry Carey's widow, Ollie. "She's a crusty old gal," he said. "She's known everyone in Hollywood from D.W. Griffith to John Wayne." When I called the eighty-eight—year old silent film actress, she responded· "Sure. As long as it doesn't interfere with the World Series."

"Oh hell, I was just a dizzy blonde back then," Ollie Carey says, brushing a wisp of graying hair from her face. She settles comfortably in her rocking chair and lights up another cigarette from the ever-present pack of Benson & Hedges.

"That was in 1912 when I was only sixteen years old." She continues, "I really didn't know what was going on in Hollywood, except the films were hiring people. So I went over to see D.W. Griffith at the Biograph Company."

Ollie Carey squints her eye away from the cigarette smoke. "D.W. Griffith, hell, I didn't know who he was, except he was a director. You have to remember this was three years before he made his epic movie, *Birth of a Nation*. When I first saw him he was sitting on this rooftop stage, with a canvas covering the whole thing—they'd pull it back to get the sun when they were ready to film. He had on a straw hat with the top cut out—thought the sun would help his hair grow—and he had several silver dollars in his hand, playing with them."

"I looked around the stage and there were six young girls, some of them the early silent stars like May Marsh, Blanch Sweets, Dorothy and Lillian Gish, and Griffith looks up at me and does a double take—I was blond and beautiful and had fairly big breasts—and he asked me, 'Can you swim?'

"I said, 'Yes.'

"He put me on the stage and told me what he wanted me to do, watched real intently, then said, 'You got the lead!' "

Ollie Carey laughs, a deep throaty rumble. The laugh ends in a cough and she looks at the cigarette. Then with an "Oh, what the hell," look, she takes another deep drag. "With all those other girls to choose from, old Griffith must have taken one look at me and thought, 'Here's a virgin I'm going to grab.' " She pauses, "Well, he didn't!"

Olive Fuller Golden (that was her film name when she headlined in the silents) chuckles and snorts a little. Crusty, gutsy, outspoken and sometimes profane, today's Ollie Carey, senior grand dame of the silent cinema, professes an "Oh, baloney!" attitude when it comes to idolizing the myths and mystiques of what she calls the "Emotion pictures." Yet she witnessed their floundering, took part in their growth, and associated with the lifeblood that made an era unforgettable. She knew and worked with Hollywood's great directors: D.W. Griffith, John Ford, Howard Hawks...she also knew first hand most of the famous faces that lit up the silver screen: Mary Pickford, the Gish sisters, Lionel and John Barrymore—and a man called Harry Carey. "Yeah, Harry," she says quietly, "I'll have to tell you about Harry. In a moment..."

At eighty-eight, Ollie Carey loves to tell stories and is able to recall names and events from a faded but flamboyant era with amazing clarity. You can almost see the image race undimmed across her mind, and through her memories, the silents speak.

The silents.

A flickering world of light that filled the screen of the early 1900s with extraordinary power. This unique and innovative method of creating substance from shadow captured the audience's imagination and transported them to a world of fantasy. It pulled each person into the story that unfolded, making the audience the final creative contributors by allowing them to fill in for themselves the voices and sound effects. The experience was magic.

"Magic—hell!" Ollie explodes. "It was just a guessing game. We made it up as we went along."

She grabs a tube of lipstick from the coffee table and dabs a little red across her lips. "Must look a wreck," she says. "Had a bunch of relatives stuffed into this little cottage yesterday. Had a lot of grand kids and great-grandkids. Cooked a turkey. I'm pooped." She looks around the small living room. There is a couch covered with an old worn Navajo Indian blanket, two leather straight-backed chairs, and in the corner, a cast iron Franklin stove. the wood-paneled walls are white, worn and fragile. "This house is stuck together with termites," she says with a laugh. "But I like it. Moved here in 1962. The house was originally used for ranch workmen."

The house is a small pink cottage set deep within a grove of avocado trees on the grounds of Rancho Monte Alegre just south of Santa Barbara. The tiny structure is covered with ivy and looks like an enchanted cottage Hansel and Gretel might have chanced upon; a cardboard pink pop-up from the page of a child's fairy-tale book.

Inside, above the dining room table is a wall covered with photographs of some of Ollie Carey's favorite people, each autographed with a personal note to "Ollie.' There are pictures of John Wayne, Richard Widmaker, Wendell Corey, Barry Goldwater, and John Ford. There is one picture of D.W. Griffith, but it is unsigned.

"That first film Griffith cast me in was a two-reeler called *Sorrowful Shores,*" Ollie says. 'They really picked weird names for those early films. It was about a shipwreck in Maine, but it was filmed in San Pedro. (The movie also starred a rising actor called Harry Carey.) Anyway, one day after the shooting Griffith said to me, 'I'll take you home in my car,' and I said, 'Okay.' He had this big touring car, a Pope Hartford. The top was down, a chauffeur was driving, and Griffith leans over to me and says, 'How would you like to have dinner with me?' I looked him over guessing what dinner might lead to. I was dizzy but I wasn't dumb.

"I said, 'I'd like it very much—if I could bring my aunt.' He scratched his head through the hole in his hat, 'You always take your aunt to dinner?' And I looked him right in the eye and told him that I had never *been* out to dinner with a man before, and if I did go, I'd have to take my aunt along. And he just sat there with the dust kicking up behind the car. He didn't say another word."

Ollie Carey smiles with a faraway look in her eye, then shrugs. She takes a drink of warm root beer—the ice cubes long melted—and adds, "That was the end of that. I *never* played another lead part for D.W. Griffith, just small parts." She chuckles, "Maybe I *should* have gone to dinner with him."

Olive Fuller Golden quit the Biograph Company after three years and went to work for

Universal Pictures as a stock player. She made $40.00 a week, a handsome sum in those days. Soon after she arrived she was cast in a film called, *If Only Jim.* "Silly name for a movie," she says. "Up until the first day of shooting, the cast didn't know who was going to play the male lead. Then in walks Harry Carey. He had left Biograph and signed on with Universal, hopefully to make westerns. That was only the second time I had really seen him or worked with him. That's when the romance took fire. I was nineteen and he was thirty-seven." She stops for a moment to study a still photo of her and Harry from a 1915 film called *The Knight of the Range.* In the photograph Harry—in a white cowboy hat—is rolling up his sleeve, eyes white hot, ready to do battle with a western villain. Ollie is by his side, grasping his arm, with a pleading "be careful" look in her eyes.

"I didn't marry Harry at first. I lived with him for five years!" She laughs, loud. "Shoot, people keep telling me that kind of thing wasn't done back then, living with someone. Well, it was—and it was done very well!

"We finally crossed into Arizona and got married by a hunchback Justice of the Peace. I figured he would bring us good luck, and it worked out real good for thirty-five years." She pauses. "Wonderful life..." She stops rocking and is silent for a moment. Then: "Harry was quite a guy. I adored him..." There is a catch in her voice, and her eyes cloud for a second.

"Harry was a New York boy, and he went to law school at New York University." She begins to chuckle. "Harry was a hell raiser. There was this whorehouse down the road from the University called Madam Moran's. One day Harry got stiff drunk and stole Moran's picnic drawers—in those days women used to wear long drawers that came down below their knees with ruffles and lace and were split down the middle. Harry tied them to the top of the flagpole at the university, and they kicked him out of school. He always called himself a 'premature alumnus' after that.

"Harry had never been west of the Bronx, but he was crazy about Western history. He decided to write a western melodrama for the stage. He called it *Montana.* He got together 3,000 bucks and had it produced. It was a big hit for five years. Then he wrote another play called, *Heart of Alaska,* but it flopped."

Flat broke, but still interested in anything theatrical, Harry Carey went to the Biograph Company's office in New York to see if he could get a job as a writer in this new-fangled thing called the "flickers." They took him on—as an actor. He made his first film in 1908, a two reeler starring the Gish sisters. The director was D.W. Griffith.

In 1915, tired of the roles he was playing for Griffith, Carey moved to Universal Pictures. There he met a young director who shared his enthusiasm for westerns. They started cranking out film with dime-novel plots and tough titles like *Bare Fists, Hell Bent,* and *Riders of Vengeance.* The movie public went crazy over them and Harry Carey became Universal's number one box office star. His salary went from $150 a week in 1917 to $1,250 a week in 1918 to an astounding $2,250 in 1919.

That same year, Ollie Carey gave up her acting career. "I quit because I was chasing around after him all the time," she says, "and that was good enough for me."

With the money flowing in Harry and Ollie adopted a flamboyant lifestyle, not in Hollywood itself, but on a 3,000 acre ranch north of Los Angeles. On the property they built a sprawling ranch house with adobe walls three feet thick, high beamed ceiling, Spanish tile roofs, and massive stone fireplaces. They surrounded this building with smaller adobe guest houses, and built a 200-seat restaurant. The ranch grounds—crowded with stage coaches and covered wagons—looked like a scene from a western epic. The corrals were stocked with fine horses. Carey even brought in a tribe of Navajo Indians to live on the ranch, paid them well, and set them to work weaving blankets ("That's one of the blankets on the couch," Ollie says) and hammering jewelry in silver and turquoise. On weekends the Carey's would stage Wild West shows, inviting friends to take part in their showcase of Western Americana.

In 1921 a son, Henry George Carey, was born "right in the big brass bed on the ranch," Ollie remembers. "I guess I was play-acting the big pioneer woman. When my son was born he had this red fuzz of hair on his head. Harry took one look and said, 'Looks like red adobe.' He's been called 'Dobe' ever since. Dobe started acting in movies in 1947, must have made a hundred of them, mostly westerns."

A daughter, Ella Ada was born a short while later in Newport Beach where the Carey's had a boat. "Harry took her aboard one day," Ollie says, "and he put her in a clothes basket and called her the 'Captain of the ship!' So, it wouldn't do but to call her 'Cappy.' She now has two sons and two grandchildren. She manages Joe's Cafe right here in Santa Barbara."

Meanwhile, back at the ranch, which was rip-roaring like a western melodrama, the Carey's lived out a lifestyle that was part fantasy, part reality. "Things couldn't have got much better," Ollie says.

Then disaster struck.

"We had gone to New York with the kids," Ollie remembers rocking back in her chair." The day after we got there—I'll never forget the date, 13 March, 1929—we learned that the St. Francis Dam above the ranch had burst."

The flooding waters leveled the ranch. The buildings vanished along with the animal stock. Seven ranch hands lost their lives. Nothing was left but sand and a few sprigs of sagebrush blistering in the sun. "Everything went down the valley," Ollie says with a sigh. "The only thing we found was the Wells Fargo safe from the trading post. It must have weighed three tons, yet it washed downstream four miles."

The loss! Over half a million dollars, almost all the Carey's had. "It was a rough time," Ollie admits. "Harry's career was at a pretty low edge, and then the ranch...I remember hearing a group of cowboy character actors sitting on a movie set talking. One of them said, 'I hear Carey's through in westerns.' And Otto Meyers—an old cowboy who used to whittle all the time—is squatted down on his haunches, and he said, 'Can't rightly tell about that guy Carey. He's got a rubber ass. He goes down, but he bounces back up.' "

And that's what Harry Carey did. He bounced back. In 1929 he starred in a picture called, *Trader Horn,* which, along with *Big Parade,* became the two biggest money grossing films of their time for Universal.

"In the movie I played a missionary opposite Harry," Ollie says, looking at a framed picture from the film. She is shown with a sun helmet on and is looking imploringly into Harry's eyes. *Trader Horn* was filmed in East Africa, and I was in it because I was the only woman to tag along with the troupe, and they decided they needed a woman actress. I hadn't worked for over ten years."

An amazing thing happened during the filming—the Jazz Singer, the first talkie, came out. Here we were making a silent, when the producer got frantic and decided to put in some dialogue. He sent to Hollywood for sound equipment, and it arrived three weeks later. When they were unloading the sound tuck at Mombasa, it slipped off the dock and into the water. We had to wait three more weeks for new equipment, but in the end the product was a 'talkie.'

"After that Harry started playing character parts," she continues. "He was getting close to fifty. He was a natural actor, like Gary Cooper or Hank Fonda, good enough to be nominated for Best Supporting Actor in the film, *Mr. Smith Goes to Washington* starring Jimmy Stewart. Harry played the part of the Vice President and he only had about four lines. He just sat there behind Stewart in the long filibuster scene making faces and showing different emotions. You know Harry never saw one of his pictures until I dragged him to that movie. But he kept playing character parts all through the late 30s and early 40s."

Then in December 1947, Harry Carey died of cancer. He was sixty-seven. To make sure that Hollywood paid the proper tribute to this endearing star of the silents and the talkies, Harry's old friend and director, John Ford, put on an enormous funeral. He also launched the actor's son in a movie career, calling him "Harry Carey Jr., and starring him in *Three Godfathers* with John Wayne.

"After Harry died, I decided to go back to work," Ollie says. "And the only work I knew was the movies." It had been almost forty years since she had made her first movie for D.W. Griffith, but here she was, as she says, "making faces again."

Does she consider herself a good actress? "Oh, hell no!" she answers emphatically. "I just made thirteen different faces, that's all."

Ollie Carey "made faces" in a variety of movies and television shows over the next ten years, playing in many westerns, such as *Two Rode West* with Jimmy Stewart and Richard Widmark. Her final movie, and no doubt her best came in 1956 with *The Searchers,* directed by John Ford. Throughout the movie Ford favored Ollie with little gems of acting business that were not written in the script. They were memorable moments. The movie starred John Wayne. "I loved Duke," Ollie says. "He was a daring man and a good friend. Everytime we did a movie together he gave me a handpainted mug with my name on it." She looks at a row of mugs on the far shelf, each with her name inscribed on it. "Yeah, I loved old Duke Wayne."

She scrunches around in the rocking chair, trying to find a more comfortable position. "Can't be getting old," she sighs, "just a little stiff. You know, I saw Jimmy Stewart on a television talk show the other day, and he looks old and tired. When you get to be my age you look at these people as you remember them. I don't believe I'm old because I don't think that way," she pauses, then adds, her voice rising, "But it annoys the hell out of me because *they've* aged!" She stops and stares for a moment. "Oh, to hell with it. Let's have a beer. There's a Coors in the refrigerator. Get me a root beer," and she smiles, a good smile, perhaps one of the thirteen faces that she does best.

I leave her there for a moment, alone, with her thoughts, realizing that she must be thinking of some of the famous faces she has known or worked with throughout seventy years of movie-making history; a montage of personalities that shine like a Who's Who of Hollywood: Clark Gable, Carole Lombard, Gregory Peck, Humphrey Bogart, Lauren Bacall, the Barrymores, the Gish sisters....

When I returned, root beer in hand, I looked at Ollie Carey, and for one brief moment I could see the face of a "dizzy young blonde" who just happened to wander into the movie business.

Clifton Fadiman

The Man Who Shook Shakespeare's Hand

This was a tough one. How was I, an embryonic writer, going to face one of the mountain-top gurus of the writing world, a man who had conversed with the best minds of the last half century! We sat down, and after half an hour of questions, he said, "You're not getting much, are you?" I gulped, looked frantically at my list of questions, then fired this one off: "Define civilization." He looked at me a bit shocked, then said, "Now, that's a good question." And then he talked 'til the sun went down and the chickens went to roost.

"The intellect is also a passion." —George Bernard Shaw

"Yes, indirectly, I suppose you could say I shook hands with Shakespeare," Clifton Fadiman says in a voice accustomed to a lifetime of civilized conversation. "Actually, the whole idea was a subtle little joke. I had discovered that with a little historical tracing I could establish a chain of handshaking that went from me back to Shakespeare. Really, nothing to it. All you need is the first link with someone of historical stature."

Fadiman looks out the picture window that overlooks the Pacific ocean, then leans back in his desk chair. He opens the drawer of the gun-metal gray Navy desk and takes a thin green cigar from a box. As he lights it he explains, "One of my friends was Cornelia Otis Skinner, and I shook hands with her many times. It occurred to me one day that she must have done the same with her father, Otis Skinner, a famous actor at the turn of the century. I then took it upon myself to look up a biography of Otis Skinner and made note of several intimate friends of his in the theatrical world. Nothing to it to trace a chain of actual touching that went back to Shakespeare." Fadiman contemplates his upturned palm for a moment, then adds, "I stopped at Shakespeare because I didn't know who he shook hands with."

A latter day Renaissance man, Clifton Fadiman has been happily in the middle of whatever excitement has happened in the world of words for the last half century. His mind has encompassed all manner of matters in the literary arena from Mother Goose to Moby Dick, from Homer to Hemingway. Writer, critic, essayist, anthologist, editor, and onetime host of radio's "Information Please," Fadiman's urbane, entertaining, and always penetrating opinions have entertained and enlightened a legion of readers.

When I arrived at Clifton Fadiman's home high on a hill outside Santa Barbara's Hope Ranch, I must admit it was with some trepidation that I knocked on the door. What questions could I ask him that would instill enough interest to enliven an interview of two hours? After all, he had conversed with the greatest literary minds of five decades. To bridge the literary gap between my meager knowledge and his expertise, I had brought along a bribe—a bottle of Austin Cellars Sauvignon Blanc wine. I knew of his intense interest in wine from reading his monumental book, *The Joys of Wine;* an interest I shared.

He accepted the wine with an embarrassed half grin. Then leading me into the living room, he asked if I would like a glass of wine, something to sip on during the ensuing conversation. "I'm afraid I'll have to forego the pleasure of joining you," he said. "I am limited now to one glass of wine a day." He picked out a California Colombard from a wine cabinet. "Sorry, nothing chilled. Perhaps a few ice cubes...?" I nodded in concurrence. He grinned,saying, "I don't think it would be a sacrilege since we both know what we're doing." He stepped, bottle in hand, into the kitchen.

Alone, I looked around the living room, trying to discern from a wall crammed with books, the essence of Clifton Fadiman. Not an easy task. His world has always been one of words, a life dedicated to dissecting and decifering what he calls, "those tiny hieroglyphics that wiggle across the printed page." His analysis of literature has not been that of a scholar's approach, rather a critical assessment laced with subtle humor.

I turned from the bookshelves and checked my notes. Clifton Fadiman: Board of Editors, Encyclopedia Britannica; book editor of *The New Yorker;* Editor-in-Chief of Simon & Schuster, and member of the board of judges of the Book-of-the-Month club since 1944.

Fadiman returns with the glass of wine, its two icecubes sparkling. He sets the glass on the white typed pages of a manuscript on his desk. I rub the palm of my hand on my trousers carefully, trying not to rub out the magical imprint of Shakespeare's hand, and mention that as a child I shook the hand of Harry Truman during one of his whistle stop train trips in 1944.

"Well, there you are." he says. "Truman would have shaken hands with Roosevelt, and with a little mild research you could establish a chain to George Washington." He shrugs his shoulders. "It's not much of a trick."

Contented that I now had a handshaking lineage to Washington as well as Shakespeare, I asked Fadiman at what age he began his obsession with words.

"I remember reading my first book at the age of three," he answers. "It was called *The Overall Boys on the Farm.* I knew at once this kind of experience was right for me. I think I immediately understood the magic of reading. It's simple; those kids I read about were *created.* I couldn't look out the window and see them; they were created on the page. And it was all done through the arrangement of little black marks on the page. That was the magic. Oh, I am sure most children feel the same magic, but possibly with less intensity."

Fadiman's feeling for the magic of the printed word was intensified many years later when he read an article in the *Saturday Review of Literature* detailing the pleasure of the publishing business. When one of his Columbia University professors, Mark Van Doren, critic, poet, and the editor of the magazine, *The Nation,* offered Fadiman the opportunity to write a book review it was just the impulse he needed to launch his lifelong occupation with words. After ten more years of freelancing book reviews, Fadiman was hired as the book editor of *The New Yorker.* That was in 1934.

"I have a rule of thumb that I made up when I was quite young," he says. "It may sound silly, but with one our two exceptions I have followed it. I never stay on a job for more than ten years. That is, unless I have to have the job to pay my bills.

"I was Editor-In-Chief of Simon & Schuster for exactly ten years. I then resigned. Of course, it doesn't always work out in ten year segments." He indicates the neatly stacked piles of typed manuscripts on the metal desk. "I've had a job as a judge with the Book-of-the -Month Club since 1944."

I glance at one of the manuscripts and notice a penned notaton that says the material is to be read and judged for the Club. Fadiman obviously enjoys his work. He says he is not adverse to spending fourteen to sixteen hours a day at his desk.

One of his favorite indulgences is collecting anecdotes. He has amassed over 4,000 of them and has combined them in an anthology. "I would like the book to become to anecdotes what Bartletts is to quotations."

When asked for a few of his favorites from the collection, he relaxes back in the chair, thinks for a moment, then says, "Here's one by Issac Bashevis/Singer: someone asked him if he believed in free will or predestination. Singer shrugged and said, 'Free will, of course. You have no choice.'

"Here's another, from Jimmy Durante. He was a wonderful and generous fellow, simple in the very best sense of the word. He and Eddie Cantor worked together in a low-class restaurant on Coney Island, where Cantor would tell jokes while Durante played the piano. Every once in a while Durante would mutter comments on his own piano playing. Cantor listened to him and finally said, 'Jimmy, you ought to work out an act. Stop playing the piano once in a while and just talk. Talk to the audience!' Jimmy's face fell and he said, 'I can't do that—they'd laugh at me.' "

Fadiman looks up at the ceiling, thinking. "Let's see, those two are funny ones. I'll give you one I think is quite different in tone. It is about Charles de Gaulle. He and his wife had several children and one of them was a retarded girl. They did everything they could for her, they were tender and loving, but the girl died early in life. As they put the child in the family crypt, Charles de Gaulle turned to his weeping wife and said tenderly, 'Now she's like all the other children.' " Fadiman pauses.

Quickly he adds, "Charles de Gaulle was the only genius statesman our time has seen, other than Hitler, and he was on the other side." I ask Fadiman to define genius and its much overrated and misunderstood counterpart, talent.

"Talent and genius," he muses for a moment. "Two vastly different things. Talent can be trained or developed. Perhaps it is another word for ability or competence. Talent is an uninteresting word.

"Ah, but genius...genius is a mysterious word. A talented man sees the world as it *is,* whereas a genius discovers what the world *is not.* The world is raw material to a genius, something he can mold, something he can recreate. Einstein must have mused about the physical world and realized the rules we live by are not quite right. So, to see it better, he placed himself in a different point at space to see how the cosmos looked. And, having done that, he saw things differently, and with his intellectual power, he not only gave us a vision of a new world, but also the equation that went with it. Any endeavor may produce genius. For instance. business. Henry Ford was a genius. He was also a very dislikable human being. But, like Einstein, he saw things differently.

"In the world of art, the genius of this century was obviously Picasso. You can't prove he was a genius but you can *feel* it. I went to see a retrospective of Picasso's work several years ago, and as I walked through the display, it became apparent that the artist had a supreme eye working together with a supreme imagination. he was able to recreate and transform the visual world in ways you and I could never conceive. His was a different vision."

And Shakespeare?

"Shakespeare is, of course, the supreme genius in writing." Fadiman says. "Yet, he was a man, not a demigod. He was not infallible. He often wrote too quickly, with his eye, not on posterity, but on a deadline. He was also a practicing theater craftsman, a busy actor, and a shrewd, increasingly prosperous businessman. He was merely—a genius.

"As far as the writing genius of this century goes, you would have to put James Joyce at the top of the list. *Ulysses* has been called the most completely organized, completely thought out work of literature since the *Divine Comedy.*"

I take a sip of the white wine, then put the glass back in the center of the damp circle it has left on the paper. I question: Ernest Hemingway?

Fadiman pauses, assessing the American novelist for a moment. "I have been rereading Hemingway recently, mostly his short stories. In a way, Hemingway was too original. He had to create his own audience. He had to make the reader see things as they had never been seen before. He was a great pathbreaker, and that was his trouble. The pathbreaker may excite us enormously at first, but he lets us down after a while. He raises us to the heights of enthusiasm from which there must be an inevitable descent." Fadiman rocks back in his chair, and clasps his hand in his lap. "I don't know whether that is a good theory or not, but it explains why Hemingway is being reassessed.

"All writers are limited. Hemingway's view of life was too. Perhaps he overvalued its macho aspects. He seemed to *undervalue* women, conceiving of them only as objects to fall in love with. I don't think he ever realized that women are three dimensional human beings, precisely as men are, no better, no worse, but just as complicated."

"Did you ever shake hands with Hemingway?" I ask. I am thinking: Hemingway might have shaken hands with...Fitzgerald certainly. Perhaps Thomas Mann. Marcel Proust? Joseph Conrad? Maybe the chain goes back to Cervantes, Dante...

"I never shook hands with Hemingway," Fadiman answers, breaking my illusions. "However, I did receive a long handwritten letter from him, six or seven pages long. Unfortunately, I did not keep it. I am not good at saving files. Yet, the letter was interesting, as he must have been a little tight when he wrote it. It was not very coherent. In it he complained that New York critics—like myself—couldn't always take him seriously. I had written a review on *Death In the Afternoon.* I am not a bullfight fan, and I thought the mysticism surrounding the sport was a bit too much, so I wrote a review in the form of a little essay on ping pong, but in the Hemingway style. It wasn't a very good parody."

And your appreciation of William Faulkner?

"I'm off his wavelength," Fadiman answers. "I was a critical minority voice for fifteen years, writing disagreeable reviews because Faulkner seemed stylistically and emotionally exaggerated to me. Too many of his books made me laugh when I wasn't supposed to. His writing just seemed a wilful reinterpretation of Southern life using the old devices of gothic romance. Now, today I think that's a little unfair. He, like Hemingway, was a great pathfinder.

"He was also a great aristocrat, and it would never have occurred to him to write a letter of complaint to me. I remember I once introduced him at a National Book Award ceremony. He was a very pleasant, quiet man, so quiet you could barely hear his acceptance speech. He was also a small man. I too am a small man, and I think I was taller than he. We tend to think of writers as giants."

I asked him if he could name a single giant in literature that he had met during his lifetime.

"Thomas Mann," he answered without hesitation. "I had dinner in his home. He was very German, very formal, very conscious of his stature as a writer. He made you feel you were in the presence of greatness."

Poets. How about Robert Frost?

"He had a ot of showman about him. He liked to be praised and applauded. He always kept an eager eye on his competitors. He was secure in his writing, not very secure in himself."

Time to throw in a clinker. Thinking back to my teenage preoccupation with The Mike Hammer detective stories, I ask about Mickey Spillane.

The reaction I expected is not forthcoming, but a better one is: "I think it a mistake to think that what we call 'sub-literature' doesn't have value. For instance, I have an interest in science fiction. Most of it is pretty trashy, but the things it can say about society can be crushing. As told from afar, in the vastness of space, science fiction can offer a penetrating social analysis."

I ask about Ross Macdonald, thinking of Santa Barbara's own mystery writer, Ken Millar, who died in 1983. "A fine writer," Fadiman answers, "Within the school started by Dashiell Hammett, he stands very high. He enlarged the bounds of the detective story by introducing a note of seriousness. Yes, I admired him greatly."

I take another sip of wine. The glass has now made a deep, wet ring on the back of the manuscript. I hope I am not destroying some precious, budding work of literature. The wine itself, now that the ice cubes have melted, tastes bland.

Yet, the wine is good, and like Fadiman, I do not believe in the pomposity of wine snobbery and the overzealousness of some wine connoisseurs. As Fadiman said in *The Joys of Wine*: "I discount the abracadabra of wine: the excesses of connoisseurship, the absurdities of finicky service, the ceremonial of a hierarchy of glasses, the supposed ability of an expert to determine from a few sips on which side of the hill the original grapes were grown. One can make excellent love in a meager hall bedroom, the requisite elements being three: two lovers and a means of support. So with wine, the requisite elements being likewise three: a bottle, which may be a country-wench Rhone, surrendering at once its all, or a magisterial Romanee Conti, calling for involved investigation; a glass, preferably thin, clear, and holding at least half a pint; and a lover. (Perhaps I should add a corkscrew.)"

I ask him about his wine book, all eight pounds of it, written in collaboration with Sam Aaron.

"A great doorstopper," he says. "It is not only a guide to wine but an omnium-gatherum of stories, a miscellaneous collection of hodgepodge about wine. I think it is the most sheerly beautiful book on wine in existence. I can say that in all modesty because the design and layout are the work of the publisher, Harry Abrams."

I finish the last diluted sip of Colombard wine, and wonder aloud about the complexity of some great wines and what makes them memorable. Is it not a little like life, I ask?

"A fine wine should have complexity, just as one's experience of life must, to make them both memorable," he answers turning to look out the window. A razor thin layer of clouds hangs over the coast like blue cigar smoke from a pool hall. "William James was fond of talking about the life's quality of *thickness*. At any one moment we are feeling a great many things. For instance, you are listening to me, and your consciousness is taking in my words, and your eyes are fixed on me—you have a certain image of an old man talking. Yet, in your consciousness other things are taking place: you are making all sorts of unconscious judgements about what I am saying, minor things, trivial things. This moment is an extremely rich, *thick* experience. It is also complicated by the perfect weather outside and the beauty of the ocean. In other words, all this makes the experience *dense*. That is what William James meant.

"Now a wine is memorable when it is thick or complex," he continues, warming to the subject of wine. "I went to Paris as a young man with my wife in 1925. She had spent three weeks in Paris previously and felt very knowledgeable about everything French. She took me to a large department store and in their restaurant ordered half a bottle of Graves. It was the first time I had tasted wine, and as I drank the stuff a whole new world opened. It didn't take thirty seconds. I said, 'Is this what wine is?' From that moment on I was a gone goose. Instant conversion. All I could say was, 'Gee, I love this stuff.' Now today, if I am lucky enough to get a taste of a great Chateau Latour that wine would make me say something more than, 'Gee, this is a wonderful wine.' I could perhaps talk about it, its complexity, its density and what I felt while drinking it."

"Candlelight and companions must add to the complexity of the magic moment," I add. "That's what William James would have said," Fadiman agrees. "That is the reason we surround fine wine with a pleasant ambiance. I don't think a great Pomerol could be enjoyed while listening to a rock band. A great wine requires the mind's full attention. It's not dissimilar to reading a complicated book. I am not denigrating rock bands, but I feel what I am saying is true. And for this reason: When we toss off a swallow of jug wine we don't bother much about the environment. We know we are going to get something pleasantly potable, good enough to drink while listening to a rock band, but the wine itself has no complexity. It requires little of our attention.

"Wine is another world. There is nothing wrong with milk, or Coca Cola, but they don't represent *worlds*. You want to see if the second glass is as interesting as the first."

He pauses, seeming to have run out of words for a moment. The tape recorder is silently spinning down to its last minute. It would be pleasant to have this moment of "thickness" continue, to feel for a few more moments the essence of the man who has made his world one of words; his own words and those of others. Instead I ask one last question: "In as few words as possible, give me the plot line of your life, a summary of eighty years."

"It's only four words: HE PAID HIS BILLS." He rocks back in the chair and laughs. "That's all I can really be proud of—he paid his bills."

The tape recorder clicks off, seemingly on cue. I rise, thank my host for a rewarding conversation, one sided as it may have been—as it was *supposed* to be, and start for the door.

He opens the door and I look up at the silent space of the sky, squinting my eyes against the brilliance. Clifton Fadiman puts out his hand and I shake it. And, there is an electricity there now, a chain that pulses all the way back to—Shakespeare.

Barnaby Conrad drawing Robert Mitchum's portrait for the 1986 Santa Barbara Film Festival. (Santa Barbara News-Press photo)

Barnaby Conrad

Gored, But Never Bored

To interview Barnaby Conrad all you need to ask is: "Who was the greatest matador, Manolete or Barnaby Conrad?" then be prepared for a week-end-long monologue. Barnaby's a bullfighting junkie. After he showed me the photographs of a Spanish surgeon operating on his near-fatal leg goring, Barnaby suddenly unbuckled his belt, dropped his pants around his ankles, pointed to the scar on his inner thigh, and said, "See, that horn damn near killed me!"

It is raining. Not in hard slashing sheets, but a soft springtime patter of raindrops. I open the gate; it squeaks agonizingly on its hinges, then slams shut behind me, and I am in a garden of glistening ferns, ivy, and purple bougainvillea. A toad garumps at me from the mossy rock of a pool, then slips under a large leaf, satisfied that it has protected its rainwashed retreat.

Through the tropical foliage I can see a weathered artist's studio. Behind the picture window is an easel, and sitting next to it is painter, author, and bullfighter—Barnaby Conrad.

I poke my head through the doorway. Conrad is hidden behind the easel, only a canvas tennis shoe, splattered with paint like a Jackson Pollock painting, peeks back at me. I clear my throat and say, "Hi."

A cherubic face with wisps of greying hair tufted behind the ears leans around from the side of the easel. Barnaby Conrad, or "Barny" or *Bernabé* (as he likes to sign his name in Spanish), smiles then rises stiffly and limps the few steps toward me. "An old horn wound from bullfighting," he says slapping the inside of his left thigh and extending the other hand in greeting.

I am reminded of the opening dialogue from Barnaby Conrad's autobiography, *Fun While It Lasted‘*

Eva Gabor (as she enters Sardi's restaurant and sees Noel Coward at a table: "Noel, dahling have you heard the news about poor Bahnaby? He vass terribly gored in Spain!"

Noel (genuinely alarmed): "He was *what?*"

Eva: "He vass gored!"

Noel (genuinely relieved): "Thank heavens—I thought you said bored."

"The horn wound is just like the one that killed the matador, Manolete," Conrad says, motioning me to a chair. "I even had the same surgeon. He had learned a lot by the time he got to me. Manolete died from his wound." The name *Manolete* rolls from Conrad's tongue with a soft Spanish inflection. The death of this tragic bullfighter in 1947 was the catalyst that soared Conrad, a struggling thirty-year-old writer, into the limelight of best-selling author.

"Manolete was the most exciting, riveting personality I had ever met," Conrad continues, sitting at the worn chair behind the easel. "I was shocked when I heard he had been killed in a bullring in Spain. Like all the other bullfighting *aficionados,* I thought he was indestructible. I knew, as a writer, from that first moment I met him so many years ago, that he was the kind of figure who could dominate a book. It was a book I had been thinking about for years, but never knew the end until Manolete provided it by dying in the bullring.

"I woke up one morning," Conrad goes on as if remembering a dream, "almost compelled by some outside force to put a sheet of paper in the typewriter and begin to write. The novel opened In the morning and ended at the end of a bullfight just seven hours later. Like Manolete, the character was a loner, ugly, over the hill, but unable to step down from being *numero uno.* In the end he died because the fight crowds kept demanding more from him. All he had left was life—so he gave it to them."

Conrad finished the book in eight weeks of furious writing and sleepless nights. Exhausted, he sent the manuscript to Bennett Cerf at Random House. Cerf turned it down.

"Bennett told me about that decision later," Conrad says. "An editor had stuck his head into Cerf's office and asked him if he wanted 365 pages on a bullfight. Cerf said no without reading it." (Cerf later apologized to Conrad and ten years later published his autobiography, *Fun While it Lasted.*)

"When Random House turned it don I thought it was the end," Conrad continues. "But I got Houghton Mifflin to take a look at the manuscript and they published it."

The book, *Matador,* was selected by the Book-of-the-Month Club as a main selction, condensed for *Reader's Digest,* translated into eighteen languages, and sold to a paperback publisher for the highest reprint rights ever paid at that time. *Matador* topped the bestseller list for a year, with two and a half million copies in print. Barnaby Conrad was a successs at age 30.

"I guess I got a lot of mileage out of Manolete," Conrad says, pushing himself out of the chair behind the easel. "Come on, let's go into the house."

I pick up my umbrella at the door and follow him up a wide wooden ramp that looks like a castle entryway, into the open door of the home. The entry hall is a hodgepodge of bullfighting memorabilia: capes and swords and posters and, on an easel, the original painting of Manolete used on the dust jacket of *Matador.* There is also the surprise of several framed surgical photographs of the ragged, but fortunately not quite fetal, horn wound that Conrad suffered in his last bullfight in 1958.

The walls of the living room are completely covered in paintings and photographs, framed letters and awards. Leaning against chairs and tables are the realistic plywood images of dogs and cats that he paints for himself of his own pets, or for others on comission.

In the dining room are more paintings, including one of a radiantly beautiful woman. "Mary, my wife," Conrad says, studying the oil painting. "I met and married her in 1962. She was a tawny, tall and glamorous divorcee with two children. She played—and still does—great class tennis and bridge and cooks nearly as well as her cousin Julia Child."

Displayed prominently in the hallway is a photograph of Ernest Hemingway. Beneath it is a cancelled check signed by Hemingway. The check is not made out to Conrad, but the signature is important to him as a symbol of the frustration Conrad went through trying to meet or correspond with the great writer. Strangely, Hemingway always spoke well of

Conrad—who was one of the few Americans who shared his passion for bullfighting—but he never communicated with him.

"I wrote to him many times," Conrad says, looking at the picture of the writer. "I never heard from him. Not even a postcard. *Nada*. Even when my novel hit the bestseller lists, *nada, nada*. Even when I was lying in that Spanish hospital, a victim of his book, *Death in the Aftenroon*—which was about a reprehensible, anachronistic, mindless, indefensible, but irresistible spectacle—he wouldn't reply to me. *Nadissima*."

Conrad shakes his head and wanders back outside to his studio. He picks up his paintbrush and starts dabbing at a wooden cutout of a dog, then says: "I do have one letter by Hemingway. I picked it up in a rare bookshop in town. I finally got my letter from Hemingway." He sighs. "Sorry, *by* Hemingway."

Looking up, Conrad accidentally dabs a little paint on my tape recorder set on the brush tray of his easel. "Whoops, sorry," he laughs, and goes back to painting the cutout of the dog. "Other than studio portraits of people, I love to paint these animals. I've always loved animals—Mary too. Ever since I can remember, I've kept animals of some kind."

Another of Conrad's early memories is his arrival in Santa Barbara. He was only three, but the city made an immediate, indelible impression on him. The date was June 29, 1925, the day of the great earthquake. "I was on the train with my nurse waiting for my father to pick me up," Conrad remembers. "When the earthquake started, the shaking didn't bother me as much as the nurse. It was the first time I had seen an adult *in extremis*. She fell to the floor of the train, screaming and kicking. I was terrified watching her."

Young Conrad grew up in his grandmother's home in Santa Barbara, surrounded by mementos of his ancestors. (The lineage includes a secretary of state, a secretary of the Navy, and his grandmother's great-great-great-grandmother, Martha Washington.)

Conrad's parents recognized in him a spark of creativiy, and nurtured his artistic and writing skills with private tutors. Finally, when he was 19, they sent him to Mexico City to study art. The trip changed his life.

"I had already seen several dreary bullfights in Mexico City," Conrad says, "but this one afternoon I went with a friend and the real bulls were there, the monsters Hemingway talked about in *Death in The Afternoon*. My friend and I were sharing a bottle of tequila, watching a luckless bullfighter flopping his cape back and forth in the ring.

" 'Why don't you go down there?' I heard my friend say.

" 'What?' I gulped, looking at him through a blur of tequila.

" 'Sure,' he said. 'The bull's a nun. He charges on rails.'

"I was trembling, and kept thinking, what if I could conquer the huge hunk of fear I had beneath my rib cage. I began to realize that it is tough to be a Hemingway hero.

"Suddenly I knew I was going to do it. I jumped up, raincoat in hand, and went down the aisle fast, jumped over the rail—and was in the ring!

"The bull saw me. Incredibly its head went down and I could hear the angry bite of its hoofs in the sand. The great horns were ivory and black-tipped in the sunlight and were aimed straight at me! I stood there petrified, which, unknown to me, was the right thing to do. The bull charged. I flung my raincoat out at arms length, and—amazing—the bull passed under my arms. I could see the great black hulk of its shoulders brush past me. The bull charged again and I swung the coat in front of its head again, and the horns impaled the raincoat and tore it from my grasp. I bolted for the fence, vaulted it, very pale of face and very wet of pants. I had decided I didn't want to be a Matador."

Not quite. The same day a young Mexican bullfighter took Conrad under his wing and taught him the finer points of the trade. Conrad got the opportunity to fight a few small bulls on ranches until one crashed into his knee, breaking it. "The sound was like a log popping in a fireplace," Conrad remembers, with a shudder. That was enough bullfighting for the intrepid American, and he left Mexico City for the calmer and cooler climes of the Ivy League, settling into the peaceful pursuit as a student at Yale.

When World War II broke out Conrad tried to enlist in the Navy, but his encounter with the bull had left him with knee troubles the Navy couldn't accept. So Conrad went to the State Department in Washington D.C., and announced that he wanted to be a diplomat. Instead, he was hired as a code clerk. Not long after, he was called into the chief's office and told, "Conrad, I'm afraid you are not made of the stuff great code clerks are made of. I am sending you to Spain—as a vice consul."

The new "diplomat" soon found himself in Seville, Spain, the picture postcard city of flamenco dancing, gypsies and bullfighting. It was there that he witnessed Manolete in the ring. Conrad met and talked to the great matador and was mesmerized by him.

Conrad also met another great matador, Juan Belmonte, who had originated the classic concept of bullfighting. Belmonte was fifty-two and retired from the ring when he invited the vice consul out to his ranch to fight a few small bulls. Conrad performed creditably for an American, and was invited back several times, learning each time a valuable lesson about the art from the *maestro,* Belmonte. Several months passed and then Belmonte told Conrad: *"Bernabé,* I am organizing a charity fight in a small town, and I am going to fight."

Conrad, who had never seen the matador perform in the real ring, was excited and asked, "Who will be fighting on the program with you?"

Deadpan, Belmonte answered, "You."

"No, really," Conrad asked again, "Who else?"

"You," Belmonte repeated with a wide grin.

After the shock had worn off, but none of the queasiness, Conrad went into the ring billed as the *Nino de California,* "The California Kid." He killed his first bull, and won the high award of two ears for his endeavor. But his biggest thrill was to hear Belmonte tell him, *"Bastante bien,"* "Not bad, Bernabé."

Bernabé continued to fight in a few small rings until the serious goring in 1958 put an end to that. After his exciting forays into bullfighting, Conrad realized he could not be content with the dull routine of a consulate, so he took up writing and wrote a book, *The Innocent Villa,* about the love affair between a beautiful Spanish girl and the American vice consul. He moved back to Santa Barbara to rewrite the book and read that Sinclair Lewis, author of such classics as *Main Street* and *Elmer Gantry,* was in town and had rented a house near his parents.

Conrad wrote Lewis, introducing himself as an "embryonic" writer who would like to meet him. Lewis agreed, and liked the brash young writer well enough to take him on as his personal secretary.

Conrad describes Lewis as, "a startling and awesome sight. At sixty-two he was tall and fiercely ugly, quite the ugliest person I have ever seen." Conrad would later write that Lewis resembled "Ichabod Crane...the backs of his skeletal hands were foxed like an antique manuscript...his breath smelled like photograph negatives."

Conrad sharpened his writing skills under the tutelage of the great author. "Characters and conflict make your story!" Lewis would roar. "Touch! Feel! Smell! See! Don't *tell* me how brave the hero is, *show* me through action and dialogue!...Don't put down one line that doesn't either advance the plot or develop the characters!" Lewis read Conrad's first draft of his book, *The Innocent Villa,* and told him to discard the first seventy-five pages and get to work with the rest of it. After Conrad completed the book to Lewis' satisfaction, it was published by Random House. The book sold 8,000 copies, a fair sale for a first novel.

Shortly thereafter Conrad left Lewis, a bit dazed by the five incredible months he had spent with "America's angry author." "My successor lasted some three days," Conrad says a bit proudly. About the same time Conrad received a telegram from a friend in Spain that read:

TERRIBLE NEWS, MANOLETE KILLED YESTERDAY BY A MIURA BULL.

The book, *Matador,* quickly followed this tragic news and Conrad became a firmly established and prolific writer. He lived in San Francisco for a while, where he opened a successful night spot called—what else—The Matador. It became one of the best known watering holes in the city, attracting such celebrities as Frank Sinatra, Ingrid Bergman, Ronald Reagan, and of course, Noel Coward and Eva Gabor. Each star signed their name in an autograph book which Conrad still treasures. He finally decided to close the place because it was taking him too far from his writing.

"I always thought I would move back to Santa Barbara when I was old," Conrad says. "Then I thought—I *am* getting old, so I moved." At his home on the beach Conrad continues to paint, and write, and for one hectic week in June, he and Mary direct the Santa Barbara Writer's Conference.

"It all began when I asked Ross McDonald, the mystery writer, and Clifton Fadiman, who both live in Santa Barbara, if they would speak to a group of writers. Then I called Ray Bradbury and he said "Yes," so armed with these authors I went to other writers and said, 'Look, I got these famous names, would you like to join them?' They all said, 'Sure, you can't leave me out.' " Conrad has persuaded everyone from William Buckley to Charles Shulz to appear at the conference. Even Alex Haley came, but he was easy for Conrad to get.

"Alex Haley was a student of mine when I taught writing classes in San Francisco," Conrad says. "He had some talent, but he wasn't sure what he wanted to write about. Then he came up with the idea for *Roots,* and the rest is history."

Conrad puts the final splash of paint on the dog's nose, gets up, and looks at the completed image. "Well, it's finished," he says and wipes his hands with a towel. "But it was fun doing it." He looks up. "It was also fun remembering. Thanks."

Conrad's life has been full of fun, and one of his rewards is remembering. He hinted at his own epitaph when he wrote his autobiography and titled it, *Fun While It Lasted.* He has also come up with another which might be more apropos: "Gored, but never bored."

Cathy Guisewite with her comic-strip double, Cathy. (Hara)

Cathy Guisewite

"Cathy!"

I interviewed Cathy Guisewite, creator of the highly successful comic strip, "Cathy," soon after her cartoon had become well known. She was vibrant, alive and totally uninhibited—and a little worried about what I would write. After I finished writing the profile, I delivered a copy to her home and handed it to her. I drove the fifteen minutes back to my own house, and when I arrived, the phone was ringing. It was Cathy. In a tearful, but relieved voice, she said, "Thank you for making me sound so coherent."

The front door swings open, "Hi!" and a hand thrusts into mine. "Whoops. Excuse me. I'm on the phone. Sit anywhere...." She motions to a couch covered in violent purple, red and pink geometric patterns.

"...Oh, I'm Cathy Guisewite."

I had guessed. She looks something like *Cathy* from the comic strip: long straight hair, eyes like big black diamonds. Except this Cathy, at age thirty-four, is attractive and slender. The cartoon *Cathy* looks more like a Hostess Twinkie. The real Cathy—Cathy Guisewite—zips into the kitchen, a disappearing act in orange T-shirt, faded blue Levis, and saddle shoes.

I sit on the couch and look around the living room: bare hardwood floors under high ceilings, a sidewalk "put-a-penny-in" weighing scale (*Cathy* "can gain four pounds on breath mints", I remember from one comic strip), an old wagon with red wooden sides, and another couch, this one stark purple vinyl.

So this is how the emerging New Woman lives.

Cathy Guisewite hangs up the phone. "Coffee?" she asks. The orange T-shirt labels her "Sunkist—Good Vibrations." "How about a cookie?" I pat my marshmallow middle and shake my head.

"I lost forty pounds," she says, answering my unasked question. "Took me six years to do it. I have an obsession with food—something anyone who has eaten a hot-fudge sundae while hiding in a closet will understsand. I let my obsession rub off on *Cathy*." ("In purple Danskins," I recall from another strip, "Cathy looks like an eggplant.") Guisewite heads out the back kitchen door saying, "Come on, I'll show you my office."

We step out the door and her dog Trolley wags up to her side; three chubby puppies wag behind. "Careful where you step," she says, walking to an outside stairway that leads to a second floor attic. I climb the stairs, she opens the door, and we step into—Cathy's world.

The old attic has been transformed from a haven for dust and cobwebs into a sparkling, modern writing workshop. The white walls slant in like the letter A, meeting at a peak above the center of the room. Sunlight streams through four bay windows, scattering light across the angled walls and far edges of the room.

Near one of the windows stands the drawing board where comic strip *Cathy's* life is continued on a daily basis. Scattered across the table is a flurry of half-completed cartoons, an explosion of creative clutter that overflows into a wastebasket filled with rejected funny faces.

"This is where I write, and draw, and think," Guisewite says. "I just close myself up in here and play depressing records—I think funnier when I am depressed." She smiles.

Cathy shows me the attic bathroom, newly refurbished in modern gothic. I almost expect *Cathy's* comic strip boyfriend, *Irving* to be leaving—the lid up.

Stepping back into the studio I have the strange feeling that *Irving,* the classic male chauvinist, is here somewhere getting ready to slouch on the sofa and watch the Rams clobber the Saints on television. *Andrea, Cathy's* girl friend—the typical hard-line feminist—should be pacing the carpet reading aloud from *The Women's Room.* And *Cathy's Mother*—the deep rooted traditionalist with a lifetime subscription to *Bride's* magazine will surely arrive any minute in an apron, to empty the wastebasket.

Each of these two-dimensional images, including *Cathy*—most of all *Cathy*—emanate like magic from the mind of the life-sized look-alike named Cathy Guisewite. It must be a unique companionship, walking side by side through life with a cardboard cutout of yourself.

"When the comic strip first began I was horrified with the idea of calling it 'Cathy,' " the real Cathy says sitting in the hardwood swivel chair by her drawing board. "Not only did the strip resemble me a little physically, but what I was writing about was quite personal. I didn't want friends calling me up the next day saying, 'Idiot, why did you say that about yourself.' '

"So I bought a baby book, *Naming Your Baby*. And I looked through the names. Nothing suited her right. She *had* to be 'Cathy' to be…well, me." Cathy tucks one leg under her, a position she assumes when she draws. "She is so close to how I think. Using the same name can be a little embarrassing at times, but it helps me keep her true to life."

Cathy's *Cathy* is amazingly true to life. Critics and fans alike have hailed the comic strip as a "chronicle of the changing woman," It's been proclaimed an "amusing portrait of the new woman torn between hard-line feminism and old-line traditionalism."

The analysis is correct and very rewarding and gratifying to *Cathy's* creator, but too much thoughtful insight about a comic strip's "secret meaning" can be hazardous to the health of any writer's funny bone.

"People have made nice, beautiful, broad statements about what I write," Cathy says touching the heart-shaped locket around her neck, "but what I am really writing about is gum wrappers, and why did I drop the hair dryer in the toilet on the day it was important for me to look perfect at the office meeting. I don't write about the big picture. What *Cathy* is doing is foundering in the middle of two ideals: traditionalism and feminism. She doesn't know which direction to go because she likes what she sees on both sides, so she is walking down the middle. Because others are walking the same line she can make the reader look at this serious subject and feel like laughing along with *Cathy* instead of ripping their hair out.

"For instance, *Cathy* is looking at an ad for 'Creamy Dreamy Lipstick,' and tells her feminist girlfriend, Andrea, that she wants to get some. Andrea screams, "That's chauvinistic capitalism at its worst. All they are selling is sex, hope and dreams!' *Cathy* grins and says, 'I'll take it.' "

For *Cathy* there is always hope, and that hope is a key part of the strip. "*Cathy* can have 440 phone calls to answer and twenty-seven projects overdue," the cartoonist says leaning forward in the swivel chair which squeaks agonizingly, "and she hasn't done the laundry in two months and the bills are stacked up and her car is out of gas and the garbage disposal is broken and yet she believes with all her heart that not only will everything be done and fixed, but she will have lost fifteen pounds by 7:30 that night!

"*Cathy* is slowly getting her life together," the real Cathy continues. "In the early days of the strip she spent a lot of time getting 'dumped on.' I was writing the strips as a kind of doormat psychology because that's the way I was at that point in *my* life. Of course, *Cathy* will never have it all together. She has her weaknesses. Her character is built on human weaknesses."

In one of the strips *Cathy* is telling Andrea about a new boyfriend she has just gone out with. "Phillip is only interested in my body" she says. Assured that Cathy is finally getting it together Andrea says, "Well, you won't be seeing Phillip anymore." Cathy says nervously, "Perhaps just one more time."

No, *Cathy* will never be perfect but then her creator wouldn't want her to be. "The problem with the concept of the 'New Woman' is that she is *too* perfect," the cartoonist says. "The women I read about in magazines and see on television are self-confident, self-assured, dynamic business people, and they are also cheery homemakers and understanding, non-sexist mothers.

"It's like the woman in the perfume commercial. She is charming at home, charming in the office, and she looks luscious when she goes out in the evening. She has every aspect of her life together, and not only that, she knows where her checkbook is. She is perfect.

"It's a wonderful ideal for us to have, but most of us feel we are not living up to it. We feel frustrated with our little failures and we want to give up and say forget it. In a nice way *Cathy* evokes a lot of empathy; when people read her they feel they are not alone with their problems."

The working out of these personal frustrations was the genesis of the comic strip. "I was working as a writer in an advertising agency," Cathy says. "I was doing quite well in business, but I was confused by a lack of success in my personal life. I kept having one pathetic relationship after another.

"My mother had always taught me that the real strength of a person was in their ability to move through a crisis, and that every big crisis has a purpose and every little disappointment has a bright and wonderful side So instead of wallowing in my own misery I would write my troubles in my diary, looking for the bright side. Unfortunately, it got to the point that I was writing down the same tragic detail over and over and it was getting boring, so I scratched out a picture of myself waiting for the phone to ring, and at the same time showing me eating everything in the kitchen." (This first idea became the basis for one of the first strips to run in the newspapers.)

"I spent a lot of evenings scratching out my frustrations. I would send them home—that was before I moved to Santa Barbara, when I lived in Michigan and my family lived in Ohio—to show how I was coping with life. The drawings were a release. It never occurred to me that I was creating a comic strip."

But it did occur to her mother. Anne Guisewite seized upon the idea that the drawings would work as comic strip. She told her daughter that the frustrations she was drawing were the same a lot of women were suffering from, and she should try and get them published. Cathy ignored her.

Her mother nagged her for months. Cathy kept sending the drawings home—they were great therapy. Finally Mrs. Guisewite went to the library and researched comic strip publishing syndicates and sent her daughter a list of them. Cathy still ignored her. That's when her mother threatened to send the drawings in with a cover letter from "Mom." That did it. Cathy sent the cartoons in herself to Universal Press Syndicate, the first name on the list.

A few weeks later she got a letter back from the syndicate saying they liked the drawings and felt that the ideas summed up the confusion of modern relationships in a very real way. In the letter was a contract.

"I was in shock," Cathy says, the wonder still in her eyes. "That was a remarkable day. Since then I've talked to other cartoonists who have literally spent half their lives trying to get a syndicate to respond to their ideas."

In that first letter the syndicate mentioned to the fledgling artist: "Work on your art a little."

"I ran out and bought several books on drawing cartoon characters," Cathy says. "I took them home and studied and practiced. I felt that I already had a natural knack for showing emotion and character in my drawings. If a comic figure felt sheepish or wishy washy, the lines I drew would be wiggly, or if someone was mad the lines would be straight and hard. If a character was happy the lines became soft and pleasant." Cathy points to her head, then draws an imaginary line down her arm to her finger. "If you really think how the character feels in your brain while you are drawing, it will work its way out to your hand."

From the frenzy of the original drawings, Cathy's style has evolved and her confidence with the pen has improved. The lines have become softer and the characters more cuddly.

Irving started out as a brute with hair on his chest, but has now been drawn down to *Cathy's* size. "I really didn't realize I did that," Cathy says. "I must have changed him unconsciously." The inter-reaction and conflict of ideas between the four main characters has remained the same.

Irving, perhaps the key character other than *Cathy,* represents Guisewite's frustratons with men. She picked the name Irving because she wanted a name she wouldn't run across in real life.

"Does *Irving* really exist?" Cathy laughs at the question. "I get asked that a lot. I don't like to pin his character on one guy. *Irving* is a composite of all the negative traits I've run across in men. He is the classic chauvinist who is frazzled by change. All his old lines are not working and he is confused. Lifestyles are changing for both men and women, but some men aren't changing with it. *Irving* is one of them."

Cathy's biggest problem is *Irving.* To simply get rid of him would destroy the core of the male/female conflict in the strip. Yet, how does the comic-strip *Cathy* justify keeping him around? Cathy pauses as if remembering a past boyfriend, and her stare is momentarily blank, then a ray of sunshine filters through and she fades back in. "Many people find themselves staying in relationships that aren't healthy. Partly because any relationship, no matter how miserable, offers some security and satisfacton. People have a tendency to think it will get better, or they think, 'I can change him.' *Cathy* has stuck herself with *Irving.*"

At the opposite end of the male chauvinistic spectrum is the hard-line feminist, *Andrea,* who represents the total New Woman. "I liked what that idea represented," Cathy says, "even though I could never get there myself. I had a girlfriend in high school called Andrea who kept trying to 'correct my vision,' and she had an influence on my life. The name Andrea seemed to fit the positive character I wanted to portray in the comic strip."

Then there is *Mother,* the antithesis of Andrea. *Mother* lingers in the old-word concept of traditionalism, yet she has learned to adapt as the strip and *Cathy* pass through lifestyle changes. "Mom" has even formed a "conscious raising" group within her bridge club. "She wrote the ten easy steps to raising consciousness on the back of a beef stroganoff recipe, and put a time limit on the group's sessions because, "the girls get cranky if they miss 'Guiding Light.'

"These women, like my real mother, see a whole new world for women that is different than the one they were raised in," Cathy says, "and they don't know quite how to handle it. My mother is the classic of confusion—she subscribes to both *Ms.* and *Bride's* magazine."

Cathy, Irving, Andrea, and *Mother,* are four comic characters drawn from the far corners of human behavior patterns. Put them all together and watch the sparks fly:

In one strip *Cathy* says to *Andrea,* "No matter what Irving says when he calls the answer is 'no.' I'm going to say 'no' no matter what he asks. The answer is 'no,no...no!' " The phone rings. It is Irving. he says, "Hi, you want to go out?" Cathy says, "Okay," puts down the phone, turns sheepishly to Andrea and says, "He caught me off guard."

Later a disgusted *Andrea* tells *Cathy,* "You and Irving have nothing in common...name one thing you have in common." Cathy says, "Both of us like him."

In one of the first cartoons *Cathy* is lolly-gagging on the couch with *Irving.* He says, "C'mon, what makes you think I don't really love you?" And she answers, "You never kiss me when we're standing up."

In another strip *Mother* is reading something from a paper to *Cathy,* "the weird, self-indulgent and crazy carefree hedonism of the '70s is giving way to a more sensible, down-to-earth kind of lifestyle." Sighing *Cathy* says, "I'm starting to feel like I missed something."

How does Cathy Guisewite plan the lives of four people? She gets up and goes to the wall where the original printers' metal plate of the first six "dailies" hangs next to a photograph of her presenting President Carter with a *Cathy* drawing. She studies the metal plate for a moment then says: "The hardest part of my job is making decisions. These are characters whose future and lives are totally in my hands. I think if someone would tell me what is going to happen I would just write it. I know I can do the words, but making the decisions is hard.

"The Mother, like my real mother will continue to change a little, but she will still cheer on my independence and my career just as feverishly as she is praying that I'll get married and begin my real life.

"I get letters from women saying they have *Cathy* strips stuck on their refrigerators," Cathy continues. "Mothers write and say they send the strips to their daughters to make a point. My *own* mother sends me *my* strip to make a point, and I say, 'Mom! I know. I wrote that!' "

Panic, depression, laughter, hard work; it's all part of a cartoonist's life. There are also rewards other than monetary. "I think this is the opportunity that writer's dream about—to write from life. That is where the richest material is, and if I can write about it perfectly..." She stops, reflecting, then continues, "One of my greatest pleasures is having someone write to me and say, 'Cathy, you said it just right!' "

Cathy stops and touches the heart-shaped locket around her neck. The comic strip *Cathy* wears one also. "I first put it on her because I liked the way it looked, but it also identifies her as the person who thinks with her heart, rather than her brains. She is a real romantic." Cathy opens the locket. There is a picture inside—*Irving.*

And the real Cathy smiles—big.

Mike Love, lead singer of The Beach Boys.

Mike Love
& The Beach Boys

Endless Summers

Co-Authored by Sheila G. Johnson

Of all the interviews in this book, the Mike Love profile is the only one written with another author. Although I like the Beach Boy's music, Mike Love, the group's lead vocalist, bored me. I thought he was aloof, affected and self-centered, a trait which I have found to be rare in the celebrities I have interviewed. Fortunately, he was glib, and a slick conversationalist.

"Catch a wave and you're sittin' on top of the world..."
From "Catch a Wave," the Beach Boys.

Their musical ingenuity—a complex tonality that rises and swells like an advancing wave—evokes the image of a laid back California lifestyle that offers an uncomplicated utopia of endless summers, surfing, and sustained happiness, a Shangri—La where youth is eternal. From the group's first national hit, "Surfin' U.S.A." to the full-fledged psychedelia of their biggest smash record, "Good Vibrations," they have continued to fit the musical mood and shifting styles of succeedng generations. The music has endured, and remains, identifiably—the Beach Boys

"There are a number of reasons our music appeals," says Mike Love, lead vocalist of the Beach Boys. "There is an intellectual level and a feeling level, but I think the important level must be the heart. We're not known for our great prose, but we do have mass appeal." As if to emphasize his point he crosses his arms and leans between two platinum records framed in the office at his Santa Barbara home. "People who grow up in middle—class America experience all the things we sing about, like on the record, 'Fun, Fun, Fun': borrowing their parents' car, going to a dance. Even the parents can identify with it, because they did it once."

"You see, there's a lot to relate to in our music," he continues. "The harmonies are intricate enough to make it interesting, the melodies are simple enough to relate to, and most of all the feeling is pleasant and relaxed. Even a fan listening to a record in Pittsburgh, a song like 'California Girls,' can take a relaxing three minute vacation in a musical vignette."

Mike Love steps away from the platinum records and sits at his desk, leaning back comfortably in his office chair, his eyes staring at the high-beamed redwood ceiling. Lean and fit in a blue jogging suit that sets off his deep blue eyes, Mike Love is in his prime at forty-one. Beach Boys fans might not recognize this cool, polished performer with his neatly trimmed strawberry blond beard, sitting behind the smooth expanse of desk.

His appearance has changed from the crew cut image of the Beach Boys twenty years ago. The white Levis, tennis shoes and striped black and white shirts that gave the the look of adolescent football referees are gone. So are the beards and beads of the early '70s. Adornments of past decades have been traded for the casualness of Hawaiian shirts and baseball hats. Their appearance seems to have had little effect on their longevity, but their music, which has dazzled the ears and settled into the senses of two decades, has. Mike Love remembers the roots of that music.

"The Beach Boys' original harmonic influence was the Four Freshmen," he says. "As a group they sang four-part harmony which is known as modern harmony and comes from the jazz influence. It really caught the ear of my cousin Brian, who is a genius in his ability to arrange and compose.

"We started out singing just for our own enjoyment," Love continues, punctuating his ideas with expressive gestures of his long, slender hands. "We sang Four Freshmen arrangements for the art of it, and the challenge of it, and the beauty of it, because they harmonized so perfectly. Those are fun songs, 'Bird Dog' and 'Devoted to You,' things like that." He stops for a moment, remembering. "The main ability our family had, and continues to have, is to sing."

Singing was always a part of family life for the Beach Boys: Mike Love, his cousins Brian, Dennis, and Carl Wilson, and their neighbor Alan Jardine. An early memory appears in the song Love wrote called "Brian's Back." The second verse lyric begins, "I still remember / you soundin' sweet and tender / singin' 'Danny Boy' in grandma's lap.

"It's literally true," says Love. "The first recollection I have of my cousin Brian Wilson singing is when my grandmother coaxed him into singing 'Danny Boy.' He sang it in a high, beautiful voice. Our families used to get together at Christmans and sing Christmas carols. After carolling the older folks would sing their songs, standards of that day and time, the '40s and '50s. The older kids—me, Brian and his brothers and our friends—would sing some of the Everly brothers songs. The little kids would just play and run around. We had as many as a hundred and fifty people singing in the house at once."

At times the Love household must have sounded like the Mormon Tabernacle Choir, and at other times like the Metropolitan Opera Company performing *Aida*.

"My mother had these friends who would come over and sing opera," Love says. "She'd also play opera records, turned all the way up to nine on the Hi-fi set. I didn't like being awakened in the morning to go to school to the sound of Renata Tebaldi hitting some high ones, or Maria Callas. So, to this day I consider operatic music an anathema because it reminds me of having to get up and go to school."

Even though constantly surrounded by music, Mike Love and his cousins never dreamed they would become singing stars; neither were they pushed by stage mothers as some talented kids have been. They weren't trained to make singing a career, yet music became their lives.

"Singing was second nature to us," Love says. "In our family music was all pervasive. We actually did it for the love of music, and I think in a lot of the early records you can hear the blend, and the warmth of it. It's not jaded and it's not canned."

He gazes out the window of his office for a moment, then chuckles at an early memory. "We didn't even know what to call ourselves at that time," Love explains. "We used to wear these Pendleton shirts that all the surfers wore, so we thought of calling ourselves 'The Pendle *Tones*.' Then a record producer suggested 'The Beach Boys.

"We said, 'The Beach Boys? That sounds weird.' But we thought about it—beach boys, and surfin'—and said, 'Well, OK, that sounds better than the Pendle *Tones*.' "

From the beginnng the recording method of the Beach Boys has been part laziness and part wanting to be spontaneous. That sound and that mood and that feeling were captured and had a tremendous life span.

"We never have been much for rehearsing," Love says. "We'd go into the studio with a song, and we'd go over it a few times, just so we'd know where we were at, but more often than not we'd be in the studio doing the harmony, and that harmony had a spontaneity and liveliness—there's an energy there."

The Beach Boys' first records, such as "Surfin' Safari" and "Surfin' U.S.A.," which were pleasant ballads about California beaches and surfing, had that "energy" and achieved an incredible degree of popularity. At the same time, these records brought financial success beyond their wildest imagination.

"You know," smiles Love, tapping a pencil against his desk top, "I had a Rolls Royce, a Jaguar, a Triumph motorcycle, a house in Beverly Hills, a house in Manhattan Beach. I bought a house for my parents and a house for my grandparents. It was a fortune, you know, all in the span of two or three years and all made in one-night stands.

"The first time I remember thinking maybe we were on to something big was in 1962. We were playing our first U.S. tour, mostly in dance halls, and I went outside between sets with my cousin Brian. We looked down the road and could see cars coming up for a couple of miles. I mean people were actually breaking windows to get into this place, and I thought 'Gee, this must have been what it was like when Elvis Presley first got started.' "

Although their collective identity attracted a tremendous following, the Beach Boys never possessed the individual charisma of Elvis Presley or the Beatles. Does Mike Love feel that he missed something by not achieving individual recognition?

"Yeah. Sure, because everybody has a personal ego," Love says. "There were reasons why we didn't have a personal identity. You see, when the Beatles came out, it wasn't just as Beatles, they came out as John, Paul, George and Ringo, which was a smart idea because the fans could follow them as individual stars. But with us, it was never that way. It was always 'The Beach Boys, the number one surfing group in the U.S.A.' It's been a void in our career. If you try to be objective about it, it's something that should have been done and wasn't, so you can't cry too much. In a way, maybe it's good, because we've been tremendously famous and successful and important, yet in every town we perform in we can go back a few months later and live ordinary lives. People know who we are, but it's not a frenetic or freaky thing. That's good, because the whole charisma of the Beach Boys is just an easygoing kind of thing anyway.

"But if I did have a public personal identity," Love says, 'I guess it would fall somewhere between what Mick Jagger is to the 'Stones' and Paul McCartney is to the Beatles. That's what Mike Love is to the Beach boys, a performer *and* a musician.

"Mick Jagger is a performer, and whatever you think of his music, or his lifestyle (and I don't think much of his lifestyle), I regard his music with—well, not awe, but respect. He's been able to keep the commercial tag going, and although there have been fantastic improvements in his music, it's certainly not art.

"Mick Jagger is the smartest entertainer in terms of projecting what he wants on the public, and manipulating public taste. McCartney's different. He's a master at mentally and musically weaving his web, and surviving and excelling musically over the years. These two, Jagger and McCartney, are the catalysts of any group. They are the Merlins; the magical wizards."

On stage, Mike Love might be mistaken for a wizard and a musical magician as he presides over his audience with the nonchalant authority of a seasoned performer. Smiling out from under the ever-present hat, in a wild printed shirt, he sings his songs of eternal summer in a nasal drone as he swings and rocks to the music. Girls in the packed audience writhe along with him, mouthing the lyrics, many from their perch on someone's shoulders.

"There's an aspect that takes over when I get in front of a microphone," Love says, rising from his chair and pacing around the office. "I don't like an entertainer who just sits there and plays the guitar and looks at his shoes. A guy like Mick Jagger, you don't have to like his style, but you can't fault the guy on the theatricality of it. He's outrageous and he's flamboyant. I'm of the same ilk when it comes to being on a stage. I run around, I jump around, I dance around, I jump on the piano, things that I wouldn't do at home." Loves sits in his chair again. 'Yeah, I'm a different personality. It's the outgoing, gregarious part of my personality. I'm at home on stage, and I'm also at home completely out of the public eye."

It is Mike Love's personal life-style and philosophy that help to determine the easygoing charisma of the Beach Boys., He learned to cope with the stress and tension that accompany stardom in 1967 when he was in Paris doing a UNICEF show for the United Nations. That night when the curtain opened he noticed John Lennon and George

Harrison sitting on either side of the Maharishi, the fountainhead of Transcendental Meditation. After the show, Love was invited to the hotel where the Maharishi was staying and received an introductory lecture.

"Since that time I've meditated," says Love. "I used to drink hard liquor to relax, but after meditating for a day, I just don't have the desire any more. I am relaxed, very much relaxed, just by meditation. You don't have to take drugs or liquor if you meditate. This is the methodology which I employ to dissolve the tension. That's why meditation is the most important thing to me. It goes hand in hand with physical fitness. The one complements the other. And also diet. I've been a vegetarian for a long time now. Once in a while I'll eat fish, but that's about it. I'm a Pisces, also, so I don't like to be cannibalistic, you know?" He stops and laughs at his joke. "I'm fine, living the way I do. This morning I had some tea, and for lunch I'll have a fruit smoothie, and it'll last me all day."

As if on cue, the phone rings. He picks it up.

"Yeah...great," he says into the phone, "but it'll be another half hour, we're still grinding away here. See you then."

He hangs up and smiles. "That's about my fruit smoothie, it's ready now," then adds, as if it needs explaining, "You see, the fruit has the energy, but it doesn't have the bulk, so you're not heavily laden down by some heavy meal. You're free to do mental or physical things."

"Like jogging?"

"Well, I don't jog along the beach," he says. "It's a long walk down, and I have a hot tub and deck up here. I look down at the beach a lot from my hot tub. I may be forced into jogging, though. I've got a new album out, *Runnin' Around the World*. I like to run better than I like to jog—I'd rather get it over with."

Love pushes the chair back from his desk and stretches luxuriously. He radiates health and energy. He's also bursting with plans for future projects. And number one of those projects is the Love Foundation. "The Love Foundation, my own foundation, is a non-profit, humanitarian, environmentally concerned organization. I'm not trying to invent a new product with the foundation, or save the snails. I'm not going to picket French restaurants that serve escargots. The Foundation is going to be able to raise a lot of money and awareness, to benefit certain causes. I'm trying to implement these plans with other people I know in the communications business.

"I met a man once, a psychic, about 1968 I think it was, who said, 'I see you in a foundation in California,' And I was thinking, if I ever make a lot of money, I'm not talking about a million bucks, you know, I'm talking about a *lot* of money; if I were ever to generate a lot of money, I'd like to do something valuable. I'd like to have a foundation that could do something positive."

Love rises again from behind the desk and walks over to the window, where he looks out at some of the amenities he's added to this three and a half acre cliff top site on the mesa. Fruit trees have been planted in front of the five handsome natural wood homes designed by Santa Barbara architect Robert Easton that he hopes to use to house members of his foundation. Below the office window a waterfall runs musically down a stone wall to the Koi pond where the brightly colored fish have been multiplying rapidly in the fruitful atmosphere.

"It's really going to be a garden spot," he muses. "Eventually I want to have exotic birds here and there, a little flora and a little fauna." He stops and savors the thought for a moment, then he says, "Yeah—the Love Foundation.'

"So far we have supported some local Santa Barbara causes like the Symphony and a prison project in Lompoc. We've helped the 'Save the Children Federation,' which celebrated its fiftieth anniversary this year. We get requests, everything from a musician who wants a certain instrument and can't afford it, all the way to someone who wants a scholarship to go to a particular school."

It was pure chance that led Love to this idyllic spot overlooking the ocean. "I was passing through Santa Barbara, and was told, 'There's this great place for sale.' And I came, and I walked down the driveway, and saw the ocean there, and all these pine trees...I rented the house that day, and moved in that night with just a sleeping bag. I was so excited I couldn't sleep."

"This was a garage," he adds, gesturing around the spacious office carpeted in beige plush. "We're still remodeling."

Love turns from the window and walks back to the chair. He adjusts the calendar spread out on his desk, on which his engagements for the next six months are recorded in an elegant calligraphy. He picks up a pencil and twirls it, stares at it thoughtfully.

"My eyes are visionary. I have pretty good perception after meditating several thousand hours. My profession has been music and it will become films, because of the audio-visual convergence that is happening.

"I think the technical capacity to do an infinite variety of sounds, both natural and synthetic, will continue and will be enhanced holographically. You'll be able to play sounds that will create 3-D images in the middle of the room, or on the walls, or in the sky. There's nothing you won't be able to do.

"Instead of Muzak, you'll have holograms. You might be in an elevator in the year 2000, which looks out over valleys and waterfalls. Why not? Why have claustrophobia? You might as well walk into an elevator and see a visual promotion to go to Hawaii on the ride down."

Love leans forward now, elbows on the desk. His glance grows more intense. "This sort of thing is very important to my life purpose. Staging those kinds of events, or contributing to a foundation for humanitarian purposes is more important to me than, 'What's your latest record doing?' or 'How's your latest album?' Those are things you do, of course, for business, for a day's work, if you're into music. But it's been a sort of long apprenticeship so far, a twenty year apprenticeship.

"Catch a wave and you're sittin' on top of the world," sang the Beach Boys at the beginning of Mike Love's twenty year apprenticeship. With that line and others like it, they captured the mood and set the style of an era. Since that time they have matured and progressed within the confines of a unique style, while appealing to a whole new generation of fans. What the future holds is anybody's guess, but one thing seems certain—the sun is still shining on the endless summer of the Beach Boys.

Neal Hefti in 1962 with a "friend"—Frank Sinatra.

Neal Hefti

The Sound of Music

When I first talked to composer Neal Hefti about doing an interview, he said, "I don't have anything to say." I bumped into him several times after that, and we began playing a rhyming game. I would feed him a word and he would find a suitable, and usually unusual, rhyme. One day, while sitting in the grandstand at a particularly boring polo game, we both ended up in hysterics rhyming "Chucker" (the different periods in a polo match). Still laughing, he agreed to the interview. I began the conversation with the rhyming game...

"Orange," I challenge, naming the one word in the English language that poet Ogden Nash said couldn't be rhymed.

Neal Hefti, musician, composer, and lyricist, rolls his eyes upward for a moment, showing white, shrugs, then says: *"Door hinge."*

Amazing.

He grins, warm and friendly, then, intrigued, tries another near-rhyme: "Let's see...on the old ranch we'd ride out to...*our range."*

Equally amazing.

His mind searches for one last perfect rhythmic combination, one final corresponding echo for "orange," and his eyes brighten as he says, "Our sister-in-law's name was Angie...but we just called her—*Our Ange."*

Even more amazing.

Satisfied by out-rhyming even Ogden Nash, Hefti relaxes back in his grandstand seat, and pulls the knot of his sweater over his shoulders. The fall air is cool at the Santa Barbara Polo Club and the sky is clear as fine crystal. On the polo grass two teams of horsemen charge across the middle of the field, their mallets flashing in the air like sabers.

Hefti stares blankly at the polo players—but he listens. To his ears, the drumming of horses hoofs and the clashing of mallets must sound as vibrantly musical as a symphony of percussion instruments. But then, the sound of music is Neal Hefti's life.

In a musical career that began at age 15 and has spanned the last forty years, Hefti has composed music for most of the finest jazz and popular singers in the world: Ella Fitzgerald, Della Reese, Frank Sinatra, the McGuire Sisters, Kate Smith, Dean Martin and Doris Day, to mention a few.

An outstanding trumpeter, Hefti also played with the Charlie Barnet Orchestra, and eventually conducted his own seventy-five pieces for Count Basie, produced over 200 LP albums for the Frank Sinatra Organization, and penned the music for dozens of movies and television shows such as "The Odd Couple," and "Batman."

"I got a lot of fan mail from 'Batman,'" Hefti remembers with a laugh. "The mail was from four and five year old kids wondering if I'd ever ridden in the Batmobile."

Neal Hefti is an easygoing, unassuming and completely unpretentious man. His name suggests he might have had a foreign background in music, perhaps he was a Viennese music master or a Swiss yodeler.

"Naw, I was born in Nebraska," he says in a voice that is still tinged with a midwestern accent. "But, my father was Swiss! When I started touring with my own orchestra, my agent thought I should change my name to something that sounded Middle American like Jones or Miller. At the time, I was also playing a lot of behind-the-scenes music for recording artists and I figured a name that sounded a bit foreign was intriguing. People would think, 'Who's Hefti? Is he foreign? If so, he must be very strict with his people and they must be fine musicians.' So, I didn't change the name. Besides, I felt it would have been an insult to my parents."

He looks across the polo field where the milling back and forth in what has become a one-sided game has lulled the onlookers into lazy gossip. Hefti continues:

"You see, it was my parents who insisted I play a musical instrument, and I took up the trumpet. That was in the early thirties during the depression, and they figured music could get my three brothers and myself through high school and out of the dust bowl. We could earn money playing at night and on weekends so we wouldn't have to quit school and take a job.

"Including my two sisters, there were eight of us living in this little one-bedroom farmhouse—we were as close to being share croppers as we would dare admit. Because the place was so crowded, I'd have to practice my trumpet outside. My mother used to get phone calls from the neighboring farmers with music requests." He turns and looks at me with a grin, "No, really! They'd say, 'Do you think Neal could play "Stars Fell on Alabama"? Does he know "Tiptoe Through the Tulips?"' ...And I could play all the requests by ear. Just by listening to the tune once or twice on the radio, I could play it right back."

"I found out very early I had good..." he pauses, searching for a word other than *talent,* "ah...predisposition for sound and how that sound works in music."

Hefti's "predisposition" for music was nurtured when his parents moved to Omaha, Nebraska, the only large city between Chicago and Denver. As such, Omaha was a mecca for traveling carnival acts, theatrical shows and territorial dance bands. Hefti's older brother had started writing music for several of these visiting bands, and when he got overloaded with jobs he passed some to his younger brother.

"The first piece I wrote was a military song," Hefti remembers. "The band wanted a tune like 'Anchors Aweigh,' so I wrote one."

Hefti's older brother also collected symphony records as well as the scores of the music. Hefti would study the music, analyze it, "absolutely dissect it," until he could write his own compositions "intelligently," so that the tunes were easy to play.

"Composing is a creative art," Hefti says, "and one of the reasons I became so good at it was that I played the trumpet. I knew the limited capabilities of that instrument, so I knew not to write music in extreme registers, too high or too low. Most composers learn to write music from a piano, and they don't stop to realize that all instruments don't have the piano's fantastic range."

At the same time Hefti was picking up the rudiments of composing music, he was given

146

the opportunity to conduct. "I had a very good orchestra teacher in high school," he says. "He was also the conductor of the Omaha Symphony, and when he was away from class he'd let me conduct the high school band. Of course, the band members didn't know if I was conducting right, and I didn't know if they were playing right," he laughs loudly, enjoying himself.

By the time Hefti was 17, he felt his teenage talents were tuned high enough to make a career in music. He packed his trumpet, scraped together a few dollars, and was off on the next train to New York.

"I got a job in a dance band," he says, then shrugs. "I was fired."

"Because of inadequacy?"

He throws up his hands. "Absolute inadequacy! The problem was I was too young. I didn't have enough experience. But I got a lot better."

"I didn't have enough money to go back to Nebraska, so I stayed in New York. I scrambled around getting enough jobs to survive." At this point, Hefti's life story read like a well-worn movie script of the starving musician locked in his room, sweating in a grubby tee shirt, his trumpet pressed to his lips, while the sound track plays a haunting melody.

"To survive, I started writing music," he says, "and, amazingly, I began to get the feeling I had some ability as a writer. I wrote a military tap tune for a dancing school, and the musicians who played the song told me, 'Neal, you really should be writing.'"

Before Hefti could concentrate on his composing, he got his "big break." He was hired to play trumpet in the Charlie Barnet band. "I was not the premiere trumpet player—at first," Hefti remembers, "but I eventually played solos." Hefti was better than he admits. During the '50s he was one of the top ten trumpet players on jazz polls.

"I also started writing original songs for Barnet," he says. "I did a little arranging, whatever he needed. I got to lead the band occasionally, mostly when we were playing music for dancers or comedians."

Up to this point Hefti's musical career had centered around doing—as he says, "a little playing, a little writing, a little conducting, a little starving, and finally a lot of getting married,"

In 1945 he met a vocalist from the Woody Herman band named Frances Wayne. For a while he wrote melodies for her, but when she became pregnant she gave up her career. The Hefti's were happily married for thirty-two years until her untimely death in 1978, a tragedy that Neal Hefti still has difficulty viewing from afar. Hefti's daughter, Marguerita, is a gynecologist, married with two children. Hefti's son, Paul, is a professional guitarist and singer.

During the ten year period from 1952 to 1962 Hefti wrote music for Count Basie, who recorded seventy-five of Hefti's tunes. Through that association the composer worked with most of the great black jazz singers of the era: Ella Fitzgerald, Dinah Washington, and Della Reese. At the same time he was writing for such "pop" singers as Theresa Brewer, the McGuire Sisters, and Kate Smith while being the conductor of SBC in New York.

"I was able to go right down the middle of the road and do all kinds of music," he says. In 1961 this ability to compose melodies across the musical spectrum from jazz to popular songs, attracted the attention of a singer named Frank Sinatra.

"I produced and conducted over 200 LP records for the Sinatra organization," Hefti says.

"I also did ten albums for Sinatra himself. He was really a great person to work for. Everyone has heard of his temper, but I never saw him throw a tantrum. I've seen him come in real quick and say 'Let's do the job,' and get out; but he never tore up an arrangement or made a fuss. I've had other singers come into the studio and blow up when the orchestra tuned up. I don't think Sinatra was the 'monster' that the public identified him with, at least he wasn't when it came to music.

"Sinatra was trained by Dorsey and Harry James, and learned to have great respect for music people. He has a great love for music and always has talented people working for him."

While Hefti was still with Sinatra, he got a call to write the score for a Warner Brothers Picture named *Sex and the Single Girl,* with Tony Curtis and Natalie Wood. The producer was so pleased with the composer's work, he contracted Hefti to do more movies. At the time Hefti and his wife and family lived in the tranquility of Connecticut. He phoned his wife asking what he should do.

"The day I called there was a big blizzard," Hefti remembers. "I said I was at the pool at the Beverly Hills Hotel, and before I could say anything else, she said: 'Stay there! I'll bring the children and join you. Don't, D-O-N-'T come back!'" And so began Heal Hefti's long association with the movie industry. He went on to make films such as *Barefoot in the Park,* with Robert Redford, and *The Odd Couple,* with Jack Lemmon.

"When I am doing a picture, I live it," he says, leaning forward, his arms crossed on the railing. On the field the polo ball has been sent spiraling toward the stadium, and the riders and horses are thundering after it. A single rider emerges from the pack, swings his mallet in a high arc over his head, and smashes the ball toward the startled onlookers. Several people in box seats down front duck as the ball careens off the wooden structure and bounds back on the field.

Hefti leans back after the near miss and continues. "In a movie, I live the parts of all the characters. I am Robert Redford for a while and then I am Jack Lemmon. In doing so I try to match the personality of the character the actor is playing with a musical instrument. For instance, Natalie Wood might be a trumpet, and each time she is on the screen that sound will be in the background. It's like a muted musical mosaic that filters into the audience's mind."

One of the most popular songs Hefti wrote for the movies was the theme for *The Odd Couple.* The song was also used in the television show. "That's the most valuable of my 'works.'" Hefti says. "'Works,' that's what ASCAP calls them. I guess I have 600 works copyrighted. Some are valuable and some didn't earn the money it took to copyright them."

It seems incredible that he's written 600 melodies with only 12 notes at his disposal.

"Those twelve notes, plus as many octaves as each instrument has, plus the different chords that can be used, can provide for an unlimited mixing of sounds." Hefti leans forward trying to explain. "It's...it's like blending different colors, almost like adding flavors to food. There is always a new, perhaps spicy, flavor to add. Just look at today's whole new synthesizer family of electronic instruments. You can see that the flavors have increased dramatically."

"Does that mean he likes today's new sounds in music?"

"I love music as a whole," he says. "Sure, I have my own tastes, and those tastes are not limited to certain categories of music. There are some rotten records today, but there were rotten ones in the '50s—I think I was responsible for a few of them myself..." He chuckles quietly to himself. The polo game is also in its last minutes, and the audience has brightened thinking of the awards ceremony to follow.

"I remember I had to play many songs that I despised," Hefti says, smiling. Perhaps that's the reason I got into composing. If I had to despise a tune, I might as well invent it."

"Still inventing?"

"Sure, I've got a whole drawer full of songs I have written since I came to Santa Barbara in 1978. I also have a music company of my own in Los Angeles that handles my works."

"I write a few lyrics for some of the tunes," he says. "I guess I am pretty good with words, but I prefer to have the input of someone else, a collaborator to feed me the rhymes."

"How about rhyming *Moon?*"

He laughs. "That's a toughie! Ah...I'd rhyme it with...how about Pat *Boone?* Or sand *dune.*"

One more, I say. Rhyme *melody.*

"That's easy. A melody is *swellody.*"

And he smiles, real big, as if he had just summed up his life in the music business—a life spent loving, working, and playing with the sounds of music.

Julia Child.

Julia Child

Inside Julia's Kitchen

Julia comes on like "Gangbusters." She was, no doubt, an assertive lady when no one knew what the word meant. When I called her on the phone, and asked for an interview, she surprised me by saying, "I'd love it! Do pop on by for lunch." While visions of sauces and souffles danced through my head, I read through her cookbooks preparing questions. Unfortunately, when I arrived at her condominium, her two ovens were . . . well, that's getting ahead of my story . . ."

"Sorry, we're having a bit of trouble with our oven," Julia Child says in a chortle that could curdle cooling bernaise sauce. She shakes my hand, pulls me through the open front door of her Santa Barbara apartment, and propels me into the living room. "Seems rather foolish, a cook without an oven," she adds, then pops into the kitchen just as the oven man pops out.

"It's not the oven, it's the electricity," the oven man says.

"Can't you do anything about it?" Julia asks.

"You'll have to get an electrical man," he says heading out the front door.

"What a bother." Then she turns to me, "Oh, well, nothing wrong with a cold lunch. I've got some left-over quail in the refrigerator, and some fresh asparagus, then there are always the sauces...come into the kitchen."

I follow this towering woman (she is six foot, two inches tall) through a swinging door and into her domain—the kitchen. The room is surprisingly small and square with a single window over the sink. But it's a chef's paradise, with two white ovens with broilers, and a white electric stove with four burners—all inoperative. One wall is covered with copper pots, aluminum pans, wooden spoons, whisks, crushers, grinders—all the paraphernalia of a well-organized cook. A massive thick oak cutting table dominates the center of the room. I sit down on a stool next to the table.

"At our other home in Massachusetts we have a bigger kitchen," Julia says as she pulls leaf lettuce from its stalk and washes the greens in tap water. "But any kitchen is fine as long as it functions as a kitchen and not something that a designer has dreamed up for *Better Homes and Gardens.* You must have the necessary cooking hardware to be able to prepare food properly." She takes the dripping leaves and puts them into a small red plastic lettuce dryer.

I watch her intently, this gastronomical giant who taught fledgling cooks—who didn't know a truffle from a toadstool—the wizardry of *haute cuisine*—and, finally, I ask, "What makes a good cook?"

"Good food and the love of eating," she answers, pulling on the cord of the leaf dryer. The lettuce whirls inside, spinning off excess moisture. "The more 'piggy' you are the better cook you are. Of course, having a bit of experience helps a lot. You need to know cooking terminology. It's like building blocks.

"And the more experience you have the more interesting cooking is because you know what can happen to the food. In the beginning you can look at a chicken and it doesn't mean much, but once you have done some cooking you can see in that chicken a parade of things you wil be able to do with it. That's when the challenge begins. That's when it becomes fun. Cooking may be a creative art, but it is also a wonderful full-time hobby."

Julia puts the lettuce in a bowl, then opens the refrigerator and takes out a small leg of smoked ham. "The problem for cookery-bookery writers like me is to understand the extent of our reader's experience. I hope I have solved that riddle in my books by simply telling everything. The experienced cook will know to skip through the verbiage, but the explanations will still be there for those who need them."

Cookbooks have been one of the key measures to Julia Child's success, as are her award winning television shows, "The French Chef" and "Julia Child and Company," but the real key has been her ability to take the mystery out of French cooking; to move it out of the bistro and into the American homemaker's kitchen.

"My idea was to take French cooking out of cuckoo land and bring it down where everybody is," Julia says. "Sure, you can't turn a sow's ear into Veal Orloff, but you can do something very good with a sow's ear."

In her monumental fourth book, *From Julia Child's Kitchen,* she reminds the reader that "French cooking isn't fancy cooking, it's just good cooking...Cooking well, too, doesn't mean cooking fancy, it just means that anything you set your hands to makes good eating, be it mashed potatoes, chicken soup, meat balls or a twelve-layer cake...A *Coq au Vin* is a chicken stew, a *Pot-au-feu* is a broiled dinner, a *Mayonnaise de Volaille* is a chicken salad, and *Soubise* is plain old rice with cooked onion, and there is nothing fancy about any of them."

Julia Child has published six successful books that echo this cooking philosophy; the original *Mastering the Art of French Cooking,* folowed by *Mastering the Art of French Cooking, Volume II.* Then came the *French Chef Cookbook,* taken from her first television series, and *From Julia Child's Kitchen,* followed by two large-format books based on the television show, "Julia Child and Company." The last two books were heavily illustrated in color. "I was getting tired of gray food," she says. "With the color there are no more gray strawberries, pale and sickly veal, livid lettuce, or pallid pickles."

In 1972 she received the *Ordre du Merite Agricole* from the French government, and in 1974 she was awarded the *Antonin Careme Medal* from the Chef's Associaton of the Pacific. She has also been the subject of a cover on *Time* magazine.

Amazingly enough, Julia McWilliams at age thirty-four could barely boil water.

"I don't think I was a born chef, but I've always been very hungry," Julia says, slicing the last of the smoked ham. "And I married a man who likes to eat. We both shared a passion for food."

She looks at Paul as he comes through the kitchen door. "Gosh, when were we married? I've got it written down somewhere...1945 or '46. The beginning date isn't as important as whether you are still together."

Paul and Julia met during World War II in Ceylon. Paul, a confirmed bachelor at age forty-two, was designing war rooms for Lord Mountbatten, and Julia was serving as a filing clerk in the Office of Strategic Services. (She had joined the OSS with every intention of achieving spy status.)

"I didn't want to marry anybody," Paul says. "Then I met Julie—I've always called her Julie. She had a kind of crazy humor, and I could see how tough she was, and how she worked like mad on projects and never gave up."

"I wasn't going to marry anyone either until I met Paul," Julia confesses, an obvious warmth in her voice, "I guess he just ruffled my nesting instincts."

"I don't know exactly what it was when we met," Paul says. "It wasn't like some bomb exploding, but there was something there, some new *fizz* about ready to go off."

A few years later they were married and Paul was assigned to the American Embassy in Paris." We got off the boat in Cherbourg and started to drive toward Paris," Paul remembers. "We stopped in Rouen, and went into a French restaurant. It was there that Julia had her first taste of French food."

"And I never got over it," Julia says putting several halves of French bread into a small electric toaster oven which, for lack of counter space, was stored atop the refrigerator. "The food in that French restaurant was so carefully prepared...I was amazed. I had never tasted anything like it before."

"She was hooked," Paul says.

Once in Paris, Julia brushed up her college French with two Berlitz lessons a day. (Paul had lived in Paris in the 1920s where he learned the language and developed a love for French cuisine.) Julia enrolled in a six-month Cordon Bleu cooking course along with twelve American G.I.s. "Some of them weren't very serious about cooking," Julia remembers. "Most of them had stayed in Paris on the G.I. Bill to be near their girl friends. For those few of us who were genuinely interested in cooking, it was easy to get the chef's full attention."

Julia was fortunate to have for a teacher Master Chef Max Bugnard, then in his late 70s, who had worked with the great Escoffier. She also met Simone Beck and Louisette Bertholle, two French women who were working on a French cookbook for Americans. Julia was taken on as the team's translator, but was soon making major creative contributions to the cookbook. The manuscript, *Mastering the Art of French Cooking,* was contracted for by Houghton Mifflin, and was finally completed in 1958, seven years after the writer-chefs started it. The pubishing company turned it down. It was too long. The three women shortened it. Still too long. Then they sent it to cooking enthusiast Alfred Knopf, who published it in 1961. The sales have soared ever since.

"I happened to be the right woman with the right book at the right time," Julia says. "It was the beginning of the '60s and the Kennedys were in the White House, and there was a lot of new talk about French food. Travel to Europe was also becoming easier and Americans had the opportunity to savor French cuisine."

The book's success propelled Julia into her first television show, an educational program on Boston's WGBH called, "The French Chef."

"They had asked me to come on a talk show to be interviewed about the book," Julia says. "During the show I beat some egg white in a copper French bowl to enliven the talk. The response from viewers was quite excited, and I was asked to tape three half-hour shows. I can remember after the first taping, I rushed home, and Paul and I dug our tiny budget television out of the unused fireplace—it was so ugly, that's where we hid it—and sat down and watched this strange woman tossing French omelettes, slashing eggs about the place, brandishing knives, and panting heavily as she careened around the stove. That's how I and educational TV lurched into its first cooking program."

Julia's success on television was not based simply on her cooking techniques or her ability to unravel the mysteries of French cooking. Her exuberance, and her passion for good food was infectious. She would take short cuts, break rules, and her audience loved her for it. She would squeeze lemons through her "Ever-clean dish towel," or sample sauces with her fingers. And if a minor disaster happened on camera, she would scoop up the wayward item, drop it back in the pan and say to the camera, "Remember, you are all alone in the kitchen and no one can see you."

"I'm not fazed by anything going wrong in the kitchen," Julia says, scooping hollandaise into a sauce dish. "Fact is some people accuse me of planning disasters. It's not necessary to plan a disaster in the kitchen. There are too many of them that happen automatically."

As if to emphasize her point the bell on the toaster dings, and Julia slides the French bread, a bit burned and smoking, off the aluminum tray. "See," she says looking at the crisp edges of the bread, "little disasters are easy....Well, it's ready. Everyone carry something, and let's go into the dining room."

I pick up the asparagus dish and lettuce tray and we all caravan to the dining table in the living room. The walls are covered with photographs taken by Paul, including one of Julia with a cat in her arms. It is his favorite photograph of Julia. A large window overlooks a small balcony with flowered sofas, and beyond is the ocean.

Julia puts down the plate of cold quail, then pours from a bottle of Burgundy. "Sorry it's not white wine," she says. "Seem to be out, but this will do fine. Wine is a compliment to any meal."

We clink our glasses together and they ring like ceramic wind chimes. Julia says, *"Le carillon de l'amitié."*

"The bell of friendship," Paul translates.

"This is an interesting sauce," Julia says, pushing a small dish toward me. "Try it. Goes well with the quail. It's got liver, butter, and cognac and port wine in it." Then, with a spontaneous touch of merriment, she adds, "I call it a 'loose mousse.'"

I spoon a bit of pale brown "loose mousse" on my plate, dab some on my cold quail, and taste. "Ummmm..." I hum as my undertrained palate tries to unravel the different taste sensations. I swallow and say, "Delicious," then, "A fabulous recipe."

"Actually, we don't really speak of 'recipes' any more," Julia says attacking the tiny quail on her dish, effortlessly separating the meat from the bone. "We speak of 'dishes.' *Recipes* make it sound awfully dry, don't you think? Perhaps it is better to simply say, 'the food' or 'the dish.'"

"Nor do we use the term gourmet," Paul Child says from the other end of the table. "*Gourmet* doesn't mean anything anymore." He cuts a piece of asparagus, fresh and green, and dips it in hollandaise.

"*Gourmet* makes it sound like someone is putting sherry wine in the cornflake casserole," Julia adds. "Which really wouldn't be very tasty. Gourmet is an overused advertising word. Someone will say to me, 'My son is going to be a gourmet cook.' And I think, what does that mean? Does he really grind the raw hamburger himself rather than getting it out of the package?"

"We say 'good food' and 'good cooking,'" Paul says, "like what we're eating."

The food in front of us is quite good, cold or not. I try a little more of everything, stuffing myself like a starving artist who may not know where the next meal is coming from. Dessert is a large plate of fruit and cheese: Brie, Camembert and cheddar. I try some of each with a piece of slightly scorched French bread and ask, "What was your biggest cooking disaster?"

"That's one of the four or five questions everyone asks." Julia says, "What disaster? I always have to answer the most recent one. Any disaster is a learning process, you just have to learn to be master of whatever happens."

"What is the second most asked question?"

"Aren't people afraid to ask you for dinner?" she answers. "Wouldn't they be intimidated? Well, not if they know us. We're nice guests to have...we're always hungry.

"Then, we are always asked what our favorite meal is. There are so many favorites—all in my cookbooks. And the last question is always, 'What would you want for your last meal on earth?'"

"It wouldn't be a monkfish," Paul says munching on a slice of apple.

"The monkfish was one of my strangest television menus," Julia clarifies. "We were in our local fish store in Cambridge, and I saw this whole monkfish. Usually it's just the tail. And I thought, what a great visual for television. It was so vicious looking."

"A monster," Paul says.

"For being so ferocious in appearance, it is a very mild tasting fish," Julia says. "It has a chewy flesh but little flavor of its own. Everybody screamed when it was wheeled into the studio on a cart. Imagine a tadpole the shape of a grand piano, no scales and a skin as loose as a puppy's."

"Filmy stuff on the top," Paul adds.

"I practically had to wrestle the fish to get the little bit of tail meat I needed for the recipe. You have to get your hands into what you are doing if you want to be a good cook. You can't approach cooking from afar with medical gloves.

"My advice to a new cook is to be fearless. And cook! And don't try the easy thing first. Really get into something like a chocolate mousse. That wil teach you how to melt chocolate and how to beat egg whites. Then, remember what you have done so it will go into your mental computer and stay there.

"Get a good cookbook and follow it seriously," Julia continues. 'Take a cooking class, but take an authorized one.

"I am a member of the International Associaton of Cooking Schools, which is trying to establish standards for cooking teachers. For a person to read a few books then set themselves up as a cooking teacher just isn't right. Our international association has over 600 members now. We are trying to standardize the cooking profession and, at the same time, make better cooks out of everyone."

Julia has become involved in a project called the American Institute of Wine and Food (AIWF), with an office located on campus at the University of California, Santa Barbara. "It's kind of a think tank for gastronomy," Julia explains. "An institute of culinary wisdom and wine appreciaton."

With Julia's help the Institute was able to acquire an exceptionally unique collection of historical cookbooks. There are nearly a thousand cookbooks dating back to the 1600s. "There are many handiwork concepts of cooking, such as pastry and bread making and sugar pulling methods that we at the Institute want to preserve, or even bring back. This library of books was just the first major step in that quest."

I stuff one last piece of Camembert in my mouth, dust a few crumbs of French toast off my fingers, and thank my two hosts for their conversation and a lively luncheon.

Outside of the apartment I bump into the electrician.

"Hear you have a problem with the oven," he says.

"Who needs an oven?" I say, softly patting my overstuffed stomach.

Julia waves from the doorway and calls, "Bon appetit!" as I waddle away.

Kathy Ireland, fashion model. (Hara)

Kathy Ireland

A Face for the '80s

Fashion model, Kathy Ireland, has long-tanned legs, a marvelously proportioned figure (she has done hundreds of bathing suit ads since this profile first appeared), and a perfectly featured face. As I sat on the couch next to her, I had to search for flaws. After all, the old cliche states that nobody's perfect. Finally, she smiled. Her teeth were too small! And her voice! Just a tiny mousebreath whisper. Whew. I relaxed.

You look at the face on the cover of *Vogue,* and you wonder what makes this elfin image stare so innocently—yet knowingly—into the lens of the camera? Is this full-face color apparition real or as hollow as a soap bubble?

"Oh, that," Kathy Ireland says, glancing at the cover of the magazine. "The photographer put these big tungsten lights right in my face. They were so bright I had to keep closing my eyes. He would say, 'Good! Now, say—one—two—three! then open your eyes as wide as you can...Now!' " She giggles, a kind of mousebreath giggle that matches the tiny, surprisingly shy voice.

And you look at her again, closer—this five-foot-ten-and-a-half-inch, nineteen year-old girl—and you wonder, how is she able to do it? How is she able to create a multi-layered image for the camera that can run the gamut from gamin to glamour girl? How? It must be magic—or just plain bunkum. Or, maybe its having the right look at the right time.

Sitting on the couch in the living room of her family's home in Santa Barbara, Kathy Ireland, internationally known high fashion model, exudes an aura of wholesomeness coupled with the mystical innocent look that has become the image of feminine beauty for the decade of the 1980s. Today Kathy is herself, relaxing in a purple T-shirt, pink cord shorts and tennis shoes. Her face is perfectly, yet softly made up, and her eyes, set deep and wide beneath the bushy eyebrows, are dazzling.

"I guess I have the Brooke Shields look," Kathys says and plops her long, deeply tanned legs on the coffee table and crosses her ankles. "To get that wide-eyed look photographers use different methods. One always mumbled. I couldn't hear him, and I'd say, 'What?' " She cocks her head quizzically. "Then, he'd take the picture—Click—just like that. If the photographer gives you too many directions it can look phony.

"At first I did a lot of work for this German photographer," Kathy continues. "One day a magazine interviewed him and asked why he worked with me so much. What specifically did he like about me? And he answered: 'I like the Russian look. Kathy reminds me of Brezhnev.' " Kathy giggles, that tiny giggle again, and adds, "He calls me Baby Brezhnev because of my bushy eyebrows."

The heavy brows are only part of what lifted Kathy Ireland to the peak of the peacock profession. To be successful in a business where youth rings eternal a model must have the perseverance of a door-chiming Avon lady, the resiliency of a rubber band, the self-discipline of a Tibetan guru, and beauty that is skin deep all the way to the bone. She also must have the right look at the right time. Had Kathy been a sleek blond with ironed hair and a laid-back California look she wouldn't have made it as an international high fashion photo model.

Fashion modeling has changed radically in the last decade. It is no longer an exclusive profession populated by tall willowy women, skinny enough to give a two-dimensional image, who have the bustline of a boy and the ideal hip measurements of thirty-three inches. The look of the '80s is back to the classic look of femininity, and is not a paragon of unattainable, glamourous perfection. No longer does fashion modeling conjure up images of an emaciated Twiggy gliding down the runway of the New York Plaza wearing Christian Dior's latest chic creation, or of some elegant flat-chested Diana wilting and yawning after a night out with the wolf pack.

"The asparagus look—white, limp, and shapeless—is out," says John Casablancas, head of the Elite Model Management Agency in New York. His competitor, Eileen Ford, house mother to the New York City based Ford Models Inc., believes the ideal beauty of the 1980s should look "sweetly sexy, romantic and authoritative—and be able to cook lasagne as well."

Strangely, Kathy Ireland, the personification of this new look, never dreamed of becoming a fashion model, and even today is not sure she likes it.

"I never really had any desire to become a fashion model," Kathy says in that soft voice. You have to listen carefully to understand. "I never looked in any fashion magazines when I was young. My older sister, Mary, wanted to be a model and I thought that was dumb." (Mary, age twenty-three has recently signed with the Elite Agency.)

Then what did Kathy really want to be I ask? "That's easy," she answers. "I wanted to be a snow ski bum in the winter and a beach bum in the summer. I kept telling my parents I wanted to be a teacher just so they would leave me alone. I was only fifteen and I really couldn't think seriously about my future. I just wanted to have fun.

"Learning about modeling was my Mom's idea," Kathy says, uncrossing those long legs and squiggling around on the couch. "I was sixteen and she paid for a class in Basic Beauty at the LaBelle Agency here in town."

The "before" picture taken the first night Kathy entered the classroom shows a bewildered young girl in baggy jeans, her face almost hidden by her hairdo.

"I can remember this mop of hair hanging into her eyes," Sheila Burch, Kathy's Basic Beauty instructor says. "She was shy and sensitive and afraid to look at you. The hair seemed to protect her, kind of a curtain draped against the outside. One night in class I pulled her hair back to show the class how it could be restyled and realized she had these beautiful, expressive eyes. She was pretty!

"She didn't talk much because of her shyness," Sheila continues, "but when she did, she had this tiny, squeaky voice."

Kathy giggles, a little embarrassed. "I have been told that too many times. Not here in Santa Barbara. I guess my friends are used to me. But in New York...they told me my voice was too high and I should take voice lessons to try and lower it. They kept telling me everyone was going to take advantage of me because I sounded like a Mouseketeer."

"One time I was so fed up about everyone telling me about my voice problem that I decided to try and talk in a deep tone to a New York taxi driver." She lowers her voice an octave, but it still comes out like a chipmunk on helium. "The taxi driver started laughing, 'What's wrong with your voice?' he said. The heck with it. My voice doesn't make any difference in my photos."

Still, fashion and glamour photographers have been shocked when Kathy steps in front of their cameras and begins to talk in her Tweety bird chirp. "I couldn't believe that fabulous voice when she came into the studio," says top photographer, Francesco Scavullo, who photographed Kathy for the cover of Cosmpopolitan. "At first I thought she was kidding—she reminded me of a child. But, you know, the girl with that tiny voice is *powerful* on film. Not tiny at all! She's a forceful presence. With her looks and that sweet voice, she'd be great in the movies."

Yet, Kathy says she really doesn't harbor any dreams of being a screen goddess. She is still "seeing how far this modeling thing goes." It was just a few years ago that the prospect of becoming a fashion model was beyond the realm of reality.

After completing the Basic Beauty class at the Labelle Agency in Santa Barbara, Kathy entered the Agency's Model Teen contest and was selected as a runner-up. She had begun to transform from a prune into a peach. And—she finally began to think of herself as pretty. "I figured something had happened when guys started asking me out," she says. At Labelle she decided to finish her training and completed classes in fashion modeling, fashion photography and commercial acting.

Then one day, Betty Mazzetti, Director of Labelle, invited a representative of the Elite Agency in New York, to drop by for a look at her crop of young hopefuls. The agent spotted a special quality in Kathy that he thought could make her a hit: "She has very childish features...young and fresh. But then she's got this massive volume of hair and a sensuous body." The agent liked the combination, realizing it would allow her to be cast both as the girl next door and sophisticate. He offered her a shot at modeling in New York. It was a golden opportunity as the Elite agency sees about 12,000 women a year from all over the world. Of these, 500 are asked back and only 150 are hired.

Kathy decided, a little reluctantly, to give it a try. "It was in New York that I began to consider modeling as a serious business," Kathy says. "I just didn't realize how much I had to learn."

The Elite agency sent Kathy to Paris, the fashion citadel of *haute couture,* and the boot-camp training ground for newly recruited models, where several dozen weekly fashion magazines are less reluctant to gamble on newcomers.

Thrust into the dazzling world of designer clothes in a flurry of flashing strobe lights, Kathy quickly learned from experience. The first experience came as quite a shock.

"This French photographer—he was really weird—told me to take off my top." She shrugs. "Just like that—off. I knew I was new, but this is not what I expected. I got mad and told him I didn't have to, that it wasn't a requirement of the job. He pulled out these magazines with pictures of some of the top models in seminude layouts, pointed at the photos and screamed at me? 'She did it...she did it!' And I said fine. Get *them* for your pictures!" And with that Kathy did an about-face and marched out. So much for day one.

Day two started the same way. The photographer asked her to put on an outfit that was brief and revealing.

"I said to myself, well, here we go again. I told him I couldn't wear the outfit. He looked at me for a moment then said, 'Fine.' And that was that. He was an established, well-known photographer. I found out later the first guy was new, and it was his first big job. He was trying to get an exclusive picture to make his name.

"Things like that don't happen anymore," Kathy continues. "The agency and photographers know what type of work I do, and how far I will go in the clothes I wear. I realize in Europe nude modeling is not such a big deal; all the deodorant ads use nudes. New York is different. The agency even lets me know if I am booked to wear bathing suits.

"Oh, I remember one job I did in a bathing suit. This German photographer took me way up in the San Bernadino mountains, and it was November and there was snow all around. It was freezing and he had me put on these swim suits. He started shooting: 'Don't look cold—look warm!' he said." She shivers, remembering. "The goose bumps showed in the pictures.

"The agency will also tell me if I am scheduled to do lingerie. They check to make sure it's nothing see-through. I don't mind doing lingerie, that pays double." She stops and says in a tiny whisper as if to reveal a secret of the trade, "that includes flannel nightgowns too."

Kathy has an enviable relationship with the Elite agency. Not only do they act as her fairy godmother, but they also bend to most of her wishes. "When I signed with Elite," she explains, "they told me I had to live in New York. I really didn't like the city, and felt I couldn't live there, mostly because it was such a different lifestyle. So, I said no. I wasn't trying to give them a hard time, but my home and family in Santa Barbara meant more to me than modeling. So they agreed to let me live in California and be on call. If they had a booking for me they would phone me the previous afternoon, then I'd jump on the red-eye special plane to New York that night and end up in Paris or the Bahamas or wherever they wanted me to go.

"One month I flew to Paris for four days, then back to Santa Barbara for three days, then again to Paris for another four and home for a couple days, then off to New York...I was like a rubber band stretched back and forth." She folds her arms across her chest and yawns. "I fall asleep in airplanes, and taxis, and sometimes forget where I am. I always have jet lag. I get lost, sometimes in airports. In Paris the streets are so windy and I can't read the signs..." She stops: a young girl, beautiful, confused, thrown into a profession she wanted no part of. The glamour still doesn't mean anything to her, nor does she care about living the exotic jet-set lifestyle associated with successful mannequins. Why does she do it, I ask?

"The money," she says, and she doesn't sound mercenary. "The money is real great! When I was a kid—I guess I was kind of a tomboy—I had this paper route for three years, and then I worked as a hostess in a pizza restaurant. I also worked at a snack bar on the beach. All at minimum wage. I can sure make a lot more than that modeling."

How much does Kathy make in front of the camera? "Right now my day rate—that's a full eight hour day—is..." and she names a a high figure, then says quickly, "You're not going to print that are you?" You have to shake your head, no. She explains: "The last time I told someone my rate everyone I knew, well, they just started bugging me about it. Asked me if I made so much money, why did I drive such a junky car. Well, I like my junky car!"

The agency sets Kathy's rate, which is determined by how much in demand she is, and how many magazines she has appeared in. "Beng on the cover of *Vogue* and *Mademoiselle* helped a lot," she says. "I have done mostly editorial work, that's layouts for magazines but eventually I should get to do advertising and catalogues which pay a lot more."

A lot more is a lot more money. The standard fee for a high fashion model like Kathy runs from $1200 to $2500 a day. A big-league stunner like Brooke Shields, Cheryl Tiegs, or Christie Brinkley can command an astronomical $10,000 a day.

Kathy's modeling takes her to the far reaches of the world. She says the most unusual place she has been is Morocco. "It was different, but I didn't necessarily like it. We stayed a week in the Sahara, traveling further and further into the desert to get the right locations. The designer draped us in big flowing scarves with real camels around us for contrast. It was weird. One day this wrinkled old nomad offered us a big plate of dates to eat." Kathy curls her lips into a distasteful grimace. "Ugh! They were covered with flies. There were more squirming flies than dates! '

"The worst place I have modeled so far was in a ghetto in Los Angeles. It was for a European magazine and they wanted all this dirt and graffiti in the background for contrast. It was uncomfortable working because this real tough gang—about a dozen guys—were standing around sneering and shouting obscene remarks. I was the only model and I had to tune them out so I could work.

"Then one time I did trash bags. The designer took Hefty garden bags and cut them into dresses and jumpsuits. That was weird too. Then once in Paris we shot in this cruddy old

160

warehouse. They had two of us costumed as motorcycle girls in black leather jackets and sunglasses, and I had to walk around acting tough." She sighs. "That's not me."

"There is a lot more acting in this profession than most people realize. The photographers are always wanting me to be sexy or sultry for the camera. And that's how I try to act it out. If I couldn't act out this other personality I would feel uncomfortable and very embarrassed in front of the camera. And I know that a model must be able to wear anything, but what I prefer is high fashion designer clothes." High fashion. That is the ultimate for any model. A fashion model is an animated clothes hanger, a mobile mannequin who enables the material to transform itself into the vibrant creation the designer envisioned on the drawing board. The fashion model *wears* clothes. Other women just put them on.

"Every photographer works differently," Kathy says. She slumps deeper into the couch. "That's what makes it so hard. It's very different with European photographers, because they have a small English vocabulary. They get mad easily. Instead of simply saying, 'Don't hold your hand quite like that,' they scream: 'That looks stupid!' "

She says that Italian photographers are the most demonstrative, talking with their hands, working models to exhaustion. "In Rome we were doing designer collections and were modeling for fifteen hours. "Because I had such bad jet lag I kept falling asleep. It was summer and it was ninety degrees, and we were wearing long fur coats. It got so hot I fainted."

Kathy isn't complaining, she's just admitting the work can be tough. "That's what I get paid for," she admits. "But sometimes the photographer will put you in these strange positions and expect you to hold them forever. *They* know how much you are getting paid, and some of them make sure they get their money's worth. They forget you are human and can be bent until you break.

"I do a lot of high fashion modeling, but I rarely remember what I wore. People ask me, 'What's the new trend in fashion?' and I don't know. During a photo session I have to change so fast, I can't remember the clothes."

She stops and thinks for a moment. "Polka dots! I remember polka dots! Well, anyway, the high fashion stuff is so weird a normal person wouldn't go out and buy it. The clothes have to be toned down a bit. I don't pay much attention to it because I won't go out and buy it myself."

She stops, run down. And I look at her one more time, and I finally figure it out. That isn't the real Kathy Ireland on the cover of all those fashion magazines. It couldn't be her, it isn't her style. She'd rather be on the beach.

"Yeah," she says hugging herself, "it's not a bad life—it lets me be a beach bum whenever I want."

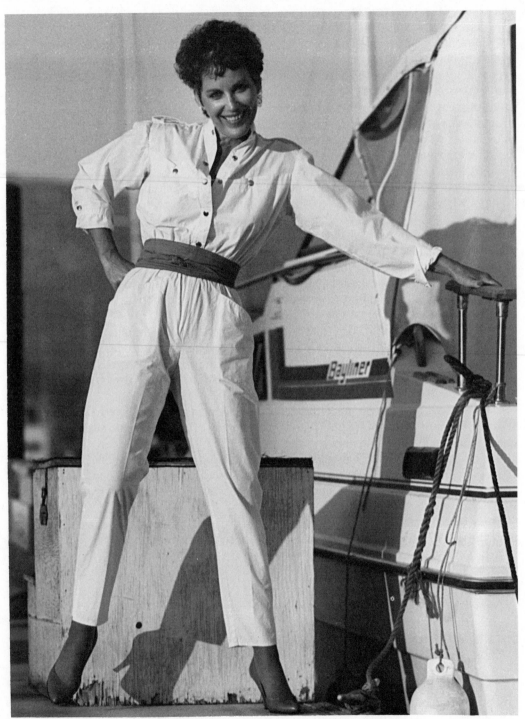

Lynda Lee, "classic" fashion model. (Lisa Ryan photo)

Lynda Lee

Model 44

Lynda Lee, "classic" fashion model, is also my wife of twenty-eight years. I still find her a fascinating interview.

"When I was twenty-five, I was the perfect mother, the perfect wife and the perfect homemaker. I drove a great big station wagon. Well, I am no longer twenty-five and I am no longer anyone's wife. My kids are grown and have kids of their own and I have a career. And that station wagon is just a rusted memory. I went out and bought myself an Alfa Romero Spider. It's red and it's got a convertible top and when I pass those ladies in their huge station wagons full of kids I wave..."

—from an Alfa Romeo commercial

"Well now, y'all, just wait ten minutes, this place will be a bedlam of bitchin'," says a pencil thin brunette model with an Alabama accent.

"Don't stand in anyone's path or you'll get mowed down," adds a strawberry blonde as she runs a brush through her hair. The thick curls fall softly back in place like undulating currents in the ocean.

She, like the other female fashion models in the room, is dressed in panty hose, high heels—and earrings. Nothing else. "Can't show panty or bra lines in these fancy duds," she says taking a designer gown off the rack and holding it in front of her.

Behind her a wall clock ticks away the last few minutes until high noon; curtain time for the runway fashion show at the Biltmore Hotel. The atmosphere is filled with energy, and you feel like you are standing in the eye of a storm, floating in a calm sea, waiting until the tempest is unleashed.

There are ten models in the cramped quarters behind stage, eight females and two males. The two male models are oblivious to the flurry of flesh around them as they prepare their clothes for the show. The female models seem to have been cast from the same mold. Each is tall—5'7" to 5'11". Each is slender, even though some of them have more curves and orbs than planes and angles. There is one major difference—age. There are several very young models, sixteen to seventeen years. But the Alabama brunette's age hovers around thirty and the strawberry blonde appears to be thirty-five. And there is one attractive and slender mature model with streaks of gray hair who is forty-four.

"That's what my car license says—MODEL 44," Lynda Lee says plucking at several tight gray curls with her fingernails. She stands in front of a full-length mirror in the middle of the room, then does a turn, arms outstretched wide like wings, the gown of gossamer whirling in cloud-like patterns from her body.

"Ummm..." she murmurs watching the flow of the gown as it billows and swirls around her. "This dress really *moves*." She stops her pirouette, and turns to a dressing table. She picks up a white, balloon-like snood that resembles a fencer's mask, and slips it over her head, a device made to protect the designer gown from her make-up. She pulls the dress off over her head, and hands it to her "dresser," a young girl in tee shirt and jeans. The dresser hangs the gown on a rack in the sequence it will be worn in the show. She also places a pair of high heels in a neat line on the foor, then arranges a pair of golden earrings in sequence on the table.

Racks of designer clothes hang in a waterfall of vibrant colors from racks lining the perimeter of the changing room. There are two full-length mirrors in the middle of the room, tilted toward one another for support; an A-frame of reflection. White bedroom sheets have been taped to the tile floor to protect skirt hems and leather shoe soles.

It seems obvious from watching Lynda Lee—the "Model 44" of this story—that fashion modeling is not simply an occupation restricted to the bikini-clad Pepsi generation. Evidently an attractive, mature woman can fit into a fashion model's thirty pair of shoes even if she is as old as Betty Furness or Bess Myerson.

There *is* life after forty, and being "mature" is no longer a netherworld for women in the eyes of the fashion industry.

"I think 'classic' is a better word," Lynda Lee says, smiling broadly. " 'Mature' makes me sound like a matron. Besides, youth and an emaciated appearing body are no longer the only criteria to be a successful fashion model. Today's model must create the image of a healthy, active, fun-loving 'natural' woman, one who represents an attainable dream for the average woman. And she can be any age."

She pauses, holding out her arms while the dresser slips a stark-white Grecian gown over Lynda Lee's head, the first gown she will wear in the show. The clock ticks slowly toward twelve noon. "Fashion modeling is not an exclusive profession populated by young women skinny enough to give a two dimensional image, who have the bustline of a boy and hip measurements of thirty-three inches," she says. 'It's all right to be over thirty, or forty, or even fifty."

The dresser helps her into gold high heels with thin straps. "I suppose I have to believe what I say, after all, I'm a Janey-come-lately in the modeling business. I didn't start until I was forty years old. I had always dreamed about becoming a model, but being married in the late 1950s left me with a family to manage. At age forty I decided it was time to chase my dream.

"I know I will never be in competition with the Brooke Shields look alikes, and I can never expect to be an international high fashion model. My goals are a bit lower, but are still fascinating enough. I do my modeling in Santa Barbara with a few forays to Los Angeles, working for the big department stores like Saks and I. Magnin."

Lynda Lee puts on a pair of earrings and goes to the mirror for a final look. She picks once again at a couple of gray curls. "When I model, I feel the older women relate to my age. They look at me and say, 'Well, if she can look like that with all that gray hair, then I can too!' The women go into the shops afterwards and say, 'I'll take that dress the older model was wearing.' "

She steps back from the mirror as Suellen, the strawberry blonde, and Laralyn, the southern brunette step up and fuss with their hair one last time. The clock on the wall shows a few seconds from twelve. The room has hushed; the models expectant.

Lynda Lee looks around at the other models. "You don't have to be a model to feel like one at any age." She says. "Everyone can be as beautiful as they want to be. You may just have to work on it a little harder. It helps if you can learn to *wear* clothes, not just put them on."

The curtain to the dressing room parts, and the show's commentator, a starkly made up model with hollow-set black eyes and a pixie haircut, walks in. The models turn toward her as if confronted by a drill sergeant.

"Okay, all you boney people, let's get the old buns in gear," she says, rattling an arms length of multi-colored bracelets. 'You have to be fast on this one. The show is timed to music cues, so if you can't make a change on time, the pacers at the curtain will send the next model in. Dressers, keep it moving back here. No screw ups. Nobody panics."

"So, who panics," Laralyn says.

"Yeah, we're pros," Suellen adds.

"Just no one fall off the runway into somebody's lap." The coordinator starts for the curtain, then turns. "Okay, pros. Have a ball."

Then, the music starts, muted tones from beyond the curtain. The models step into an orderly line, Lynda Lee first. The dressers stand by their clothes racks. It is time.

"Go," a pacer says and Lynda Lee vanishes beyond the curtain and into the limelight. There is the muffled sound of the commentator's voice and then applause. Another model is sent beyond the curtain, and another. The line shortens.

Lynda Lee scurries back into the room, undressing as she heads for her clothes rack. The dresser takes the falling dress, throws it over her arm, and at the same time holds out the next gown as Lynda Lee pops the snood over her head. One foot up and the dresser removes a high heel and slips on another, then the other foot. The snood is dropped to the table, and zippers are pulled up on the back of the dress.

"Earrings," Lynda Lee says, and the dresser snaps two pink prisms with gold clips into the model's hand with surgical precision. Then with a quick glance in the mirror it's off to the exit curtain. The last model in line has just stepped out. The fast change would have been something to make an Indianapolis 500 pit crew cheer.

Models rush in and out of the room, in blurs of gossamer, brocade and silk, baubles and beads. They slip hurriedly out of dresses, peel off panty hose, and toss blouses, shirts and ties over their heads with practiced efficiency. There is no panic, just an occasional warning: "Damn! Those are the wrong shoes." Or: "The zipper, it's stuck."

Lynda Lee enters the second time , the dresser dabs a bit of perspiration from under her lip with a Kleenex. Lynda Lee swiggles into a tight pair of slacks that slide smoothly over the panty hose. Around her the swirling flash of material and glints of gold continue unabated, as the stormy scene increases its tempo. The minutes snap past, as if a camera recording the scene had been set in fast motion.

The room is suddenly filled with models. The pacer says in a hushed whisper, "Finale, line up." The models step quickly into line for this final parade of fashion, and as they exit through the curtain the applause rises in volume. As the clapping begins to fade the models return, laughing, chattering, relaxing.

"I got my heel caught in the carpet," a junoesque teenager with knee-weakening blondness says. "God, I lost my shoe, and almost fell off the runway!" And you wonder how she can even walk in those staggeringly high heels, let alone maneuver them on a carpeted runway.

"That zipper broke, came open on the runway," Lynda Lee says, her eyes glazed from the excitement of the last forty-five minutes. "I had to stuff my hands in the pockets to keep the dress up." She slips off the last gown and helps the dresser hang up the clothes. She is breathing heavily. "I guess I get a little high on runway modeling," she says. 'Can't help it. I *love* it." She takes a deep breath and lets it out slowly. "Yeah...I love it."

A half hour later, over a cool glass of wine, we sit on the outside terrace of the Biltmore overlooking the ocean, and talk about this "love," and its genesis

"Many women dream of becoming fashion models," Lynda Lee says, relaxing. "I did when I went from sweet sixteen to a svelte seventeen, even to the point of enrolling in modeling courses. But marriage, two children, and the addition of enough flab to make me tip the scales at 155 pounds, slowed me down until I learned to 'hover' around 125 pounds. Then suddenly the children were teenagers and I had more time to myself, and most of all—I turned forty.

"I was also going through a major lifestyle change. My husband, who was a Navy pilot, had just retired after twenty years of service, and I began to get the bug to do something, a career of my own. I had taught a basic beauty course for military wives at our last duty station, and I had also done a little fashion modeling for the wives' club. So, after we moved to Santa Barbara, California I went for an interview with the local modeling agency. I thought I could teach beauty courses, but much to my surprise, I ended up as a fashion model.

"Turning forty didn't bother me," she continues. "Age is something that is natural in life. I look in the mirror and see a few wrinkles that weren't there the year before, but I accept that as my own personal aura of maturity."

"How beautiful do you have to be a fashion model?" I ask.

"I am a case in point," she replies. "I can hardly say I have a beautiful face, but there are a few good bones. When I look in the mirror I see recognizable flaws: my nose has an unfortunate ripple in it, my mouth is too wide, and I have hair that humidity pincurls. At five feet, seven inches my figure is sleek enough to fit in to a size eight. And, at age forty-four, I figure I have been around about as long as the modeling industry itself."

(A little research unearthed the fact that fashion modeling got its start after World War II with the rapid rise of ready to wear dresses. Industry advertisers realized that dresses looked better on live mannequins than plaster dummies. At first actresses were engaged to show off clothes, but demand outdid supply, and schools for modeling had to be organized to train girls. The fashion model quickly came into being.)

I wonder: what's so incredible about being a fashion model?

"The clothes, for one thing," Lynda Lee says sipping from the crisp wine. "There is a euphoric feeling when you are on the runway and you can feel the press of a designer gown against your skin, and see the blur of chiffon as it billows and swirls around you. There is also the added compensation of working in front of a live audience—like today—and hearing their 'oh's' and 'ah's.' Listening to the applause gives a fashion show a theatrical first night atmosphere.

"There is also a vast amount of creativity in what the model can do with a certain gown on a runway. I think the design of a gown can touch off a spark in the model—I know it does in me—then she adds her own personal creativity—her own style. That's what the model can do for clothes. It is a melding of talents."

She looks up at the late afternoon sun low in the sycamore trees, and continues, "Fashion modeling can also be an incredible second career—and an exhilirating way of earning extra money.

"The pay won't get you a Rolls Royce or enough prestige to 'tea' with the queen, but being a model can clothe you with new confidence, add to your wardrobe, and get you invited to great parties. And that is fun—even at forty-four!"

Lynda Lee takes the last sip of her wine, and pushes the empty glass away. Behind her the yellowing afternoon sun highlights the gray-white streaks in her hair. "You know, I'm having the time of my life," she says. "I drive around in my little sport car with the convertible top down, and when people stop and look at the license tag that says MODEL—44, I turn to them and smile."

"And wave...."

(Santa Barbara News-Press photo)

Kym Herrin. (Bill Boyd photo)

Kym Herrin

Santa Barbara's Playmate

When Kym Herrin, Santa Barbara's Playboy centerspread arrived for the interview, she said, "I've been trying to think up answers—but I don't know the questions." I found her relaxed, eager and honest. She carried on a running commentary as we leafed through her portfolio of nude photographs and bikini shots. She stopped at a Playboy cover illustration which showed her wearing a revealing aerobics outfit. "I got the Playboy cover because of my small nipple size," she said. "They can't show nipples on the cover, and with those thin straps on the outfit, I just fit." It was that kind of interview.

"Nope, that's not me," Kym Herrin says brightly, holding up the centerfold of the March 1981 issue of *Playboy* magazine. "I mean, it's very artistic and outdoorsy—and I am an outdoor girl, sun and surf and all that—but look..." She dangles the three-page foldout by its corner. "They stood me next to this red Ferrari, put me in thigh-high boots, and a fur coat—and I hate furs, I never *wear* furs—and then they stuck these wild sunglasses on me. It's not a Southern California girl. It's a Hollywood and Vine girl." She drops the centerfold on the table and laughs, kind of an embarrassed little girl laugh. "I mean, look at *that girl,* she looks like a rich whore."

You look at the nude centerfold one more time, and you have to agree. *That girl* is not the real Kym Herrin. It isn't even close. Kym Herrin is the quintessential laid-back Santa Barbara girl, a fresh-faced blonde, tanned, long-legged, athletic, "Hey, I got it made" girl. She is a world apart from the jet-set *Playboy* portrayal. So far apart that she detaches herself from the photograph, referring to the girl pictured as *it.* The glossy girl on the printed page is only a fantasy image.

"I seldom really look like I do in my modeling photographs,' she says, smoothing her light summer dress across her legs. The curve of her body gives the material movement and life. "I don't have a high fashion look. Those models have turned up noses, and I have this little round nose." She trails an index finger down the bridge of her nose, and around the curved tip. She laughs lightly again. "The nose is not the greatest, but I'm not heartbroken about it."

The most striking thing about the *real* Kym Herrin is her hair, a sun-bleached shimmer of flaxen gold; silken tresses that would have driven Rumpelstiltskin into a frenzy. Her eyes are briliant green and her skin naturally the color of a Southern California suntan, a legacy from her mother who is half Philippino. She is slender; lithe might be a better word for her 5'8" frame. Her figure has the almost magical ability to transform itself into celluloid images of athletic sensuousness.

Photographers can sense this and hover around her. "I can't even walk into Von's because a Brooks photography student will be at every aisle asking me to do a photo test with him."

She picks up a large model's portfolio, unzips the case, and starts thumbing through page after page of photographs. There is a series of bikini shots for Santa Barbara-based Yanah Swimwear, as well as photo clips from magazine advertisements in which Kym posed in a variety of athletic attire, from skiing outfits to scuba diving suits.

There are cover shots from such magazines as *Skier's World, Fitness and Diet,* and *Fit.* There are also two covers from *Playboy,* the September 1982 and September 1983 issues. "I really like the *Playboy* cover shots," she says pausing at the tear sheets. "They are more like me. Besides, not every Playmate gets to do a cover, and I got two."

She flips past a few pages until she comes to a full-face "head" shot of herself, a strikingly beautiful black and white photograph which accentuates her features. "That's a new shot," she says. "Pretty good, huh?" She slowly zips the portfolio shut. "I've really got to update some of these pictures. I don't have anything in here from *Romancing The Stone.*"

In that blockbuster of a movie, which starred Michael Douglas and Kathleen Turner, Kym had a part in the opening sequence. She played Angelina, a fantasy heroine who inspired the transformation of the Turner character. "I didn't realize that Angelina was such a good part when I was called to Hollywood to audition," she says. "Besides starring in it, Michael Douglas was also the director. He auditioned me. That was an extra foot in the door, because he also lived in Santa Barbara until recently. People seem to be local oriented here, and I think that helped. But what really won it was my hair, which is kinda naturally styled in that loose-flying romantic novel look that fit the part.

"I think the whispy hair also helped when I was chosen for the part of the ghost in the Dan Akroyd movie, *Ghostbusters.*" She shakes her head and the hair falls lightly on her cheeks. "Look, I'm not really pursuing acting, I don't even have any acting training, but I'm not afraid of the camera. I think all my photo modeling has helped me be more natural. I guess, if I really was into a serious movie career, I'd wake up every morning with the gut feeling that I had to be an actress. *Then,,* if I landed a big part, I'd have to move to Los Angeles and I'd hate to do that. How can I sacrifice my lifestyle? I'm a sunshine Santa Barbara girl and always have been. LA gives me a headache."

"I get a lot of casting calls from Hollywood—'Oh, come on down, it's a good part,' they'll say. One time I went down only to discover the part was a ridiculous nude scene which was terribly tacky. The women in it were really treated like sex objects. So, I said, 'No way, I don't do nudes for movies.' I still get asked all the time. I guess that's my Playboy legacy."

At age twenty-two, Kym was thrust into the national spotlight when she posed nude for the *Playboy* centerfold. How did this modest surfing enthusiast get involved with *Playboy?*

"It was kind of funny how it started," she says smoothing her skirt with the palm of her hand. "I was going with this boy, and his mother was a photographer who had subimmited a lot of photos to *Playboy.* She had recently photographed another girl who had been accepted for the centerfold. 'Look at this girl,' she said to me. 'She made it. Don't tell me you couldn't.' So I agreed to take some test shots, but I said no one was to know about it. The big problem was I had to pose in front of my boyfriend's mother! It was real embarrassing."

Playboy liked the pictures so Kym and the photographer were asked to take a second series of shots. The editors liked them too, so much so that Kym was invited to Hugh Hefner's mansion for a personal interview.

"The first time I drove up to the Playboy Mansion, there was Hugh Hefner, just as I pictured him," Kym remembers. "He was small, thin and had a pipe in his mouth. And he had on silk pajamas. He always wears pajamas in his house, for entertaining, for business I guess, for parties. He looked at me and said, 'She's a gatefold. Shoot it.'" She shrugs. "That was it."

And if she had to do it all over again...?

She pauses for a long moment. "Playboy seems different to me now, almost four years later. Now they show—more. I don't want to bad mouth the magazine, because it's been very good to me, but the photos seem to be getting more risque. Now, I didn't think much of my own centerfold shot because it wasn't me, but, at least, it was *clean*.

"The big problem is you don't have any control over what picture is used, although you can refuse to pose for certain types of shots. They can use the photos whenever they want and as many times as they want. I mean, if I were to become famous, they could pull out a series of terrible shots and print them. They grade them according to how much.. ah..shows. There are three categories: 'A'—'B'—'C'. They could pull out a bunch of 'Cs' that showed—everything."

One of the enticements to be featured in *Playboy* is the money. "Oh yeah," Kym says. "I got $10,000 for the centerfold. I also did a lot of promotional work for the magazine afterward. I'd go on tour, all expenses paid, and sign autographs for four hours a day. I liked signing the cover photos, but I always put my hand over the breasts when I signed the centerfold. But it's fun work, and you get paid $300 a day."

Posing for *Playboy* spawned a wide variety of modeling jobs for Kym, all of which take her far away from Santa Barbara. "I traveled over 100,000 miles last year, and I am getting a little tired of it. I have contracts from several companies to model their sportswear, usually on a percentage-of-sales basis. It's a bit of a gamble but all expenses are paid, and so far it has worked out pretty well. I've even modeled with underwater video equipment. It's the kind of work where I can scuba dive, relax on the beach in a swimming suit, and eat anything I want. I have low-calorie taste buds, and prefer salads to sweets. I seldom gain an ounce."

"I have been travelling so much that everything else in my life is on hold," she continues. "Now that I am getting old..." She laughs. "I'm twenty-six—the body won't last forever—and I have to do something else with my life. So I've started designing women's clothing and am really excited about that. I am working with soft lamb and deer suedes; I feel it is the really big material right now and will get bigger. I don't want the Indian look. I want to do something in these materials in the style of the '50s. I'll design reversible garments like making the back of a blouse so it can be turned around and worn in the front.'

"I thought of all the French words to name my line of clothes, but everyone uses French names. So I decided to use my own name, Kym, then add a *z* to the end—*Kymz Designs*. Unfortunately, everything is on hold right now because of my traveling. I want to get it all underway as soon as I have a few months clear." She sighs. "I guess I'm just going to have to decide what is the most important thing in my life and then put all my energies into it. I may never surf again.

"Someday I just want to plant a garden. I am a real homebody at heart, I love to cook. I love domestic life. No, really, I love it." She stops and holds her hands up like a stop sign. "But, I am not a housewife! I just don't want to be so overwhelmed by a career that I don't have time to come home and be domestic, or to play at a sport I love."

And marriage? "Sure, eventually."

Family? "I always told myself I'd be pregnant by the time I was twenty-six. So—I'm twenty-six. I've been looking for the ideal man for quite a while."

On her *Playboy* biographical sheet, Kym described that "ideal man" as being "tall, broad-shouldered, with an ethnic background." She wonders about this now. "Ethnic? Where was I coming from at the time? But amazingly enough, that was the exact description of the next man I met, and went with."

In the same biography, under the question "turn ons" she wrote: "Live entertainment, fresh snow, Mom's home cooking and hot oil massages."

She defined her "turn offs" as being: "Critical people, cruelty to animals, and the saying, 'You're pretty for a girl.' "

Being a "pretty girl" as well as being *that* girl who posed for *Playboy* gets her continual stares from admirers. "Yeah, the guys stare a lot," she says. "It doesn't bother me—when they stop staring, that's when it will bother me. At first I was nervous and couldn't handle the stares. I kept thinking 'Is something showing?' It seemed like everybody watching me had their score cards out and were making a list of my good and bad points. I heard this girl say, 'Oh, I don't think she is pretty at all.' And the guys were saying, "Oh yeah, her, I've been with her.' " She smiles. "After the *Playboy* thing *all* the guys were saying they had been out with me. But I hadn't even had a date in a year! Everyone was afraid to ask me out. I finally took a guy to dinner and even paid for everything."

Obviously, not all of the responses for doing the *Playboy* spread have been positive. "I've had women come up to me and say, kinda stuffy, 'Well, *I'd* never do it.' I always feel like saying, 'You don't have to worry about being a Playmate, so don't strain your brain.' Of course, I never say anything."

Even though she remains mute in the face of criticism from her peers she is worried that she is too open, too honest about herself. "Yeah, sometimes I am too open. I say things about myself that I shouldn't. But, if I had three wishes just for myself, I'd like to see my career in dress designing take off successfully." She pauses, thinking about one last wish, then brushes the streaming cascade of golden hair away from her face, and smiles a big friendly, smile. "Most of all, I'd like to live long and laugh often."

So far, she's off to a good start.

Roscoe Tanner.

Roscoe Tanner

First Serve

Roscoe Tanner is the All-American boy—honest and clean-cut; what every mother and father would want in a son. He loves tennis, but unfortunately, his dream of a comeback after his shoulder operation never became a reality. His serving arm had taken too much abuse in his career on center court. However, he will be playing on the senior circuit—thirty-five and over—and they'll know he's there.

"He can beat anyone on the court when his serve is humming...if he's on, I lose."
Bjorn Borg, Tennis Champion

Bjorn Borg, the "Ice Man" of tennis, waited at one end of the court at Wimbledon, England. His back was bent like a question mark. He held his racket in front of him in both hands, pointed like a sword at his opponent across the net. Nervously he shuffled his weight back and forth...waiting...

I could see deep in his eyes—he was scared. He was called the "Ice Man" because he never showed any outward emotion, but at that moment I knew he was scared to death.

On the other side of the net stood his challenger, Roscoe Tanner, a six-foot, 170-pound tennis machine with the most devastating serve in the game; a human machine that could spew balls across the net at blinding speeds of 144 miles per hour.

I could feel Borg's emotion. He didn't know what would happen in the next few moments, whether he would win or lose. I felt good. I was going after him.

Tanner looked steadily at Borg as if trying to see through him, then in a practiced motion tossed the ball above his head and cocked his racket behind his back. Lashing forward, he sent the ball blazing at Borg.

The strawberries and cream crowd at Wimbledon's Center Court turned their heads in a sea of motion to watch the blur of white as the ball crossed the net. The spectators were hushed, feeling the energy and tension in the air as these last few points were played out.

The match thus far had been a masterpiece, a classic pairing between the three-time champion, Bjorn Borg, a methodical counter-puncher with impenetrable nerves, and the aggressive challenger, Roscoe Tanner, the all out "Let's go for it!" attacker. Borg had told Tanner, "I am the champion. You have to beat me; I won't beat myself." Tanner was convinced he *would* beat Borg. He would win the most prestigious championship in tennis—the Wimbledon.

Tanner's serve bounced on the grass surface, and Borg, in a wonder of reflex action, jabbed sideways with his racket and the ball bounded back across the net.

I watched the ball coming at me, and everything changed to slow motion. And there was the silence, it was as if the sound had been turned off. I waited—then hit the ball—hard.

The ball crossed the net by a few inches and bounced on the baseline, kicking up a puff of white. The ball was clearly in. Tanner's point.

Then, amazingly, the linesman called—'Out!"

The crowd sighed like a whisper of wind in rushes. Tanner stood silent.

"Even at that crucial point, I knew I could still beat Borg," Roscoe Tanner remembers as he squints his eyes against the brilliant Santa Barbara sun. He is sitting on a white metal lawn chair next to the practice court he uses on an estate in Montecito. From the court he can see the Santa Barbara Channel partly enclosed by its girdle of islands. Tanner, as would be expected, has on white tennis shorts and tennis shoes. He wears a pale blue sweat shirt pushed up at the sleeves. Parked near the court is his Mercedes convertible with the license plate—1ST SERVE.

Tanner stretches his left arm, his playing arm, over his head and rubs his shoulder. His arm doesn't look lethal, and the hand reaching in the sunlight would fit any athlete of his size. He winces a little as he moves the arm around. "I've just finished having surgery on my arm," he says in a soft, modulated voice with just the hint of shyness. "They had to dig out some cartilage and bone chips. But the prognosis is that the arm will be normal again, and if it is...well, there's always Wimbledon again." He grins a little, that good-looking, mild-mannered, All-American grin, and you know that Wimbledon is something special to Tanner.

But, then, Wimbledon is something special to all tennis players. Center Court at Wimbledon is the greatest tennis arena in the world; it is like the Masters, the Super Bowl, the World Series. To have played there, and to have played for the championship, is the dream of any six-year old who first clutches an oversized racked in an undersized hand.

"Wimbledon has a marvelous, almost mystical tradition," Tanner says, crossing both arms over his chest. "Each year the Wimbledon Champion comes back to claim *his court.* No one has been allowed to play a match on Center Court since he won. The champion returns to play the first match, the first Monday at 2:00 P.M." He smiles. "Well, they *do* let a few of the lady members of the club on the court to, as they say, 'warm it up a bit.' "

"When you walk out on Center Court for the first time, you say to yourself, 'This is it, this is the most hallowed spot in the game of tennis.' And you have a real gut feeling, you're all tied up inside, and the nerves are fluttering, and you walk up and bow to the kings and queens and princes and princesses in the Royal Box. I have a list of who was there the day I played for the championship—the king of Greece, princesses from the Netherlands, some other queens and princes—bunches of them." He casually crosses one ankle over his knee. "Borg and I even joked that God was there—Charlton Heston was in the stands."

To play before "God" and "bunches" of royalty was an impossible dream for young Roscoe Tanner when he first picked up a tennis racket. Born in Lookout Mountain, Tennessee, Tanner was given a racket by his father who was a lawyer. "He figured I'd become a lawyer too, and tennis would be a good recreational activity." But natural talent and that awesome serve soon lifted the mild-mannered teenage tennis player high on the amateur tennis ladder. By age eighteen, Tanner was the number one ranked amateur player in the country.

Still not sure of his potential, Tanner enrolled at Stanford to pursue his law degree. There he played on the tennis team and attained All-American status in 1970, '71, and '72. He also found time to test his abilities by playing in several professional tournaments against some of the world's top players. When he beat Jan Kodez, who had just won the prestigious French Open, Tanner began to think, "Maybe, just maybe, I *can* play this game."

The heart of Tanner's game is his serve which a Washington Post sportswriter once described as the "quickest, most deceptive and most electrifying in tennis." "I spent a lot of time working on my serve in terms of timing and rhythm," Tanner says. "In practice I decided to try and hit the ball harder and harder. I also had to get the accuracy, so I put tin cans in the corners of the practice court and tried to hit them with a spin serve and a flat serve. If you can hit all the corners when you want to, you can confuse any opponent. The fun part is seeing if the opponent can figure out my serving plan. The day he does, he wins. If he doesn't, I win."

Tanner flexes the fingers of his left hand, as if reaching out for the grip of a tennis racket. "There isn't a guy playing right now that I haven't beaten. I feel confident when I go out on that court, if I do what I *can* do, I *will* win."

Because Tanner's early professional matches were heavily dependent on that "big serve," his performances were often erratic. The bad days were far too frequent. It took a few lean years perfecting the rest of his game, but when he began to get it all together, he began winning the "big ones."

In 1976 he beat Jimmy Conners, the number one player in the game, at a Wimbledon quarter-final match. In 1979 he destroyed Bjorn Borg in the U.S. Open. His blistering serve accounted for an astonishing thirty-one "aces," or points made with no return. He kept Borg so far back of the baseline that one writer wondered if "the usher might ask Mr. Borg for a ticket." In 1981 he blitzed a formidable field to capture the U.S. Pro Indoor championships. He won over such great players as John McEnroe and Ivan Lendl. He had become the Giant Killer.

When Tanner first started the pro circuit, he set two goals. The first was to win one of the Grand Slam titles; Wimbledon, the U.S. Open, the Australian Open or the French Open. He achieved this by defeating top-ranked Guillermo Vilas in the Autralian Open in 1977. His second goal was to be a winning player on a winning American Davis Cup team. In 1981 he achieved that goal. Still, the tournament he really wanted to win was Wimbledon. He would get his chance at the Championship in 1979 against Bjorn Borg.

"I play better in the major tournaments like Wimbledon," Tanner says. "I get hyped up. I prepare myself better. The only problem is that it gets harder to prepare yourself each year." Tanner, who turned thirty-four in 1986 realized the game is for very young men. Most top professionals drop out after age thirty.

"There are two things that can stop a player from continuing to play," he says. "One is getting old. You slow down physically, and each year it gets harder to get back in shape. The body just doesn't come back as quick as it did. The second reason for quitting is injuries." He tests his left shoulder again, feeling the joint carefully. "My serve has been hard on my left arm, yet the operation indicates it will be fine, maybe even as good as before. However, there are also indications of an arthritic condition at the joint and I don't want to aggravate that. I'd rather quit."

"The problem with continuing to play is that I am not as *hungry* as I used to be. I have achieved my goals and I have made all the money I need." (Tanner's estimated annual earnings have been "between $500,000 to a little over a million." On top of that he has promotional contracts with Jantzen sports clothes, Hart, Schaftern & Marx leisure wear, and Pony shoes.)

"To keep playing you have to practice thirty hours a week," he says swinging the palm of his left hand through the air in a smooth backhand motion. "You always have to be keyed up, you have to keep feeling that you *will* win. Look, all the players out there can hit all the shots, but can they hit that shot when all the money is on the line, or when the match is down to the big points. When they are backed up against the wall, can they say: 'I can come out of this!' " He leans forward, elbows on his knees. "You have to *know* you can win. It isn't good enough to *think* you can."

"The game of tennis is sixty-five to seventy percent mental. I know when I walk on the court whether I am going to have a good day. A great player will win even if he's playing terribly. He'll just grub around until he finds something that works. When I walk out on that court, I fully believe I can win. That I *will* win."

Even with a will to win, Tanner has lost frequently at the top level of competition. But, no matter how he loses, he always does so with dignity. On the court he remains in tight control of his emotions. He is one of the few "gentlemen" left on the court today. His impeccable manners are a far cry from the bawl-baby antics and abusive explosions of some of today's bad-boys of tennis: Conners, McEnroe, Nastase.

"As professional players we have the responsibility to maintain the tradition of good sportsmanship," he says. "Unfortunately, some players swear at the officials and make obscene gestures; others whine and scream at the umpire. Now, I'm not a pilgrim, but I think it's a shame when the game gets so X-rated from verbal abuse that parents are afraid to bring their children."

"Sure, it's an intense game," Tanner continues. "But all the players should learn to control their emotions. The problem is, they don't feel they have to. After all, what is the umpire going to do to them? Fine them a few dollars which they can easily afford? Perhaps take away a few points? One thing the official should do, but will never do, is default the offending player from the match. Legally he could, but the promoter needs that top player, and the crowd wants to see that player. The high-ranking players have become bigger than the game."

Tanner relaxes in the chair, wound down for the moment. He has said his piece abut the game he loves, the game that takes him all over the world. He admits that travel has taken him away from home and family too often. The stresses of his professional lifestyle led to a divorce from his former wife Nancy.

He pauses to gaze at the mountains for a moment. "You know, as a tennis player, I can live anywhere. But of all the places I have traveled in my career, Santa Barbara is *the* place to live. It has great physical beauty, with the mountains and the sea and the trees—most of all the trees. I also love the people, so warm and friendly..." He pauses and grins. "I even married a Santa Barbara girl in 1985, Charlotte Brady. Yeah, it's tough to leave this place, even to go play tennis."

Unless it's to play at Wimbledon. His 1979 confrontation with Borg at Wimbledon is still fresh in his mind. That year Borg was the number-one tennis player in the world. He had won the Wimbledon championship three times and to the fans he was like Lancelot in shining armor—invincible. Tanner, the number four player in the world, was a knight of the tennis roundtable too, and a winning one. But woe to him that would dare joust with Lancelot.

"As far as the sportswriters were concerned, I didn't have much of a chance," Tanner says. "At the press conference before the game I knew that they would expect me to come out and tell all the ways I felt I could win. For fun, I decided to agree that Borg was unbeatable. 'Roscoe,' they said, 'you're getting ready to play the top tennis player in the world. What do you think about that?'"

"And I said: 'Well, quite frankly, I've been reading what you guys are saying, and I agree—he's absolutely unbeatable. I don't have a chance, and I don't want to be embarrassed, so I'm thinking about going home.' Suddenly, everyone was telling me, 'Well now, wait a minute, you can do this with Borg, then this...' Finally, I said, 'Yeah, maybe you're right, I guess I'll stick around a bit.' Then they started laughing."

For the championship game Borg and Tanner arrived in the locker room at 11:30 a.m. Both practiced for an hour, then showered, and dressed for the game. All the other eliminated players had gone. The two finalists were left alone, together. "Neither of us tried to psych the other out," Tanner remembers. "We were friends, we had traveled together, played jokes on one another. Yet, we both knew that we would soon go head to head trying to beat the other guy's brains out, tring to *kill* the other guy..." He pauses, and corrects himself. "Uh—trying to *beat* the other guy. We knew that after it was over, we'd go out to dinner together and have a good time."

So there they waited, in a cold room that smelled of steel and sweat. They waited—and read each others fan mail. "'The mail was all very similar," Tanner says. "Borg would get a letter from a little English girl, maybe thirteen or fourteen, and she'd write him exactly the same thing she wrote me. We read the letters out loud and laughed together." At the same time butterflies fluttered away deep inside.

"There was a locker steward who used to tell me jokes before each Wimbledon match to calm me down," Tanner says. "His name was Leo and he would carry my rackets on the court. On this final day he told me of an unusual superstition known only to a few people. It seems that for the last five years the player who had won the championship had sat on a chair on a specific side of the umpire. Then he whispered to me that he would put my rackets on that chair, the winning chair."

"There are a lot of superstitions in the game," Tanner continues. "I have my fair share—a bunch of them. I always wear white on the court, but with a particular color trim. I walk on the court in a certain way not stepping on any lines." He grins sheepishly, as if confessing that he knows these step-on-a-crack-break-your-mother's-back rituals might sound a little ridiculous. "I don't know whether it helps, but they are all programmed in. If I pass something by, I'll have a bad game."

That day at Wimbledon, Leo carefully placed Tanner's rackets on the winning chair. Then, the man who carried Borg's rackets moved Tanner's and put Borg's on the winning chair. Tanner, not knowing which chair was which, never knew he was sitting in the losing chair until the match was over.

Ah yes, the match...

I knew my serve was working, so even after the crucial bad call when the ball hit the chalkline, I knew I could still win.

Borg won that crucial game. He also won the next. Tanner served and won. The score of the final fifth set was Borg—5 games, Tanner—4. Borg served for his sixth game—and the championship. He quickly won the first three points. It was now three championship points. Tanner's back was against the wall.

All right Roscoe, you've been out here almost four hours, and now is not the time to ease up and play carefully. Just start gunning everything. Go for winners!

And he did. Incredibly, he won the next three points and tied the game. The next two points were long and tight, each player dueling against the other—and, in the end, Borg prevailed.

Tanner sat down in the loser's chair.

"People think it has been a nightmare for me because I lost," Tanner says. "But I know I played a great match, in the greatest arena in tennis, against the greatest player of his time. I fought and played my best. I didn't blow it. And that, for me, is success."

Yet, you sense that deep inside he is still thinking of Center Court and something that *might* have been.. He pauses and for a moment, turns and looks at the Channel Islands far in the purple distance. Finally, he says: "I guess the thing that keeps me in the game is Wimbledon."

He'll be back, walking softly onto Center Court carryng that big serve.

And they'll know he's there.

Mayor Sheila Lodge and husband Judge Joseph Lodge. (Donald Cyr photo)

Mayor Sheila Lodge

The Mayor and The Judge

"Mayor Sheila," as she is referred to, is a dedicated, and hard-working public servant. She also looks more like a school marm or a librarian than a mayor. (The same could be said of Queen Elizabeth.) I first met Sheila Lodge at the LaBelle modeling agency. She was running for mayor and had decided she needed "glamourizing." After a lengthy session with a makeup analyst and a clothes expert she emerged looking like—Sheila Lodge.

Sheila Lodge tucks one leg under the other and rearranges a strand of hair into the bun on the back of her head. She smiles and says, "As mayor, so far my favorite letter was from the prime minister of Rarotonga, the capital of the Cook Islands in the South Pacific. It was addressed to 'Your Worship Mayoress Lodge.' "

She laughs and settles back into the cushions of the couch, and her features relax behind the familiar steel-rimmed glasses. "Of course, I told the city council afterward that I expected them to refer to me from then on as 'Your Worship.' "

On the couch next to the mayor in the living room of the Santa Barbara home they share with daughters Helen, 17, and Amy, 20, is her husband, Judge Joseph Lodge, at one time a Goleta attorney, and for the last twenty years a judge on the Santa Barbara Municipal court. At the age of 52, he is tall and lanky in the Gary Cooper style, his voice softly modulated and articulate. He curls an arm affectionately behind his wife's shoulder and says, "I suppose Sheila's proper title, her official title, is simply Mayor Sheila Lodge or Madame Mayor. It really gets confusing when we get a letter addressed to both of us using our official titles. Do you say the Honorable Sheila and the Honorable Joseph . . .? Of course there is no question she outranks me—at least in terms of protocol.

"It's a little strange at times being a Mayor's husband," Judge Lodge continues. "People will come up to me and say, 'Oh, you must be *Mr.* Sheila Lodge!' And they mean it very seriously, they are not laughing. And to a very great extent I am *Mr.* Sheila Lodge." He pauses, then adds—as if he is not quite sure he believes it himself—"I enjoy it!"

"As a judge, Joe has his own very strong identity," Mayor Lodge says, "but I think he has been able to gain an insight of what it is like for women to be cast in the shadow of a husband."

"It's funny, but the night of the election everyone was asking me, 'How does it feel to be the first woman Mayor of Santa Barbara?' I really, honestly hadn't thought about it that way. I was just pleased to be *the* Mayor. The fact that I am a woman is irrelevant.

"I really haven't noticed any prejudices as Mayor," she continues. "I think I am being treated with equal consideration, and I think the reason for that is personal attitude. If you play games, act coy and bat your eyes, you're not going to be treated with respect."

"The judge and the mayor have been Mr. and Mrs. Lodge for twenty-one years. They met at a friend's house, just two of a group of civic-minded people who gathered occasionally to discuss political issues and community problems.

"When I first met Sheila," Judge Lodge says, "she was sitting on a fireplace hearth..." he pauses, trying to remember, "knitting, I think..."

"I really don't recall," Mayor Sheila Lodge says. "We just seemed to attach ourselves slowly to each other. We both had the same interests, he was a judge and anything to do with the functions of government fascinated me."

Born in Arcadia, California fifty-five years ago, Sheila Lodge's fascination with politics was nurtured by her parents who constantly discussed the issues that affected their community, state and nation. When she was twenty-seven, she joined the League of Women Voters, a step that provided a background for the intricacies of city government, and an insight about how a citizen could serve a community. Yet, she did not attempt to participate as an elected member of government.

"When I was 41 my mother died," Mayor Lodge says. "She was 82, and suddenly I realized that if I lived to be as old as my mother, I still had half my life to live. I began to wonder what I would do with the rest of my life, the next forty-one years."

One of the first things she decided to do was build a house, a massive, elegant home sheathed in redwood. Its natural wood exterior is a sharp departure from Santa Barbara's typical stucco and tile facades. The interior has high-beamed ceilings and large cathedral windows, a design that fills the home with light and air. When Mayor Lodge designed the house she took its architectural origins from the late 1800s era of naturalism in San Francisco.

"I wanted to study architecture when I went to college many years ago, but that never happened," Mayor Lodge says. "So I cut pictures out of magazines for most of my life, then, finally, I went to City College in Santa Barbara and took a drafting class and an architectural drawing class. With that knowledge I designed this house."

Mayor Lodge gets up from the sofa and goes to the huge front window that overlooks a garden and an acre of orange trees. "I love to work outside, just to dig in the garden..." She sighs and reluctantly turns from the window. "There are some days, when the problems of being the mayor seem overwhelming, and I will come home and sit by this window and think about building a wall around this home and never going outside. I'll just work in my garden and forget about the problems of the city." She walks back to the couch and settles by her husband.

"There is a staggering amount of time she has to put into her job," Judge Lodge says. "She is the type of person who reads all the reports. She pours over them, then asks questions over any point that might be a little vague. Time and time again she is up until midnight or two in the morning. When she gets a day off she can be found at her desk working. She has to do it out of a labor of love because the pay is miniscule." (A Santa Barbara mayor's salary is $700 a month.)

"I'm doing this because I care," Mayor Lodge says. "I think Santa Barbara is a special place, with its climate, its mountains, beaches and beautiful parks. What I hope to do as Mayor is insure that all of the city's special qualities are preserved—forever."

To preserve the "special qualities" of Santa Barbara was the driving force that motivated Sheila Lodge to serve on the city's planning commission starting in 1973. Her opinions about the growth restrictions of the city were so strong that she decided to run for City Council in 1975, where she would be able to actively participate as a voting member. She served on the Council for six years, and from there the mayorship was only an election away.

"Santa Barbara is a relatively old city," Mayor Lodge says, beginning to explain her philosophy. "The city is basically landlocked. There is simply little space to build on. We are in such a tight squeeze between the mountains and the sea that we must ask ourselves—at what population level would Santa Barbara lose its special qualities?"

She pauses, warming to the subject that she feels is the most critical in Santa Barbara's history. "In 1975 the zoning commission, of which I was a member, discovered that with the zoning laws on the books, if every scrap of land was developed to its fullest, the population within the city limits could grow to 170,000 people! Just think of the traffic problems alone! It's desperate now with a little over 70,000 citizens.

"So, predicated on water usage, air pollution, and how many cars the city could handle the commission surveyed different zoning concepts and came up with the maximum population that would fit within our resources. That figure was 85,000. Quite simply, the city cannot be allowed to grow so big."

To work on this problem and the hundred of others that beset the city, Mayor Lodge meets with the city council once a week. "Every Tuesday," she says. "It takes up the whole day. We start at nine in the morning, break for lunch, have an afternoon session, then frequently have a meeting in the evening. There are always new projects for the city—from fountains to freeways."

The council meetings are broadcast live on the government access channel on local television, but so far Mayor Lodge hasn't seen herself on television. "I would like to see it just to see what I look like," she says. "But then I'd probably worry and say, 'Oh, I look awful,' or 'Why didn't I comb my hair more carefully?' or even worse, 'Why did I say it *that* way?' "

One of Mayor Lodge's concerns is her fear that Santa Barbara will become a community for the rich alone. Wealthy citizens are drawn to the city, not only by the warmth and beauty of its Mediterranean-like setting, but by its aura of affluence. In actuality that aura is a myth, as Santa Barbara has a lower per capita income than cities like Oxnard. Almost a quarter of the population is over the age of 60 and living on retirement incomes. (It must be remembered that the wealthier enclaves of Montecito and Hope Ranch are not within the city limits.)

"Tourism is another problem," Mayor Lodge says. "There are simply not enough accommodations for the influx. Some hotels have been torn down and others, like the Carrillo have been turned into retirement homes. That is one reason why the council finally decided it could handle the Fess Parker project on Cabrillo Boulevard—on a reduced scale from the original proposal that is."

She also worries about transients and the homeless as well as the abundance of hitchhikers, bums and derelicts that wander into the city. Drawn to the beaches and to the shabby comfort of lower State Street doorways, they live with the attitude that, as long as they are not bothered by the authorities, it is better to starve in a warm climate. Their presence is a disturbing factor to many citizens, not so much from fear of physical harm— although that is always an underlying concern—but more from the distastefulness of their grubby physical state and haphazard life-style.

"It's an easy place for them to land," Judge Lodge says, moving from the sofa to a straight-backed chair. ("Bit of a back problem," he explains.) "They get off the freeway at the stoplight, or at the railway station, and hibernate in the nearest doorway with a paper bag and a bottle. Because the typical skid-row derelict is passive, most of them are harmless, but some of them may get a little too much booze and want to punch someone out. Sometimes they go a little crazy and steal things, and scare people, and since it isn't their permanent home, and they are never coming back, they feel free to deface the city."

"Many people have told me they have a fear of walking in the lower State Street area," Mayor Lodge says. "So I decided I would walk regularly in that area for a while. Early in the morning I would walk from city hall to the beach and back up again. No one bothered me, but I could see what was going on. Derelicts would sit in doorways and start drinking as soon as they awakened, and by noon there would be fifteen or twenty of them drunk.

"The city can, and is, providing officers to patrol this area, and this is a deterrent," she continues. "The officer is not there for the purpose of issuing citations or making arrests, but his presence is valuable because it creates a sense of order. People feel more comfortable. I have also discovered that simply not having space for a large group to gather is an added deterrent. One of the hotels on lower State, that was plagued by drinking parties of derelicts, simply boxed in the front steps so they couldn't be used as a parking place. When we extend the State Street Plaza, sitting room for such gatherings must be eliminated."

Unfortunately, there is a tendency to think that Mayor Lodge can simply snap her fingers and make things happen. The power of the Mayor is much more limited than most people imagine. Santa Barbara, like most California cities, has what can best be termed as a "weak mayor" form of government. There is a professional city administrator who is responsible for administering the policies of the city council. The Mayor "chairs" the meetings of the council but has only one vote.

"I am the chief spokesperson for the city and for the city's programs and policies, but the power to implement these policies is limited," Mayor Lodge says. "I have talked to mayors of Eastern cities, like the mayor of Jersey City, New Jersey. He heads the political party and in effect appoints leaders from his congressional district to Congress. He can also hire or fire anyone in the city. He has that kind of power. The East Coast brings to mind the big city political bosses. I'm afraid that is far from what we have here."

"A great many of her functions are ceremonial," Judge Lodge adds.

"And there are so many ceremonial functions for me to attend," she says. "Just recently there was a Scandinavian picnic, and at the same time there was a Chumash Indian picnic and right after that I was to attend a function for the Philippine community—three functions actually—and I know they felt disappointed that I couldn't attend all of them."

Ceremonial considerations aside, Mayor Sheila Lodge is deeply concerned about preserving the life-style and dignity of the city. At the same time her husband, in his judicial capacity, earnestly strives to implement the myriad of legislative rules levied by an unwieldy justice system.

"I am concerned with the judicial system and how it works and how it serves society," Judge Lodge says. "Sheila is part of this and is doing her job extremely competently. She is constantly seeing the fruits of her work. But in my position there is a terrible frustration. I feel that the judicial system is getting worse, so much worse that it is about ready to collapse."

Judge Lodge pauses for a moment, then begins to explain, "Under the law, we have given the people so many rights that these rights have become entangled. Our constitutional protections have become too complex. Now, by comparative studies, we are one of the roughest sentencing countries in the world, but so many defendants—who are really guilty—get off on flukes, that the public is incensed. When Hinkley was found not guilty for his attempted assassination of the President, the people were appalled. But, in a sense, I was glad to see it happen. You see, the rules that let Hinkley off have been around for years. If he hadn't been found 'not guilty for reasons of insanity' then people might think our criminal justice system is in great shape. What the people have to understand is that the Hinkley kind of thing is *no* exception.

"Part of the problem is that the justice system has become too much of a game," Judge Lodge continues. "An attorney can stand in a court room and pull one trick after another out of his bag. I mean, let's say you get a middle-aged man in court who has always been a law-abiding citizen, and let's say he was arrested for exposing himself. There he is, scared, embarrassed, and he doesn't know whether to leave town or not. Then you call his name, "The People against John Doe.' and you say that he is charged with 'child molesting.' All the bright lights are on him, the flags are hanging in front of him, and the bailiffs are standing before him in uniform, and the judge is staring down at him in a black robe—and the man breaks down crying.

"Now, that man is ready to listen, to be counseled, he needs help. And the judge leans over to talk to this tormented person—and the attorney shunts the client aside and says, 'We're going to plead not guilty, and we want a jury trial, and we are going to file motions...' I don't mean to knock lawyers who use their procedural rights, but if we could have held off and talked to the man, to counsel him, then we might have solved something and it would have been a wonderful experience for everyone."

Judge Lodge stops, takes a deep breath and then slowly adds, "I'm afraid that for both of us, Sheila and myself, our powers are a lot more limited than most people imagine."

Judge Lodge gets up from the straight-backed chair and returns to the sofa and sits next to his wife. "With my job as judge and her's as mayor we seem to see little of each other lately, and I am jealous of the city for that. I like talking to her. I like listening to her play the piano. She is a marvelous cook, and she loves to work in the garden..."

Sheila Lodge, surrounded by the warmth and affection of her husband, says she realizes that the duties she cherishes as the mayor of Santa Barbara will eventually end. "I know that when I am no longer in an elected office, I won't be able to just stay at home." Then she laughs and adds, "I'm too much of a busy body. I would be down there at the council meetings as a member of the audience—complaining."

The garden will have to wait.

Cork Millner, author. (Lora Yates photo)

Cork Millner

Before he began to write professionally, Cork Millner was a U.S. Navy aircraft carrier pilot. He terminated that career after twenty years because—as he says—"I was terrified!" Opting for a safer, more sedentary existence, he now writes screenplays, theatrical stage comedies, film documentaries, wine books and magazine articles. Cork Millner's celebrity profiles have appeared in the *Saturday Evening Post, Seventeen,* and twenty five issues of the *Santa Barbara Magazine.* Millner is also completing a book titled, *The Art of Interviewing.* His newest book is called, *Looking Great! Without Diet or Exercise.*

Millner presently lives in Santa Barbara with his wife, Lynda and two children, Kim and Dane. His book on the wines of Santa Barbara County, *Vintage Valley,* was published in 1983 and revised and updated in 1985. In December 1985, Millner's new wine book, *Recipes by the Winemakers—Cooking With Wine,* was published.

Prior to coming to Santa Barbara in 1976, Millner and his family lived in Jerez, Spain, the sherry wine citadel of the world. After seven years of personal and enjoyable research tasting his way through all the old bodegas of the city, learning in minute detail the age—old process of sherry making, he wrote a loving and romantic look about this unique wine titled *Sherry—The Golden Wine of Spain.* James Michener called the book," . . . a joy . . . most evocative . . . with a nice combination of the author's observations and historical references."

Mr. Millner has a Masters of Arts degree from the University of California in Theatre Arts (emphasis Playwriting), and a Bachelor of Arts degree from the University of Maryland. He completed his U.S. Navy military flight training at Pensacola, Florida in 1954. He presently teaches writing for Santa Barbara City College Continuing Education, and the University of California, and is also on the literary staff of the Santa Barbara Writers Conference.

Mr. Millner is featured frequently at wine appreciaton seminars on cruise ships (such as Cunard Line's five-star Sagafjord,), and at social functions and professional club meetings, where his knowledge and wit both enlighten and entertain.